THE JOHNS HOPKINS UNIVERSITY PRESS

This book was composed in Press Roman Medium. It was printed by Universal Lithographers, Inc. on 60-lb. Sebago stock and bound by L. H. Jenkins, Inc. in Holliston Roxite Vellum cloth.

from Public Water Project Investment. Unpublished Ph.D. Thesis, Michigan State University, 1972.

30.   Yang, W. Y. *Methods of Farm Management Investigations for Improving Farm Productivity.* Rev. ed. FAO Agricultural Development Paper no. 80. Rome: Food and Agriculture Organization, 1965.

Good source for a discussion of techniques of analyzing farm accounts as a basis for preparing farm plans and making financial projections.

ECONOMIC
ANALYSIS
OF
AGRICULTURAL
PROJECTS

J. PRICE GITTINGER

The Economic Development Institute
International Bank for Reconstruction and Development

THE JOHNS HOPKINS UNIVERSITY PRESS
Baltimore and London

Copyright © 1972
by the International Bank for Reconstruction and Development
All rights reserved
Manufactured in the United States of America
Library of Congress Catalog Card Number 75-186503

ISBN 0-8018-1386-7 (clothbound)
ISBN 0-8018-1403-0 (paperbound)

CONTENTS

FOREWORD

This book is the first of a series of Economic Development Institute publications derived from and used in its teaching programs that we feel should also be of interest to a broader audience. The EDI plans, in addition, to publish another series consisting of case studies and other teaching materials prepared for Institute training programs that should be of interest mainly to those undertaking courses of a similar nature.

The purpose of this book is simply to sharpen the decision analysis tools of those people in developing countries who must decide on how to spend scarce money on agricultural development. It discusses practical, not-very-complicated ways to help insure that when investment decisions are made resources will be used economically and efficiently. It outlines means of comparing the yield or return of one agricultural investment with other agricultural investments and with investments in other parts of the economy.

The approach of the book reflects its origins in lectures and teaching materials prepared for the Agricultural Projects Course offered for officials from developing countries at the Economic Development Institute of the World Bank. As a result, the style tends to be less formal than might otherwise be the case but also as a result, we hope, more readable and easier to grasp.

This book deals primarily with the straightforward application of what are known as "most probable outcome" evaluation methods to compare alternative agricultural development projects. The book is not a treatise on agriculture, nor even on those very important aspects of project preparation and evaluation that rest on the skills of agronomists, livestock specialists, irrigation engineers, and the like. The assumption is that readers already have such professional qualifications. All that is attempted here is to make it possible to add economic analysis to an existing kit of professional tools.

This book is not an "introduction" to an occult science. It is expected that anyone who has education and experience enough to be entrusted with administration of agricultural development regardless of his professional background will be able to do all the analysis we discuss. Hence, the discussion is aimed primarily at agriculturalists, not agricultural economists. It is hoped, however, that agricultural economists may find this book useful to them, too. (It is surprising how many people with very good economic educations have never had an opportunity to become familiar with applied project analysis methodologies.)

The economic theory underlying most project analysis is quite simple. It is certainly not enough to deter a noneconomist. In any case, the most necessary theory is touched upon in this book. The formal analytical tools introduced are not complicated. The mathematics do not go beyond addition, subtraction, multiplication, and division. The approach is too tedious to be done well by hand, however. Normally a desk calculator will be needed--but not a computer.

Although the economic analysis tools outlined are not complicated, but they are effective. They are commonly used by international lending institutions (including the World Bank) for the economic analysis underlying millions of dollars of investment decisions every year. Thick volumes of economic analysis backing up proposed investments usually involve nothing more complicated than is discussed in the following sections--although large investments may require extensive elaboration and involved intermediate steps to accommodate all the ins and outs of a complex agricultural project. A big project is commonly no more than a grouping of small projects, each of which should be subjected to its own analysis. (It is only fair to note that some very large projects are evaluated by methods more complicated than those discussed in this book. Such projects are very much the exception, however.)

It is impossible to acknowledge the assistance of all those who have contributed to this work, but special appreciation is due to George B. Baldwin, Hans Adler, P. D. Henderson, Frank H. Lamson-Scribner, and David H. Penny, all presently or formerly with the Economic Development Institute; to numerous staff members of the Agriculture Projects Department of the World Bank, especially Lionel J. C. Evans, Willi A. Wapenhans, and A. Robert Whyte; and to the participants in the Agricultural Projects Courses in Washington and in project courses in developing countries who have criticized in detail earlier drafts and the original lectures and exercises. Particular mention is also due to K. S. Krishnaswamy for his personal help in this project and for the fact that the work was begun and substantially completed during his term as Director of the Institute.

March 1972   Andrew M. Kamarck
                                                    Director
                                      Economic Development Institute
                                             World Bank Group

ECONOMIC ANALYSIS OF AGRICULTURAL PROJECTS

1. PROJECTS: THE "CUTTING EDGE" OF DEVELOPMENT

Projects are the "cutting edge" of development. Perhaps the most difficult single problem agricultural administrators in developing countries face is implementation of development programs. Much of this can be traced to poor project preparation.

Clearly, project preparation is not the only aspect of agricultural development or planning. Identifying national agricultural development objectives, selecting priority areas for investment, designing effective price policies, and mobilizing resources are all critical. But for most agricultural development activities, careful project preparation in advance of expenditure is, if not absolutely essential, at least the best available means to insure efficient, economic use of capital funds and to increase the chances of on schedule implementation. Unless projects are carefully prepared in substantial detail, inefficient or even wasteful expenditure of money is almost sure to result--a tragic loss in capital-short nations.

Yet in most countries the capacity to prepare and analyze projects lags. Administrators, even those in key planning positions, continually underestimate the time and effort needed to prepare suitable projects. So much attention is paid to policy formulation and planning of a much broader scope that it is often overlooked that much development cannot proceed unless there is a specific project on which to spend the money available. Ill-conceived, hastily planned projects virtually improvised on the spot are too often the result.

What is a project?

In this book, we will discuss how to compare the stream of investment and production costs of an agricultural undertaking with the flow of benefits it will produce. The whole complex of activities involved in using resources to gain benefits constitutes our "project." Of course, there is an enormous variety of agricultural activities which may legitimately be cast in project form. The World Bank itself lends for agricultural projects as widely varying in their nature as irrigation, livestock, agricultural credit, land settlement, tree crops, agricultural machinery, and agricultural education.

Generally, in agricultural projects we are thinking of an investment activity where we expend capital resources to create a producing asset from which we can expect to realize benefits over

1

an extended period of time. In some projects, however, costs are incurred for production expenses or maintenance from which benefits can be expected rather quickly. The techniques discussed in this book are as applicable to estimating the return from these types of projects as from more common investment type projects.

Indeed, the boundary between an "investment" and a "production" expense in an agricultural project is not all that clear. Fertilizer, pesticides, and the like, are generally thought of as production expenses. A dam, a tractor, a building, or a breeding herd is generally thought of as an investment from which we will realize a return over several years. But the same kind of activity might well be thought of as a production expense in one project and an investment in another. Transplanting rice involves a production expense. Planting rubber trees is an investment activity. Agronomically and economically they are not different kinds of activities at all – in both cases we put out young plants grown in a nursery from which we expect to receive a benefit when they mature. The only difference is the time span during which the plants grow.

Often, projects are the first, concrete portion of a larger, less precisely identified "program." The whole program, of course, could be subjected to analysis as a single project, but by and large it is better to keep projects rather small, close to the minimum size which is economically and technically feasible. If "projects" approach "programs" in size, then there is a real danger that high returns from one part of the project will mask the low returns from another. A 100,000 hectare land settlement program may well be better analyzed in terms of five 20,000 hectare projects if the soils or slopes in some areas are markedly different from others. Analyzing the project as a whole may hide from us the fact that it is economically unwise to develop some areas in the entire 100,000 hectare block instead of moving on to an entirely different region.

About all we can say in general about a project is that it is an activity on which we will spend money in expectation of returns and which logically seems to lend itself to planning, financing, and implementation as a unit. It is a specific activity with a specific starting point and a specific ending point intended to accomplish a specific objective. It is something you draw a boundary around--at least a conceptual boundary--and say, "this is the project." It is something which is measurable both in its major costs and returns. Normally it will have some geographic location or at least a rather clearly understood area of geographic concentration. Perhaps it will have a specific clientele group which it is intended to reach. It will have a relatively well defined time sequence of investment and production activities. It will have a specific group of activities which we want to finance, and a group of benefits for which we can identify and estimate values. Often it will have a partially or wholly independent administrative structure and set of accounts. Hopefully, after reading this book, your projects will also have been subjected to an analysis of their economic justification and financial results.

Sometimes people become concerned that they cannot define a "project." Don't be. In practice, the definition works itself out; there are much more important aspects of project analysis to grapple with than trying to formulate an academic definition of a project.

The project investment decision

Even though the analytical methods we will be discussing can be of great help in identifying which project alternative will increase social income most rapidly, they will not make the project investment decision for us. That decision is one on which many, many factors other than quantitative or even purely economic considerations must be brought to bear. A settlement project and a plantation project may have roughly similar economic benefits, but we may choose the settlement alternative on the grounds that it has better income distribution effects. Or, our analysis may reveal that the plantation project is more profitable and give us some quantitative idea of just how much more remunerative it is. We may then ask ourselves if the social benefits of the lower paying project are worth the loss of future wealth foregone from the higher paying project. In the end, any national investment decision must be a political act summing up the best judgment of those responsible. The function of project analysis is not to replace this judgment; rather it is to provide one more tool (a very effective one, we hope) by which judgment can be sharpened and the likelihood of error narrowed.

The place of economic and financial analysis in project evaluation

It should be clear from the outset that the kind of economic and financial rate of return or benefit-cost ratio which we will be discussing in this book is not an end in itself; no single measure can be. Economic and financial analysis provides a framework within which all aspects of a proposed project can be evaluated in a coordinated, systematic manner. Careful project analysis will point up unrealistic or questionable assumptions and indicate ways in which a project can be modified to improve its wealth generating capacity or to increase the noneconomic or nonquantifiable values which we expect to gain from it. A project carefully analyzed and revised in the light of this analysis has a much improved chance of being implemented on time and of yielding the benefits we seek. The rate of return or the benefit-cost ratio when computed is a useful measure of a project's wealth creating capacity, but it is the whole system of evaluation which justifies the time and effort devoted to a project analysis and from which comes the payoff in terms of better projects.

Projects in overall development

Clearly, projects which a nation chooses to implement should be of high priority in the national development program. They should be selected only after thorough consideration of alternatives in the economy as a whole and within the agricultural sector itself. Since capital is limited and techniques of project analysis approximate at best, many alternative projects of roughly comparable economic return will be candidates for investment. Often high priority projects are well known to political leaders and to agricultural experts, but most countries undertake more formal sector studies or agricultural plans to set forth priorities and objectives clearly. Only if attention is focused on their overall development strategy can governments be sure their investment programs are well balanced.

The range of systematic efforts to study the agricultural sector may go all the way from a continual review of agricultural development policies by cabinet officers to a formal agricultural plan framed on the basis of sustained and careful research and preparation. To some degree or another, all these approaches will incorporate a strategy for the sector as a whole and point out the principal broad areas of investment needs with some idea of their relative priority. Agricultural sector studies will help assure that there is a suitable balance between alternative investments in the agricultural sector and that proper attention is paid to the linkages between growth in agriculture and growth in other sectors. They will draw attention to institutional modifications needed if agricultural development is to proceed and propose changes in policies affecting prices, inputs, and taxes. Sector studies may point out the need for basic resource inventories, river basin surveys, agricultural research programs, and similar fundamental studies. From this broad strategy approach should come identification of those specific projects on which initial feasibility studies will be undertaken to be followed, if the indications are favorable, by the detailed project preparation necessary before investment can proceed.

Points of view in project analysis: economic and financial

In project analysis, there is a critically important distinction to be kept in mind between two complementary points of view.

For any project, we are interested in the first instance in the total return or productivity or profitability to the whole society or economy of all the resources committed to the project regardless of who in the society contributes them and regardless of who in the society receives the benefits. This is the social or economic return of the project and we determine it by applying what we will term economic analysis.

In contrast, the individual financial entities which participate in a project--farmers, businessmen, entrepreneurs, private corporations, public agencies, or whoever--each is properly concerned about the return to the equity capital he contributes. We may consider this the financial return to an equity participation in a project and we determine it through what we will term financial analysis. Some economists term the financial return the "private" return, although financial analysis may quite properly be used for analyzing public sector investments of quasipublic agencies or even the return to the government treasury. (Sometimes financial analysis may be applied to estimate the return to all equity capital or all capital of whatever nature used in a project. In these cases, the purpose of the analysis is to determine the financial viability of the project rather than to estimate the return to the capital contributed by one or another of the participants.)

Policy makers must be concerned about where scarce capital resources can best be directed to maximize economic growth--that is, they are concerned to know which among alternative projects yields the higher social or economic return. This is true whether the resources committed are being invested by the government directly or by individuals within the economy. The economic analysis techniques in this book will help identify those projects which make the greatest contribution to overall economic growth. The economic analysis basically allows for remuneration to labor and other inputs at market prices or shadow prices which are intended to approximate true opportunity costs. Everything left over is then compared to the capital stream necessary for the project. That project which maximizes returns to capital is given the highest rank. Inherent in this approach is the assumption that capital is the most important limit to faster economic growth. What is not implied, however, is that capital causes the economic growth. All the productive factors employed in a project contribute to the new wealth which is created and the methods we will be discussing do not address themselves to the question of just what is the proportionate contribution of each factor. An entirely different analytical approach is necessary to study that problem.

Note well that the manner in which we will apply the methodologies discussed in this book in economic (not financial) analysis makes this analysis neutral to income distribution and neutral to capital ownership as well. Although the analysis will determine the amount of the income stream generated over and above the costs of labor and other inputs, it does not specify who actually receives it. Part of the surplus income is normally taken through taxes for social purposes outside the project. Part is generally made available to compensate capital owners for the use of their money. Part may become the basis of an income transfer as would be the case if we decide to charge farmers benefiting from a land settlement project less than the full cost of establishing their holdings. Economic analysis is silent about this distribution.

Because economic analysis of a project tells us nothing about income distribution, it is neutral as well to capital ownership. The value of a capital asset arises from the right to receive the future income which it generates. Since our economic analysis methodology does not specify who in the economy is to receive the income which our project earns, it is neutral to who owns the capital. Economic measures of project worth are equally valid to help choose the most remunerative alternative from the social standpoint whether the capital is to come from public revenues or from private sources, whether there are income taxes or not, and whether the project is to be in the public sector or to be operated by individuals on their own behalf.

In financial analysis, on the other hand, we are very much concerned about income distribution and capital ownership. Although we will be applying exactly the same discounted cash flow methodology in financial as in economic analysis, the way we normally set up our analysis and the elements we normally will include in the cost and benefit streams mean that the result will be a measure of the return to the equity capital contributed to the project by each of the various participants, public or private. It is then a policy decision as to whether we wish to affect that return through income taxes, special lending terms, price subsidies, or any of the other tools open to the society.

Financial analysis may be applied to the costs and returns of the various public entities which participate in a project. A government credit agency, for example, is a failure as a development activity if it cannot recover the funds it lends to farmers. When preparing the financial analysis of the credit agency, this will be kept uppermost in mind as its accounts are projected. These accounts will, in turn, be related to an analysis of individual farmer accounts. Will the farmer be able to invest the money he borrows profitably enough in a new enterprise or practice that he will be able to repay his loan? Will his sales come at the proper time to enable him to meet his repayment schedule?

Financial analysis may show the public entity responsible for operating a project will not have receipts large enough to recover all the capital--or even operating--costs it incurs. Even so, it may still be worthwhile to carry out the project because the economic analysis shows the total return to the society to be favorable. One might think of an irrigation authority operating a project where the increase in farm output is enough to make the project economically attractive from a social standpoint but where a policy decision has been taken not to assess farmers a water charge high enough to repay all the costs of the authority. In this case, a public subsidy will be involved and financial analysis will give us an idea of how much this transfer payment will amount to, who will receive it, and how it will affect the financial return the recipient realizes on his own equity capital contribution.

Financial analysis is important when we turn to a consideration of the incentive structure associated with a proposed project investment. It will do us no good to have a project which is profitable from the standpoint of the whole economy if individual farmers are unable to earn a living from their participation.

Timing of returns, which the financial analysis will reveal, is also important. A society may be able to invest in a land settlement scheme which will be profitable over a twenty-year period but for which there may be no return at all for the first five years. A peasant farmer could rarely continue on in a scheme of that sort without outside assistance.

In many agricultural projects the proposed investment includes a commercial component--say the establishment of producer cooperatives, the participation of commercial banks, or the development of storage and processing facilities. In that case the financial analysis is no different from that for any other commercial activity and must concern itself with questions of return to the enterprise's own capital, past performance, cost of new facilities in relation to their ability to earn new income, estimates of future earnings, cash flows, balance sheets, and the like.

There are three very important distinctions between economic and financial analysis to be kept in the back of your mind as you read the discussion in the following pages (they are given here in very summary form; we will return to each point in greater detail in later chapters):

1. In economic analysis, certain prices may be changed to reflect better true social or economic values. (The adjusted prices are often termed "shadow" or "accounting" prices.) In financial analysis, market prices including taxes and subsidies are always used.

2.   In economic analysis, taxes and subsidies are treated as transfer payments. The new wealth generated by a project includes any taxes the project can bear during production and any sales taxes buyers are willing to pay when they purchase the output. Taxes are part of the total project "benefit" which is transferred to the society as a whole to spend as it sees fit and are not treated as a cost. Conversely, a subsidy is a "cost" to the society since it it an expenditure of resources which the economy incurs to operate the project. In financial analysis such adjustments are unnecessary; taxes are treated quite simply as a cost and subsidies as a return.

3.   In economic analysis, interest on capital is not separated out and deducted from our gross returns since it is a part of the total return to capital available to the society as a whole and it is that total return including interest which our economic analysis is designed to estimate for us. In financial analysis, interest paid to outside suppliers of money is treated as a cost and repayment of money borrowed from outside suppliers is deducted before arriving at the benefit stream. Interest imputed or "paid" to the entity from whose point of view the financial analysis is being conducted is not treated as a "cost" because it is a part of the total return to the equity capital contributed by the entity and, hence, is a part of the financial return which that entity receives.

The methodology of comparing costs and benefits discussed in chapter 4 is the same whether we are seeking the economic or the financial return. Only what is defined as a "cost" and what is considered a "benefit" is different. For the moment, it is enough to recognize that there is a difference between economic and financial analysis and that most of the discussion in this book is directed toward applying economic analysis to estimate the economic return.

The underlying facts

Project analysis rests on a broad range of technical information and an equally broad if less precise range of judgments about organization and administration. The technical information will require the specialized professional skills of a whole group of specialists--agronomists, civil engineers, soil scientists, and so forth. Putting all the individual parts of a project together in such a way that the project can have a good chance of success requires the skills of experienced administrators who know their society and the region where the investment is planned. Before you can proceed with the kind of economic and financial analysis we will be discussing, you will have to have the summary information of many, many other professionals. Gathering and verifying these underlying facts is more time consuming than is generally realized; be sure to allow enough time in your planning.

One kind of information needs particular attention. That is the economic information based on farm accounts which gives a picture of individual farms in financial terms. From this information you can proceed to the economic analysis which has a broader horizon than just the individual farmer. This is normally called "farm management" information by professional agricultural economists since it was first developed to help farmers improve their management skills. Although better management is important, for our purposes it is not so much the management aspects which concern us as the necessity to look at the timing and amount of returns to individual farmers in proposed projects. Perhaps this kind of information is better called "farm business analysis" or "economics of farming" information. No term I have found seems to say the same thing to different kinds of specialists.

Generally, farm management information will be gathered by survey from individual farmers and supplemented by careful, informed judgment about likely future changes as a result of new investment. This requires--once more--a combination of technical information from agronomists, civil engineers, soil scientists, and the like, plus judgments about how effectively farmers will be able to use new techniques and how fast they will accept new practices. The importance of detailed attention to gathering this kind of information is often overlooked. Quite often the practice is simply to assume x increase in yields multiplied by y hectares in the project area and let it go at that. This can be quite misleading. We must determine whether farmers consider the possible increased farm family net benefits--both in cash and in kind--would justify a new practice. (Farmers, too, do benefit-cost analysis.) We must examine individual farms to see if new practices will fit into existing cultivation patterns. We must know whether the capital investment farmers themselves are expected to make will be profitable enough to induce them to act. We must find out what farmers think about risks of new techniques. All this is a specialized kind of economic science of its own, and one on which project analysis in agriculture rests quite heavily. In its absence, we have to make such sweeping assumptions as to cast doubt on our whole analysis.

Once the underlying technical facts have been marshaled and the organizational and management judgments made, economic and financial analysis has a critical contribution to make. Good project analysis enables us to make better judgments about which among alternative development opportunities is likely to accelerate the growth of incomes most rapidly. It helps us judge if there is adequate income to enable individual farmers to earn a good living and sufficient incentive that they will exert their best efforts. Economic and financial analysis has another usefulness: because it rests on the summary of so much technical information and judgment, it helps specify where the underlying analysis has been forgotten or is inadequate.

Kinds of agricultural projects for which analysis is appropriate

The World Bank in its lending program considers it convenient to group agricultural projects into four main categories. Other people would have other categories. For our purposes, it is enough to note that even for such a broad range of classifications as the World Bank's, the analytical techniques discussed in this book are appropriate and, indeed, are in regular use.

Water resource development. Water resource projects include those for irrigation and ground water, land reclamation and drainage, salinity prevention, and flood control. Bank experience has led to particular emphasis on several key factors. High priority is attached to the organization for construction, operation, and maintenance of the project with emphasis on coordinating use of the physical works with overall agricultural development. Not only bringing water to the project area is important, but also proper drainage to be sure any excess is carried away and that soil salinity does not build up. Careful investigation must verify the suitability of soils to sustain production over a long period of time under irrigation. Adequate administrative arrangements must be developed. The operating organization in the project has to be able to manage water resources so that water is available at proper times and in correct amounts. It must also be in a position to help cultivators manage their soil and water efficiently. If farmers are to realize the benefits of irrigation, there must be such supporting services as extension, marketing, credit, and transportation, both for handling the crops produced and for the inputs needed. Water resource projects normally are capital intensive. The economic analysis must take full account of all the attributable costs and benefits as well as the timing of the cost and benefit streams. Appropriate arrangements will be needed if the project is to recover costs--or at least the operating and maintenance costs--from the farmers whose incomes will increase when their land is irrigated. In multipurpose projects, costs must be allocated among power, irrigation, and other uses, and there must be agreement among the users on the water regime.

Agricultural credit. Agricultural credit projects--sometimes called "on-lending" projects--are intended to provide a large number of farmers with the resources they need for on farm investment to improve their level of living and to raise the production of the economy as a whole. Credit projects by no means are limited just to those farmers who produce entirely for the market. Often they are designed to reach small farmers producing largely for their own families on subsistence holdings but who can be helped to modernize their farms and in the process become market oriented producers.

Agricultural credit projects aim at making agricultural credit a viable commercial operation, not a welfare activity. Projects in agricultural credit need to be defined in terms of the broad categories of on farm and ancillary industry investment contemplated. They may include a variety of activities or may be limited to specific investment programs such as livestock or small machinery. The best basis for evaluating both the use of the credit and the benefits which will be generated is a set of pattern farm plans which trace the effect of "typical" investments using agricultural credit on a particular farm. These give an idea not only of the timing of investments and the amount and kinds of the returns, but also an evaluation of the repayment capacity of the borrowers.

Modern lending to farmers should allow credit applications to be appraised on the productivity of proposed new investments rather than on the physical collateral borrowers can pledge. The terms and conditions of the repayment schedule should dovetail with the timing of new income from the investment.

A range of institutions can be used for agricultural credit projects, but careful attention must be paid to managerial and administrative questions and to the organizational problems which loom particularly large in credit projects. Possible credit channels can be a specialized agricultural credit institution, a multipurpose development bank, rural banks or cooperatives, the commercial banking system, or some combination of several of these institutions.

In general, the operating policies of agricultural credit institutions should result in a financially viable program which will not need special subsidy. Even subsidy through interest rates at less than market levels should be avoided since it leads to misuse of investment resources.

Agricultural development programs. These include such projects as those for regional development, land settlement schemes for small holders or estates, and range development. Frequently these require a substantial technical assistance component to enable farmers to adopt new production techniques. Efficient organization and management often require establishment of new or improved administrative arrangements. To judge whether such projects will, in fact, make a contribution sufficient to justify the investment, particular attention needs to be paid to commodity markets for the products from the project area; coordination of contributing administrative, financial, and technical services; links between production, processing, and marketing; distribution of income among the various participants in the project and the government; and incentives for farmers to respond to the services and opportunities provided by the project. While development projects of this sort may at times be comprehensive and diverse in nature, they generally tend to emphasize a specific product such as tea, cotton, palm oil, or livestock.

Agricultural industries and commercial development. Projects for agricultural industries and commercial development either improve the adequacy and timeliness of input supplies and specialized contractors' services to farming, forestry, and fisheries, or else help improve the storage, processing, and marketing systems. Both kinds of projects play a key role in commercialization of agriculture and they become increasingly important in national investment priorities as emphasis shifts from primary production for home consumption to commercial production. A key question in such projects is that of appropriate technology. In most countries, emphasis should be given to projects which make effective use of abundant raw materials and labor and bring high returns to capital, foreign exchange, and managerial ability. Introduction of more advanced technology sometimes requires replacement of small and scattered processing units by modern industries with a larger scale of operations–and more complex administrative and organization problems. If farmers are to produce high quality specialty crops, it may be necessary to arrange special incentives and to direct the flow of production inputs through various forms of contracts between processing industries and farmers. Especially important in agricultural industries are marketing and price policies which can permit sufficient incentive to suppliers and satisfactory operating margins.

A useful "check list" of the more important components of various kinds of agricultural projects will be found in Outlines for Projects to be Presented for Financing prepared by the FAO/IBRD Cooperative Programme (7).[1] This publication suggests elements to be considered in preparing projects for irrigation, credit, livestock, tree crops, grain storage, agricultural education, fisheries, and forestry.

---

1   The figures in parentheses refer to the references cited in the bibliography beginning on page 216.

Aspects of project evaluation

Out of its experience with lending for development projects, the World Bank has come to distinguish six aspects of project preparation which it feels should be carefully considered in any project (15, pp. 3-14). Not all of these are equally applicable to all projects and some are only rather indirectly applicable to many agricultural projects, but all need to be considered.

Technical aspects. The technical analysis will concern itself with the inputs and outputs of real goods and services. Clearly technical analysis is extremely important and the project framework must be tightly enough defined to permit the technical analysis to be thorough and precise. Good technical staff are essential for this work--perhaps drawn from consulting firms or technical assistance agencies from abroad--but they cannot work effectively if they are not given adequate time or if they do not have understanding cooperation and informed supervision on the part of administrative officials.

Managerial and administrative aspects. Management and administration are very difficult to evaluate but they may be the key to success or failure of a project. In agriculture, our concern must be directed to two levels. On the one hand we must examine the ability of the project staff to administer such large-scale public sector activities as a water project, an extension service, or a credit agency, including arrangements to train the necessary personnel. On the other hand, we are concerned about whether farmers will have the opportunity to learn the new management skills they need if they are to adopt new practices or cropping patterns. Obviously both kinds of management skills can only be evaluated subjectively; but unless careful attention is given to making the best judgment possible, the chances of making a realistic decision about a proposed project are greatly reduced. When we consider the managerial and administrative aspects of a project, not only are we concerned that eventually managerial and administrative problems will be overcome, but we must also make a realistic assessment of how fast they will be overcome since the contribution of an investment to creating new wealth is very sensitive to delays in implementation.

Organizational aspects. Closely related to the managerial and administrative considerations are the organizational aspects. Some, indeed, would say they are all part of a single, inseparable judgment about how well a project can be carried out. In breaking out the organizational aspects, the intent is to focus on the relationships of the project administration to other parts of the government. Are authority and responsibility clearly linked? Are there ample provisions to report up-to-date information about how the project is progressing? What about training arrangements? Can disbursements be promptly made? Without proper provision for these organizational arrangements, even the best manager or administrator is frustrated.

Commercial aspects. The commercial aspects of a project include the arrangements for marketing the output produced by the project and the arrangements for the supply of materials and services needed to build and operate the project. Clearly, in agriculture the marketing aspects are of great importance. Attention must be given to the proposed outlets for the products which the farmers will grow and to the efficiency of the marketing channels. Indeed, some projects may simply be marketing projects wholly concerned with improving the marketing process. On the input side, there must be appropriate arrangements for farmers to secure their supplies of fertilizers, pesticides, and high yielding seeds if they are to be able to adopt new technology or new cropping patterns. Commercial aspects of a project may also include the arrangements for procurement of project equipment and materials and for competitive bidding if there are to be major construction works.

Finally, there are the two aspects of project analysis to which this book is addressed: the financial and the economic.

Financial aspects. The financial aspect deals primarily with the revenue earning considerations of a project. It is concerned with whether the project will be able to secure the funds it will need and be able to repay these and whether the project can become financially viable. We have noted earlier that in agricultural projects financial analysis must address itself to two distinct phases. On the one hand, it must look at the financial results on individual farms to be certain there will be sufficient farm family income and enough incentive for participating farmers. On the other hand, financial analysis must concern itself with the results of public entities or commercial organizations such as cooperatives, banks, and private input distributors or processing companies.

Economic aspects. The economic analysis is directed toward determining whether the project is likely to contribute significantly to the development of the economy as a whole and if the contribution of the project is likely to be great enough to justify the use of the scarce resources which will be needed.

2. IDENTIFYING COSTS AND BENEFITS OF AGRICULTURAL PROJECTS

If the object in economic analysis of agricultural projects is to compare costs with benefits to determine which among alternatives is more remunerative, then the costs and benefits will have to be identified. Obvious enough, but tricky.

Furthermore, once the costs and benefits are known there may be problems of valuation. Money prices are not always the most appropriate to use for economic analysis (although they are for financial analysis). We will turn to the question of selecting proper values--including the complex topic of shadow prices--in the next chapter.

Our treatment both of identifying costs and benefits and of valuing them is directed toward practical, operating approaches to agricultural project analysis. It is necessarily highly summary and professional economists may find it oversimplified. For a discussion of "some unsettled issues" about costs and benefits and their values, you may wish to turn to Henderson (11).

"With" and "without" test

An extremely useful rule of thumb approach to identify the overall return arising from an agricultural project is to ask yourself what will be the impact "with" and "without" the project. The difference is, in general, the net additional benefit arising from the project. You can then proceed to verify that the specific costs and benefits you have identified do add up to the difference "with" and "without" and that none are missing. Note that the question is not posed as the difference "before" and "after;" it is easy to miss some of the less obvious costs and benefits if the question is asked in that form.

Costs in agricultural projects

In almost all project analysis, costs are easier to identify (and value) than benefits.

Goods and services. Rarely will the goods and services employed in an agricultural project prove difficult to identify. For such things as concrete for irrigation canals or bulldozers for land clearing, it is not the identification which is difficult, but the technical problems associated with planning and design to find out how much will be needed and when.

Labor. Neither is the labor component of agricultural projects difficult to identify. From the highly skilled project manager down to the farmer maintaining his orchard while it is coming into production, the labor inputs raise less the question of what than of how much. Unskilled labor, however, while not difficult to identify, does raise special valuation problems and a shadow price may be appropriate. We will take this up in detail in the next chapter.

Cost of land (net value of production foregone). Determining a proper value to place on land in an agricultural project is often extremely difficult, but at least the basis for reaching the value can be made clear if we view land costs as the most important special case of the more general question of the net value of production foregone.

In most agricultural projects the land where the development is to occur already produces some amount of agricultural produce. An area to be irrigated may now be cropped on a dryland basis or an area to be converted to fruit may now be planted to wheat. If we take a new orchard as an illustration, the whole net value of the new fruit crop cannot be considered as a net benefit. Rather, to reach the incremental net benefit we must reduce the net value of the new fruit production by the net value of the wheat crop--that is, after deducting the value of the labor, seed, and fertilizer needed to produce the wheat--since the net value of the wheat which formerly was available for remuneration for the use of the land is now lost. The situation is not one of "before" and "after," but one of "with" and "without."

The economic cost of land in agricultural projects grows out of this concept of the net value of production or opportunity cost.

If there were a perfect market such that economic considerations were the sole determinants of land values (and no land market anywhere fits that description), the purchase price of land would be the present worth of the future net contribution of that land to the value of production. In turn, the net contribution of the land to production would be equal to its rental value, since in a perfect market that is the point at which rents would settle. Thus, the purchase price of land would equal the present worth of the future stream of rent which would be equal to the present worth of the future net contribution of the land to production. In this perfect market, we would be indifferent if we chose to value land at its purchase price, at its rental value, or at the value of its net contribution to production; each would be the equivalent of the other. Similarly, if we wished to use the land for some new purpose in an agricultural project its cost to the economy would be the loss of the net value of production in its present use and we could choose to express that value either directly, as an annual rent, or as a purchase price.

Unfortunately, of course, markets are not perfect and we cannot be indifferent among the theoretical alternatives for valuing land in an economic analysis. Much more than just economic values enters peoples' decisions about the price they will pay for land or the amount they will pay for rent. There are innumerable considerations of prestige, security, personal preferences, imperfect information, and the like which influence their choices. However, we can draw on our theoretical understanding of land values to decide how to value land in project analysis by choosing that alternative means of valuing which we feel most appropriately estimates the true contribution of the land.

To allow for the value of land in an economic analysis of a project, then, there are three alternatives:

1. Value the land at its purchase price entering the cost of land purchase as a lump sum capital item incurred one time only at the beginning of the project. This is the simplest approach, but it makes the inherent assumption that the price of land is a fairly good reflection of the present worth of the contribution that land would make to the value of the future crops which would have been produced in the absence of the project. It implies, too, that the land market is relatively competitive and open and that the price of land is not too far from what would be its equilibrium price in a perfect market. This might be a good alternative if land actually is to be purchased for an agricultural project--say, for dairy farmers who will establish new holdings or for right-of-way for an irrigation canal. In many situations, however, the assumption that the land market is reasonably competitive is not plausible and an alternative valuation approach will be needed. It might also not be a very appropriate analytical technique if there is to be only a land use change in a project and no actual change of ownership rights is expected. (It should be clear, of course, that in financial analysis if land is to be purchased then the actual market price to be paid is the proper purchase price to enter into the accounts, whatever its true relationship to economic worth.)

2. Value the land at its rental cost and enter it into the project accounts year by year as the project proceeds. This would be a suitable alternative in a land market where sales were thought to be strongly influenced by

noneconomic considerations but where there was a relatively competitive market for rental land. The rental value then becomes a convenient and rather easily determined proxy for the net value of production foregone and can be readily used. This might be a convenient alternative even in cases where there was to be no change in ownership or management pattern, but only in an enterprise within a farm. If pasture land were to be converted to sprinkler irrigation for crop production, the rental value of the pasture might be a rather good estimate of the net value of production foregone. (Again, it is clear that in a financial analysis if rent is to be paid then that is the appropriate means to value the land in the analysis. Even when rent is not to be paid, the rental equivalent may be a convenient proxy to use in the financial analysis for the net value of production foregone when there is a change in land use.)

3.   Value the land at an estimate of the net value of production foregone or opportunity cost entered each year as a cost to the project, thus reducing the incremental benefit which is realized. This method of using an imputed cost or price for land is usually the most defensible alternative in economic analysis and sometimes--even in financial analysis--is the only means to allow for the value of the land. It is not, however, always an easy value to calculate. Using the net value of production foregone directly is often the best approach to allowing for the value of land for both the economic and financial analysis when the project envisions a change in land use on farms without any change of ownership or management. (It may be noted that in an analysis of a project where land use was to be changed you would not use both an imputed cost of land and then also deduct the net value of production foregone. That, of course, would be double counting.) Using the net value of production foregone is probably also the best means in an economic analysis to value land which is publicly owned since both the purchase price and the rent charged for use of public domain is generally an administered price, not one competitively determined. When land is to be cleared for settlement, the net value of production foregone may well be so little it may be ignored, but in that case the basis for taking the land into the settlement project at zero value is clear.

Sometimes the problem of increases in the value of land during the life of a project causes concern. The argument here generally is related to an assertion that speculative increases in land value or increases due to increasing urbanization are somehow not "real" increases. However, for both financial and economic analysis, a change in the value of land relative to other values is a real change and should be included in the analysis. If a dairy farm is established on the outskirts of a city where the price of land is expected to rise during the life of the investment, then the value of the land at the end of the project--the salvage value (see page 106)-- must reflect this change. This is because the alternative uses of the land will change during the life of the project and so the opportunity cost of the land will change. When the project begins, the land may really only be useful for dairying or some other farm enterprise; by the end of the project the land may be quite valuable as a factory site. The change in the price of the land reflects a true change in the contribution of the land to production. The fact that no "investment" was needed to make the land appreciate in value is beside the point. In fact, one alternative for an individual is to invest his money in land speculation, so that in financial analysis terms the treatment of land appreciation is perfectly clear. In economic analysis the fact that the opportunity cost of the land has changed during the life of the project must be included in the analysis. Otherwise, the alternative investments in the economy will not be correctly compared with the project and an erroneous choice among alternatives may result.

Taxes. Taxes are a transfer payment which require special treatment in project analysis.

In financial analysis where we are undertaking our analysis from the standpoint of an individual entity or enterprise all taxes are treated as a cost and there is no analytical problem.

In economic analysis, however, where we are considering the return to the whole society, we must allow for the fact that taxes are a transfer payment--a part of the net return from the project which is turned over to the government to spend on behalf of the society as a whole rather than by individual farmers or by the project management. Hence, taxes in economic analysis are not deducted from the income stream as a cost. This applies to all forms of taxes: income taxes, duties on imported items, and any local taxes which may be levied. Sometimes identifying the tax component in the prices which are available to you is difficult; this may be true, for instance, for imported machinery where the duties are generally not separated out in the market price. (Note that social security payments, which are often called "taxes," are really a form of deferred labor remuneration and are treated as a cost in the economic analysis.)

Subsidies.   Subsidies also pose a special problem when considering the costs of a project. They amount, in effect, to a transfer payment to the project (or to the farmers in a project) from the rest of society. A subsidy on fertilizer reduces its cost to the farmer and thereby increases his income. Of course, this may well be justified on grounds of increasing incentives to adopt new technology or perhaps even on income distribution grounds.

In financial analysis terms, subsidies raise no problems. The subsidy reduces cost and the money transfer goes to those who participate in the project.

In economic analysis terms, however, we must adjust market prices to reflect the amount of any subsidy. If subsidies operate to reduce input costs, then we must add the subsidy to the market price of the commodity. If fertilizer is subsidized so that it sells at only 80 percent of its true cost to the society, then if we are to compare our agricultural project with alternative investments in the society, we must add one-fourth to the cost of the fertilizer used in the project. If the subsidy operates to raise prices, then in economic analysis we must deduct the amount of the subsidy from the market value of the product before entering it in our economic analysis.

Benefits of agricultural projects

Benefits in agricultural projects can arise either from an increased value of output or from reduced costs. The specific forms in which benefits appear, however, are not always obvious and valuation problems may be exceedingly difficult.

Increased value of output. The most common form of benefit in agricultural projects is an increase in the value of output.

Greater physical production. Increased value of production can most obviously arise from increased physical production of a crop or livestock product--providing the market and price relationships are such that the greater physical volume does not simply trigger a more-than-offsetting fall in price. Since most agricultural projects are not large enough in themselves that they will significantly affect price relationships, the interrelation of prices and production increases is usually not a problem in project evaluation. It can be, however, where projects are large relative to their proposed market or where there may be a rapidly growing supply of the commodity to be produced by the project.

The ways in which projects can increase physical production are virtually unlimited. An irrigation project is proposed to permit better water control so that farmers can obtain higher yields. Young trees are planted on cleared jungle land to increase the area devoted to oil palm production. A credit project makes available capital resources so that farmers may increase their expenditures both on production expenses--fertilizer, seeds, or pesticides, for example--and on investment--a tubewell or a piece of agricultural machinery. The benefit is the increased production from the farm.

In a large proportion of agricultural projects the increase in production will be marketed through commercial channels. Identifying the benefit from commercial production is easy although there may be problems of valuation when you try to determine the appropriate price.

However, in many agricultural projects the benefits may well include increased production which is eaten by the farm family itself. The economic value of this home consumed production is just as much a real return to the economy as if the production had been sold on the market. We could think, for example, of a hypothetical case of a farmer selling his output and then buying it back. Home consumed production is part of the total wealth available to the nation for the use of its citizens in exactly the same way as is commercial production. It enters into national accounts just as if it were marketed. Hence, despite difficulties of valuing home consumed production, it clearly belongs among the project benefits. Omitting it will tend to make projects producing commercial crops seem relatively too profitable and lead perhaps to poor choice among projects. Failure to include home consumed production will also tend to understate the value of agricultural projects relative to investments elsewhere in the economy.

When home consumed crops bulk large in a project, the importance of careful financial analysis is increased. Farm family net benefits -- including both the value of home consumed production and money from off farm sales--will, of course, be estimated. But so, also, will net cash surplus. From the estimate of cash income one can determine if farmers will have the money they need for purchasing modern inputs or will have the cash in hand to repay credit obligations. It is quite possible to have a project in which home consumed output increases enough that the return to the economy as a whole is attractive but where so little of the increased output is sold that farmers will not have the cash to repay their loans.

Quality improvement. In some instances, a benefit from an agricultural project may take the form of a quality improvement. In Ecuador, for example, one analysis for a credit project to make loans to beef cattle producers assumes not only that ranchers will be able to increase their cattle production but also that their new investments will enable them to increase the quality of their animals so that the average live price of steers per kilogram will rise from

5.20 sucres to 6.40 sucres in constant value terms over the twelve-year development period. Loans to dairy farmers may be intended to permit them to switch from producing market milk for processing to milk of a high enough quality for fresh consumption. Most often in agricultural projects both increased output and quality improvements are expected, but this is not necessarily the case. One word of warning: be careful when estimating quality improvement benefits since it is easy to overestimate both their rate and extent.

Changes in location and time of sale. In some agricultural marketing projects the benefits will arise from improved marketing which changes the location and the time at which the product is sold. A grain storage project may make it possible to hold grain from the harvest period when the price is at its seasonal minimum to a time later in the year when the price has risen. The benefit of the storage investment arises out of this change in "temporal value." Other marketing activities may include transportation to carry products from the area where they are produced and prices are low to distant markets where prices are higher. The benefits of the project arise from the change in "location value." In most cases the increased value arising from marketing projects will be split between farmers and marketing firms as the forces of supply and demand increase the price at which the farmer can sell in the harvest season and reduce the monopoly power of the marketing firm or agency. Many projects are structured to assure that farmers receive a larger part of the benefit by making it possible for them to build storage facilities on their farms or to band together in storage cooperatives, but an agricultural project could just as well involve a private marketing firm or a government agency with much of the benefit accruing to someone other than farmers.

Changes in form (grading and processing). Loans to agricultural processing industries anticipate a benefit which will arise from a change in the form of the agricultural product. Farmers sell paddy to millers who, in turn sell polished rice. The benefit arises from the change in form. Canners preserve fruit, changing its form and making it possible to change its time of sale or location more cheaply. Even such a simple processing activity as a grading shed gives rise to a benefit through changing the form of the product from run-of-the-orchard to sorted fruit.

Cost reduction. In addition to increased value of output, benefits in agricultural projects may arise from a reduction in costs.

Gains from mechanization. The classic example of cost reduction is investment in agricultural machinery to reduce labor costs which may happen where tubewells substitute for hand drawn or animal drawn water, pedal threshers replace hand threshing, or that favorite example, tractors, replace animal draft power. Total production may not increase, but there is a benefit arising because the costs have been trimmed (providing, of course, that any labor displaced can be productively employed elsewhere).

Reduced transportation costs. Cost reduction is a major source of benefits in agricultural marketing projects where transportation is a factor. Better transportation may reduce the cost of moving produce from the farm to the consumer with a resulting benefit which may be distributed among farmers, truckers, and consumers.

Losses avoided. One kind of cost reduction benefit may arise because of a loss avoided. This kind of benefit stream is not always obvious, but it is one which the "with" and "without" test tends to point up clearly. In Jamaica lethal yellowing is attacking the Jamaica Tall coconut variety. A large-scale investment is being undertaken by the Government of Jamaica to enable farmers to plant Malayan Dwarf coconuts which are resistant. Total production will change very little as a result of the investment. Yet farmers and the economy will realize a real benefit because of the loss of the former income which is avoided through the new investment. Projects for irrigation system maintenance or soil conservation may not envision any increase in production. Instead, the benefit arises from the loss of irrigation water avoided or the soil erosion prevented. Simple storage projects may avoid rodent damage.

Sometimes a given project increases output through avoiding loss--a kind of double classification by this listing but one which in practice gives no problem. Proposals for eradication of foot and mouth disease in Latin America envision projects in which the loss of thriftiness or outright loss of animals through death would be avoided. Beef production, of course, would be at the same time increased.

Other kinds of direct benefits. Those concerned with agricultural development may find other kinds of direct benefits arising from their projects. In agricultural education projects, one means of valuing the benefit is to make an assessment of the increased earning capacity of an agricultural vocational school graduate over what would have been the case had he gone to work with only a primary education. It is assumed that the investment in his education will give rise to a flow of benefits to the better educated individual which will continue over his working career. Transportation projects are often very important for agricultural development. Benefits may arise not only from cost reduction in marketing--as noted earlier--but from time savings, accident reduction, or new development activities induced in areas opened for the first time by reasonably priced market access.

If new housing for farmers has been included among the costs of a project, as is often the case for irrigation and land settlement projects, then among the benefits will be an allowance year by year for the rental value of the housing. Since this will generally be an imputed benefit and not a competitively determined market price, it may be difficult to establish an appropriate value. There is a tendency to plan for housing which is unduly expensive. If this is done, the benefit which the housing produces is considerably above the rent which farmers would be willing or able to pay, given the level of their incomes. Generally, it is inappropriate to provide for expensive housing in planning a project and then to allow a high imputed annual benefit from the housing. Although this might not affect the economic analysis significantly, since farmers would not be able to pay the full cost of their housing they would gain the benefit without paying for it, requiring a housing subsidy from the government. In some cases this might not be considered undesirable, but because farmers on new irrigation or settlement areas are already expected to benefit substantially from being able to participate while equally deserving farm families cannot, it seems inappropriate to plan an additional benefit in the form of subsidized housing. (There are difficult questions about appropriate design for housing which we cannot touch upon here except to point them out as technical problems and to note that many authorities suggest the best approach to housing is to provide new settlers with building materials and to permit them to construct their own houses. Not only will the houses then be of a design acceptable to the settlers, but the costs of the housing will be kept down, perhaps making it possible to provide a high standard of housing without the need of a subsidy.)

Secondary costs and benefits

The realization that projects can lead to benefits being created or costs being incurred which arise outside the project itself has led to the argument that economic analyses should allow for "secondary" costs and benefits to be attributed to project investments. (Of course, this would be important only in economic analysis; the problem does not arise in financial analysis.) Both identifying and valuing these secondary effects has been the subject of a substantial and continuing exchange among economists. A good place to begin reading about this debate is the survey article on benefit-cost analysis by Prest and Turvey (22) from which much of the following discussion is drawn. Another discussion of a highly technical nature is found in Mishan (20), and I have benefited greatly from the discussion in Ward (29) (and from Professor Ward's assistance with this section).

Contemporary discussions of secondary effects generally distinguish among three varieties of such benefits: (1) the "customary" variety of "stemming from" and "induced by" generally treated analytically by adjusting price relationships to reflect opportunity costs more adequately but sometimes treated by considering a project investment to have "multiplier" effects; (2) those due to scale economies; and (3) "dynamic secondary effects" which actually change the form or productivity of the resources involved. While it may be true that in terms of the economic development aspects of public investment the scale effects and the dynamic effects hold the greatest potential for large-scale impacts on the economy, they are by nature so difficult to evaluate that few attempts have been made to deal with them empirically. Analysts still do not have enough information about scale effects in projects to be able adequately to predict their magnitude or occurrence. Dynamic secondary effects prove extremely difficult to analyze given the existing state of economic development theory. Thus, the attempts which have been made to analyze scale effect and dynamic secondary effects have been of a largely theoretical nature and have little operational significance. Faced with these theoretical obstacles, economists concerned with secondary costs and benefits have spent most of their time and effort attempting to identify and measure the "stemming from" and the "induced by" effects.

Even a definition of secondary costs and benefits has given the profession difficulties. The most common example of secondary benefits which is used to illustrate "stemming from" and "induced by" effects--and the one which Prest and Turvey cite--is that of the new values which arise as a result of increased grain production from a new irrigation project. The direct benefit (in these discussions often termed the "primary" benefit) is the value of the increase in the grain output less the associated increase in the farmers' costs. The increased grain output, however, will involve increased activities by grain merchants, transportation concerns, millers, bakers, and so on, and, hence, give rise to an increase in their profits. If these new profits total, say, half the increase in the value of grain at the farm gate then it is argued that secondary benefits equal to this amount should be credited to the irrigation project investment. This is an example of "stemming" or "forward" linkage secondary benefits; "induced" or "backward linkage" secondary benefits, in contrast, are the extra profits made by firms which sell inputs to farmers.

The most commonly mentioned secondary benefit in developing countries is that of employment. It is argued that in many countries substantial unemployment and underemployment exists. By investing in a project new employment opportunities are created, and new wealth is generated. Further, as newly employed people spend their wages additional employment is created as new service and production opportunities open up--a "multiplier" effect arising from the project investment which could properly be attributed to the project as a secondary benefit.

When there is a properly functioning price mechanism--one which accurately reflects the true values of the commodities--the argument in favor of including secondary costs and benefits in a project analysis becomes highly questionable. Taking the example which Prest and Turvey give, the market demand for wheat is a "derived" demand--one which arises from a "final" demand for bread from consumers--and so reflects the value of extra bread and the marginal costs for transportation, milling, and baking. In such a price environment, the values of wheat, transportation, bread and so on are properly estimated, as is the value of the increased grain produced and the increased farm costs. All capital resources and all labor would be productively employed. The estimate of direct benefits obtained by using the price of wheat and the price of farm inputs is an adequate reflection of all the project benefits and no secondary effects would arise.

The problem is, of course, that such perfectly adjusted market structures only rarely exist, at least in developing countries. When market prices fail to reflect true costs and benefits and where there is unemployed or underemployed labor then project investments can lead to benefits not incorporated into an analysis based solely on market prices. There are two ways to deal with this in order that projects can be ranked appropriately taking into account both the primary and secondary benefits. The more straightforward and simpler is to impute a new price for those items which are not properly valued by the price mechanism and to use these prices--the "shadow" prices discussed in the next chapter--in the economic (not financial) analysis of the project. In effect, this means that at least the largest part of all the effects which can be identified whether "primary" or "secondary" are incorporated directly into the project analysis and imputed as direct benefits to the project investment. Projects can then be ranked by their relative effectiveness in utilizing resources and no further adjustments need be made to allow for secondary effects. This is the method which most international lending agencies, including the World Bank, employ and which is outlined in this book. It is also the method proposed by Little and Mirrlees (17) although their adjustments in the market prices are much more extensive than those commonly in use (see pages 43 to 46).

An alternative approach to allowing for secondary benefits is to increase the benefit derived at market prices by some factor which represents the "multiplier" of the investment. Since different kinds of investments (or, at least, public sector investments as opposed to private sector investments) could have different secondary effects, this adjustment would permit ranking different projects according to their overall impact on the economy including both their primary and their secondary effects. (An incidental advantage to such an approach is that all values are stated at market prices so that the implications of a public sector investment for the government budget become immediately apparent without needing to adjust the figures used in the project analysis. This has obvious advantages for those concerned with national planning.)

In the professional literature discussing this approach, attention has been focused for the most part on aggregate demand relationships and the Keynesian "multiplier" concept.[1,2] Indeed, in most such discussions the very definition of secondary benefits has been that of an aggregate multiplier effect. "Multipliers" in this context generally refer to the relation between some welfare-related dependent variable and an independent "policy" variable subject to manipulation from without, in this case generally the project investment.

It turns out, however, that there are many such relationships and thus it is simplistic to think in terms of "the multiplier," although most discussions tend to make that assumption. The basic approach to secondary effects analysis through the multiplier effect has tended to revolve around the estimation of aggregate changes in output resulting from the secondary impacts of increased expenditures due to a public project. A multiplier concept in some form has been derived to estimate these impacts. Yet the conditions under which the full multiplier effects of an agricultural project as they are typically estimated would constitute a real net change in welfare are specific and operationally very limiting: (1) the public expenditure is not financed out of tax revenues so that the multiplier-creating expenditures are not drawn away from the private sector; (2) the conditions of supply for all factors stimulated to employment by the investment are perfectly elastic at prevailing prices; (3) the opportunity costs of those factors in the absence of the investment are zero; and (4) the outputs which result do not simply substitute for other products in the market place and, thus, do not result in unemployment for other factors of production. That none of these conditions hold fully in the general case should

---

1   Formally, the Keynesian investment multiplier is defined as the reciprocal of one minus the marginal propensity to consume, $(\frac{1}{1 - MPC})$

2   This section closely follows Ward (29) and is used here with the author's permission.

be apparent, although, of course, some or all partially hold in many cases. Attempts to quantify the impact of multiplier effects, have, however, tended to assume that all of these conditions are fully met, and thus the "secondary benefits" which have been generally estimated using secondary impact analysis are really not net secondary benefits at all, even from the viewpoint of the factors being employed, but rather are gross changes in the demand for these factors. As a result, empirical estimates using multipliers have exhibited a consistent tendency to overestimate the real welfare effects of secondary impacts. The gross change in demand for a factor could be taken as fully a secondary benefit only if its supply curve were perfectly elastic at zero price--that is, it had absolutely no other alternatives. Given these very restrictive conditions, secondary effects estimated from most projects will be grossly miscalculated using multiplier analysis alone without substantial adjustments.

The literature on secondary effects shows a marked reticence by economists to admit of any net national project benefits beyond primary benefits computed by estimating multipliers. While most of this reticence is based on logical deductions from economic theory, much of it appears to have been motivated by the observed misuse of multiplier concepts by field analysts. Attempts to use multipliers to estimate secondary benefits for use in water resources projects in the United States, for instance, have tended to result in estimates which greatly exceeded the proportions which theorists had expected. At the same time, however, most theorists have been particularly concerned about the secondary effects in regions having severe unemployment problems. As a result, professional discussions regarding secondary effects have tended to emphasize the possibility of secondary benefits in instances of severe unemployment while playing down the possibility or at least the importance of a secondary benefit in all other situations.

A case where secondary benefits may be important and which is of particular interest to those concerned with agricultural projects arises when development roads are to be built into hitherto inaccessible areas. It is argued that the production arising because of the induced investment activities of otherwise unemployed new settlers should be considered a secondary benefit of the road investment. This would seem to be a case of dynamic secondary effects and it proves extremely difficult to deal with in project analyses. One way of avoiding this problem is to view such a case as a land settlement project of which the road forms a component part. New production is then properly included among the direct benefits of the project, can be valued at market or shadow prices, and no attempt need be made to allocate the benefits between the road investment and the other kinds of investment which must be made by settlers and the government if settlement is to succeed.

A group of what have been called secondary costs have also been the subject of discussion in the professional literature. These have been termed "technological spillover" or "technological externalities." An example is the increased cost for dredging which arises downstream when a dam reduces river flow. These costs have been termed secondary because they occur away from the project site, but a better approach is to consider that they are direct costs of the project wherever they may occur and to include them as such in the economic analysis. In recent years adverse ecological effects have been mentioned as among the secondary costs of projects. Again, these are technological spillovers and when they can be valued (or the costs of averting them can be estimated) they should properly be incorporated as among the direct costs of the project even if they do not occur at the project site.

Although the debate about secondary benefits persists in the economic literature and attempts continue to be made to incorporate some notion of secondary effects in project analysis through the use of a multiplier--especially in the United States--the weight of professional opinion remains skeptical. It seems best to conclude that for the present for most projects in developing countries it is better not to try to allow for secondary effects through the use of a multiplier. The major kinds of secondary benefits which are agreed to exist are better incorporated into the economic analysis by using shadow prices to reflect true opportunity costs. This appropriately treats the resulting benefits as being primary in nature and as arising directly from the project investment. The practice of the World Bank and that of most other international lending agencies reflects this conclusion.

Intangible benefits

Almost every agricultural project has a group of costs and benefits which are "intangible." These may include better income distribution, national integration, national defense, or just a better life for rural people. Such intangibles are real and reflect true values. They do not, however, lend themselves well to valuation, although an attempt is sometimes made. (In the United States, irrigation projects will sometimes include among their benefits an allowance for improved recreation.) In most cases it would seem economic and financial analysis is an inappropriate tool to use for dealing with intangible effects. In any event, the final selection of a project depends on a whole range of considerations which must of necessity rest on subjective judgment. In one sense, that is what we are saying when we say that projects give rise to intangible effects. The best practice seems to be to acknowledge that intangible effects exist and are important but not to attempt to value them nor to include them in the economic analysis computations.

3. SELECTING PROPER VALUES

Once costs and benefits have been identified, if they are to
be compared they must be valued. Since the only means to compare
differing goods and services directly is by giving them a money price,
this comes down to saying we must find the proper prices at which
to enter costs and benefits into our analysis of agricultural projects.

Prices reflect values

Underlying all economic and financial analysis is an
assumption that prices reflect values or can be adjusted to do so.
Unless you have delved into economic theory a bit, it may not have
occurred to you to worry much about this, but the fact is that
market prices do not always do a good job of reflecting economic
values.

Basically, economists hold that a "perfect" market--one which
is highly competitive with many buyers and sellers--will wind up
with every economic commodity priced at its marginal value
product. That is, the price of every good and service will just exactly
reflect the value the last unit utilized of that item contributes to
production. Whenever a unit of goods or services can produce more
in some other activity, its price will rise and it will be attracted
there. When the economy is in "equilibrium," the "opportunity
cost"--the best use in an alternative production process--the marginal
value product, and the price will all be equal. Resources will then
have been allocated through the price mechanism to that use where
the last unit utilized of every good and service in the economy is
at its most productive use; no transfer of resources could result in
greater output. Obviously, however, "perfect" markets do not exist,
and, hence, prices do not always reflect values.

Without trying to push any further into price theory, we can
turn to some direct implications for agricultural projects of this
assumption that prices reflect values.

First, let it be noted that although markets are imperfect and
prices subject to question, there is a large nugget of truth in the
theory. Generally, the best approximation of a "true value" of
a good or service which is traded is its market price. Put another
way, if you can find a market price for an item, that is normally
the best price to use in valuing either a cost or a benefit. In financial
analysis, as we have noted, you <u>always</u> use the market price or your
best estimate of it. In economic analysis, on the other hand, you

may feel some price other than the market price is a better indicator
of the value of a good or service--a so-called "shadow price," a
subject to which we return below. Remember, however, that the
burden of proof is on you. In most instances, it is better to devote
your time to trying to find the appropriate market price--not always
an easy task, either--than to trying to determine a shadow price.

In all project evaluations it should be kept in mind that
economic and financial analyses primarily deal with considerations
of costs and benefits which are quantifiable in money terms. There
are many, many other, nonquantifiable or noneconomic values which
must be considered in a final judgment about whether to go ahead
with one project or another. These values range all the way from
considerations of national identity or national defense to such values
as reduced water pollution, recreation benefits, or the advantages
of literacy. Economists keep trying to enlarge their ability to attach
monetary values to these benefits since the resources they require
for realization must compete with alternate uses for clearly
quantifiable benefits--increased rice production for hungry people,
say, versus a better environment. But in the end, every project
must ultimately be accepted or rejected on the basis of a subjective
judgment about its worth; economic and financial analysis contribute
to improving the quality of that judgment, but they do not replace
it. The inadequacy of prices as a measure of values is only one
more reason why this is the case.

Which price to use?

If some sort of market price is probably the best
approximation of the "true" value of a good or service in an
agricultural project, which price should we use? Often, even in a
relatively good market, the problem of choosing the right price is
not all that easy.

Point of first sale and intermediate goods. Other things being
equal, perhaps the best place to value the output of a project is
at the point of first sale. If the point of first sale is in a relatively
competitive market and we can accept the price as a relatively good
one (that is, a relatively accurate reflection of its true marginal value
product) or if we can find an acceptable shadow price, then this
provides a good measure of the value of the output.

During the production process there are often important
intermediate goods--items used primarily as an input for some other
production process--which are not freely sold. In that case, we may
find we must define our project in such a way as to carry the
production process forward to the point of first sale. Irrigation
water is a good example. The "product" of an irrigation
system--water--is, of course, really intended for use to produce

agricultural products and the price is generally determined administratively, not by any play of competitive market forces. If we were to try to separate out the irrigation system from the production it facilitates, we would be faced with a very difficult problem of determining the value of irrigation water. Hence, it is not surprising most irrigation projects take the value of the agricultural products which are offered on a relatively free market at the point of first sale as the basis for the benefit stream. Again, pullets might be valued as the output of the rearing enterprise on a farm and "sold" to the egg production enterprise. But if there is no active market for pullets, how are they to be valued? Note, however, that in many countries where pullets could not be valued, there is an active market for feeder cattle, an "intermediate good" economically quite comparable to a pullet. Each project will simply have to be defined in terms of its own market situation.

Farm gate price. In agricultural projects, the point of first sale at which it is generally desirable to value new production (or production foregone) is the "farm gate" price--the price the farmer receives when he sells the product at the boundary of his farm. The additional value added to the product as it is processed and delivered to a market for sale arises as payment for marketing services. This value added is not properly attributed to the project investment for production but rather to the labor and capital engaged in the marketing service.

If, on the other hand, the project is a marketing project or has a marketing component--perhaps because there is no competitive market channel reaching down to the farmer level for the unprocessed output--then we become concerned with both the farm gate price if that is the input into our marketing project and the price at which the product is sold in a market.

In projects producing for organized markets, the farm gate price may not be too difficult to determine. This is the case for palm oil in Malaysia or for milk in Jamaica where the price quoted the farmer is the price on his farm and the person responsible for the marketing comes to the farm and picks up the product. In many cases, however, the prices which we can find recorded include services which we will not properly be able to attribute to the project itself. This may happen, for instance, when the only price series available for a product is that at which it is sold in a central market--such as the price for eggs in Madras, for melons in Tehran, or for vegetables in Nairobi. In that case, if we are thinking of a production project, the project analyst will have to dig deeper to find out how to adjust the time series available to him to reduce it to the farm gate price.

The farm gate price is generally the best price at which to value home consumed production. In some cases it may be extremely difficult to determine just what is a realistic farm gate price for a crop produced primarily for home consumption because rather little of it really appears on markets. This is the case, for example, for manioc and cocoyam in Africa where some argue that the true value of the crop is overstated if the market prices are used as a basis for valuation. Even so, home consumed production should be valued at your best estimate of a valid farm gate price and included in your project analysis.

The farm gate price itself may be skewed in terms of economic analysis. In Ghana the Marketing Board takes off some proportion of the cocoa price as a tax for development purposes. In Thailand, until recently a rice "premium"--that is, a tax on rice exports--effectively kept the domestic price well below that which the international market would have paid. In these cases, the true value of the product will have to be considered higher than the actual farm gate price--you will have to select a "shadow price." In other instances just the opposite happens. In Mexico the price of corn is maintained at a high level to transfer income to ejidatarios, the small farmers. In Malaysia the rice price is supported to encourage local production and reduce imports. In these cases, some amount of the price does not really reflect the economic value of the product, but rather an income transfer to small farmers. Again, you may have to resort to shadow prices to reflect the true value of the product.

Seasonal fluctuation. Agricultural commodities generally are subject to substantial seasonal fluctuation. If this is the case, then you must make some decision about the point in the seasonal fluctuation at which to choose the price you will use for your analysis. A good starting point is the farm gate harvest price at the peak of the harvest season. This is probably close to the lowest price during the cycle. The argument here is that as prices rise during the cycle, at least some part of that rise is a result not of the productive activity of the farmer but of the marketing services embodied in storing the crop until consumers want it. But, markets being what they are, there may be an element of imperfection in the harvest price level. Market channels may become so glutted that merchants are actively trying to discourage farmers from marketing their crop immediately. The need to sell immediately to meet debt obligations may force farmers to offer their crops at artificially low prices. In some cases, therefore, you may wish to select a price higher than the farm gate harvest season price. But there is an obligation here to justify the price chosen as more valid than the harvest price. (One way to resolve this problem in certain projects may be to include an element of credit in the project design. This will permit farmers to store their product on their farms until prices have had a chance to rise from their seasonal lows.)

Grades. Prices vary among grades, of course, and picking the proper price for project analysis may involve making some decisions about grades. Generally, it is possible to assume farmers will produce in the future much the same quality as they have in the past, and will market their product ungraded. In many agricultural projects, however, one objective is to upgrade the quality of production as well as to increase the total output. In this case you may want to assume that small dairy farmers will be able with the help of the project investment to meet the fluid market standards of sanitation and command a higher price, or that reduced delivery times. will hold down the sucrose inversion in sugar cane, or that better pruning will increase the average size of the oranges Moroccan farmers can offer European buyers. Then the proper price to select is the average price expected for the quality to be produced.

Predicting future prices. For most agricultural projects you will be faced with the task of predicting changes in commodity prices over the lifetime of the project. For many crops the likelihood of a relative change in prices is not as great as the likelihood that the relative price will remain much as it has been in the past. Hence, the best general guide to future prices is those of the past decade or so. Only when there is a clear-cut case for changing the relative prices would it seem justified to abandon the assumption that the relative prices of agricultural commodities will remain the same. Future prices for food grains are probably the least difficult to estimate. Although grain prices will vary some in relation to other prices, the production of food grains is so large and so basic that probably you can use a "conservative" price based on the past decade or so to predict prices for the next twenty years. In the case of a number of other commodities, however, predicting future prices may not prove so easy. At this writing, for example, the price of palm oil, which has been hovering at rather high levels, is expected to move sharply downwards because of rising world production of vegetable oil. In such a case, obviously, you would have to estimate the benefits of your project on the basis of declining prices.

Where can you turn for information about future price trends? For domestic food crops, the chances are there will be no systematic studies you can use, and you will have to seek out knowledgeable people and ask them their opinions. On the basis of these conversations you may be able to judge whether the relative prices will drift downwards or tend to rise. In Iran, for example, it seems likely the relative price of food grains will not rise much over the next two decades because of the availability of new technology to increase production and the likelihood of plentiful supplies of wheat on the world market which could be imported if wheat prices begin to rise too sharply. On the other hand, the already seriously overgrazed pastures will not permit much increase in sheep numbers even though rising per capita incomes point to a rapid growth in the demand for mutton. Clearly, the relative price of mutton will rise. How much? Some idea may perhaps be available from a look at the income elasticities (that is, the proportionate increase in the amount spent for meat when there is a rise in incomes), but the chances are that in most countries--like Iran--no formalized studies have been carried out. You will have to make a guess based on informed judgment--meat prices, say, will rise relatively by a fourth compared to wheat over the next twenty years.

In the case of internationally traded commodities, there is more help available. Countries which depend to an important extent upon a major export crop probably should have a small group somewhere in the government whose responsibility it is to keep on top of commodity production and price trends. These people may be able to suggest a plausible trend to be expected for the internationally traded commodities important for your country--rubber for Malaysia, cocoa for Ghana, coffee for Brazil, and the like. You will also want to turn to the price and production projections of the major international agencies. FAO maintains an elaborate structure of commodity studies and publishes periodic projections of future prices. These are available to any member government. The World Bank also has a commodity group which studies likely future trends in production and prices, and the results of its research are available to member governments for project analysis, whether or not you expect to finance the project with a World Bank loan. The major international commodity associations also maintain groups which study production and price trends. The Rubber Study Group, the International Coffee Secretariat, and the secretariat of the International Grains Arrangement are examples. Research results from these groups are readily available to members of the organizations, and you can use their reports to form a judgment about what may happen to future prices. Finally, agencies in some of the developed countries undertake studies of production and price trends of commodities of interest to them and these projections are usually available without charge or restriction to governments of developing countries. The United States Department of Agriculture--probably the most important example--publishes elaborate and detailed commodity studies for most major crops traded in international markets.

A problem similar to that of agricultural commodity price changes will face you when you consider if the prices of inputs are likely to increase or decrease relatively to all other prices. The problem does not seem so difficult, however. Industrial products have less of a tendency to fluctuate, but you may wish to consider whether you think the long-term relative price of labor may rise or perhaps whether the long-term price of nitrogenous fertilizer will rise as the current overcapacity is absorbed by growing world fertilizer demand.

Year-to-year fluctuations. As for the problem of year-to-year and longer term price fluctuations, it is likely that for most economic and financial analyses they should be ignored. It is true, of course, that agricultural commodities tend to be subject to rather marked price swings from year to year, but since the discounted measures of project worth which we will discuss really estimate an average return to capital over the whole of the life of the project, such price fluctuations are averaged out in the analysis. In any event, who is brave enough to predict price swings?

Inflation

Most countries have an experience of inflation and the only realistic assessment of the future is that inflation will continue. This raises the question of how to cope with inflation in project analysis. One means would be to inflate all costs and returns by what you expect will be an average rate of inflation. However, this is cumbersome and unnecessary (and may sidetrack discussion of your analysis to a discussion of probable rates of inflation). Much the better solution if it accurately reflects your expectation of reality is to assume that all prices on both the cost side and the benefit side will rise uniformly by the same proportion and that therefore they will not change their relative values. Then your analytical procedure can be simply to value all future prices at today's levels, knowing full well that future money prices will rise. This is equivalent, of course, to deflating all costs and benefits by some kind of price index, say, keeping all prices constant in terms of 1972 dollars.

Of course, if it is your expectation that inflation will have a different impact on some prices than on others, then your analysis will have to reflect the change in relative prices. Such differences might occur, for example, if you think the domestic rate of inflation will be different from that of world inflation or if you think inflation will affect costs to a different degree than benefits. In such a case, it is likely the best procedure is to assume constant prices for all items except the ones which you think will be affected to a different degree by inflation. Then the prices for those items you think will

be influenced differentially, can be increased or decreased to reflect
your views about relative changes in prices arising from the differing
impact of inflation. (The use of a contingency allowance in a project
analysis to allow for inflation is discussed on pages 100 to 104.)

There is a special problem introduced by inflation in credit
projects. Although this is not an analytical problem, it becomes
very serious for farmers and administrators. If inflation is expected,
what can be done to maintain the value of money lent to farmers,
especially in the form of longer term loans? If farmers are lent
money at a "reasonable" interest rate--one, say, thought to be close
to the true opportunity cost of capital--then the real value of their
loan may fall if there is inflation. To avoid this windfall to
borrowers, some countries arbitrarily increase the rate of interest
charged--say, from 12 percent which is thought to be a "true"
opportunity cost to around 18 percent which will allow for a fall
in the value of the currency. Such adjustments tend to be arbitrary
and inaccurate. Other countries--Brazil is an example--have worked
out an index based on agricultural prices. Repayments of certain
long-term loans in Brazil are pegged to this index, and no allowance
for inflation is included in the interest charges.

Shadow prices

Shadow prices (which some economists prefer to call
"accounting prices") are a very tricky and controversial aspect of
the economic analysis of projects. In this brief discussion we will
hardly deal with the theoretical problems that are raised; instead
I will suggest pragmatic solutions to some problems of shadow
pricing applied to agricultural projects. More theoretical economists
will not agree, probably; but we must get on somehow with our
project analysis and with the development program. (Note that the
whole question of shadow prices refers only to economic analysis.
In financial analysis, as we noted, use the market prices actually
to be paid, whatever the "true" value and, hence, the shadow price
might be for purposes of economic analysis.)

For various reasons, markets are imperfect. There may be
institutional rigidities, price controls, imperfect information about
prices offered by competing sellers or buyers, monopoly elements,
"traditional" prices, and so forth. The list is endless. Because these
imperfections exist, the use of market prices may introduce a
significant error into the economic analysis of a project. The price
of foreign exchange may be too low, for example, tending to favor
projects with a high import content. Or the wages paid to labor
may be too high, tending to favor capital intensive projects over
labor intensive projects. To avoid these biases in the analysis of
projects, we may use instead of the market price, a shadow price

which is intended to reflect the "true" value of the commodity or service. For purposes of operational project analysis, a shadow price may be defined as that price which would prevail in the economy if it were in perfect equilibrium under conditions of perfect competition.

The rub, of course, comes in trying to find out what is the shadow price. Theoretically, it would be possible to work out a giant econometric model for the economy and to use that to define all the prices in the system, but only the most ambitious computer enthusiast would want to embark on such an effort. So, in practice, a much less elaborate approximation of the shadow price is used in project analysis (and in national economic planning, too, I might add).

In agricultural projects there are generally only three areas where I feel anyone trying to do an economic analysis should consider the use of shadow prices rather than market prices. These are for foreign exchange, for commodities which are important in world markets, and for unskilled agricultural labor.

Foreign exchange. For those concerned with analysis of agricultural projects the easiest shadow price to dispose of is that for foreign exchange. My suggestion is simple: use the shadow price (that is, rate of exchange) which the central planning unit is using. For one thing, if some projects use one shadow price for foreign exchange and others use another, the whole point of using shadow prices to value import content correctly and uniformly in various alternative investment analyses is lost. Furthermore, trying to estimate the foreign exchange shadow price yourself is time consuming and tricky. If you use the shadow price for foreign exchange which the central planning unit uses, then any questions about how the rate was set may be passed on to them, and you can proceed with the problems of agricultural projects.

There may, of course, be cases where you disagree with the central planning unit and think some foreign exchange rate other than the one they use would be more appropriate. My suggestion in that instance is that you take the question up with them and try to persuade them of the validity of your case, not that you arbitrarily change the exchange rate you adopt in your economic analysis.

World market prices. The second kind of shadow price which seems to make good sense in analysis of agricultural projects is the use of world market prices in place of domestic prices in protected markets. The reasoning here is that world markets--whatever their drawbacks--are more nearly perfect markets than protected markets. Thus the world market price for wheat is more nearly a true measure of the "value" of wheat than a domestic price. In the last resort, you could always choose to import wheat rather than to increase domestic production.   If your shadow price for foreign exchange is right, this would not introduce a bias into your analysis.

All the kinds of problems we touched upon in discussing which price to choose reappear here when we try to decide which world market price to use for project analysis.   The same kinds of considerations apply: the appropriate grade, the allowance for costs of marketing from the farm gate to the point where the world market price is offered (at the port, for example), and the imperfections introduced into the world market by the existence of commodity agreements.

A point to be mentioned is that shadow prices for agricultural products should not be limited to those crops which are intended for export.   A better measure of the worth of an investment to a country may be obtained by shadow pricing the output of an agricultural commodity to be produced in a project than by using a domestic price, even if the commodity is expected to be largely locally consumed.   Thus, it would seem to me that rice in Malaysia should be shadow priced at the world market price rather than the higher domestic support price for exactly the same reason that I think cocoa should be shadow priced in Ghana rather than valued at the domestic price depressed by the Marketing Board margin.

For many crops, of course, the question of world markets hardly enters and these would have to be priced at the domestic price level--vegetables, cassava, meat, and the like.

Labor.   Now we turn to what seems to me to be the most difficult problem of shadow pricing: agricultural labor.

The price of labor in a perfectly competitive market would be determined by the marginal value product of the labor.   That is, the wage would be equal to that amount of product which an extra laborer hired would produce.   This is because it would pay a farmer to hire an additional laborer--for harvesting, for example--as long as the worker increases total output by more than the farmer has to pay for the additional labor.   If labor is short and there is an active labor market, then the wage rate is probably a fairly good approximation of the real marginal value product of labor, although imperfections in the labor market are more prevalent than for any other item for which we try to establish a price.

The problem is, of course, that in many crowded countries the addition of one more laborer may not add anything at all to the total product.   That is, if there is a surplus of agricultural workers there may be no productive outlet for their energies.   In the jargon, we may say that the marginal value product of such labor--the amount that it adds to the gross domestic product--is zero.   Since the marginal value product is also the opportunity cost of labor in equilibrium, we may make another statement: if we take labor away from a farm community where it is producing nothing and put it to work producing something, then we do not have to forego any production in order to realize the new product. If an agricultural laborer was adding nothing to the production in his community, then we lose nothing by transferring him to productive labor elsewhere. This being the case, we need not consider that this labor has any cost attached to it. Its true wage is zero because that is what it could otherwise produce. Following this line of argument, the proper price to charge in the economic (not financial!) analysis of projects would be zero. And if the labor in an agricultural project is properly priced at zero, then it is likely the rate of return will look very favorable in comparison to, say, a capital intensive alternative project which uses labor saving tractors.

Note that the validity of this argument is not changed by the fact that agricultural labor is, in fact, paid a wage. This may well be due to a "traditional" concept of the "proper" wage, or to social pressures on the farmers who are better off in a community to share their wealth with their less fortunate neighbors. In parts of Java, for example, social custom prevents even quite small farmers from harvesting their own rice. Instead, they must permit landless laborers to do the work, even though the farmer himself may well have the time to do it. This is consciously seen by the community as a means to provide at least a little something for the poorest agricultural laborers.

A common example where a "wage" is paid even though no productive work is available is found in the case of family labor. Older children and the farmer's wife will most certainly be entitled to a share of the family income, even if the family farm is too small to give them an opportunity to be productive. In this instance, if an older son were to find productive employment elsewhere, the total production on the family farm would not be reduced. Alternatively, if we can help the farmer add a new enterprise or make available irrigation to permit him to double crop, the new production comes at no expense of other production foregone. From the standpoint of the labor, the additional production represents a net addition to wealth at zero cost. (Of course, there may be other costs associated with double cropping and these would be real. The concrete used to line the irrigation canal, for instance, could have been used to build an urban building, and thus would not be shadow priced at zero).

At one time there was a large body of professional opinion which held marginal value product of labor in a number of Asian countries was, indeed, zero. More recently, professional opinion has swung to the view that the marginal value product is not quite zero, but often very close to it. A good discussion of the whole question of the marginal value product of agricultural labor will be found in Kao, Anschel, and Eicher (14).

Now in practical terms where does this leave us? The problem of determining the "true" marginal value product of agricultural labor in an economy is extremely difficult. For purposes of project analysis, it would seem this question can be simplified without doing undue harm to the economic realities.

In some crowded communities the marginal value product of agricultural labor may be so close to zero as to make zero a good approximation of the real value. This would be the case where there is thought to be widespread disguised unemployment or where family labor cannot be adequately ultilized. In these cases, it seems justified to shadow price unskilled agricultural labor at zero.

In other communities, there may be a very seasonal pattern to agricultural employment. During the harvest, for example, farmers may not be able to hire enough labor to bring in their crop as fast as they would like to. In rice producing countries there may well be a shortage of labor at transplanting time, too. Under these circumstances, virtually every agricultural laborer can find employment at the peak season--and casual labor from urban areas may return to their home villages to help out. Surely at these peak times, the marginal value product of agricultural labor is not zero. Thus, for purposes of agricultural project analysis, it would seem reasonable to suggest that the price of labor in these cases be valued on an annual basis at a price which is determined by multiplying the wage when labor is scarce by the number of days in a year when it can be considered that labor is reasonably fully employed. This might mean, for example, that where the going wage is Rs. 5 a day and labor is scarce for 50 days a year during planting and harvest, that the annual wage for unskilled agricultural labor for a project analysis could be shadow priced at Rs. 250, even though it was expected that the labor would work 200 days a year and be paid an annual money wage of Rs. 1,000.

The third position is to value agricultural labor at the wage it commands. This is equivalent to saying not only is the marginal value product of agricultural labor more than zero, but in fact laborers produce additional output worth something near the value of their wage. In this case there is no shadow price.

The case where farmers create their own capital items by direct investment, such as building their own houses, digging their own irrigation canals, or clearing their own land may raise questions about shadow pricing the farmers' own labor at zero. The argument is that the farmer builds his house in his spare time and consumes no more food as a result of his efforts. The house, of course, is not considered to be costless--the value of the materials is a clear cost; only the labor cost is shadow priced. In cases where farmers are working full time to create capital, as may be the case in land clearing or maintaining perennial crops until they are in production, the normal practice is to value the labor at the consumption level of the farmers. In the case of Federal Land Development Authority projects in Malaysia, for instance, the labor of farmers maintaining their own holdings before they come into production is priced at the maintenance allowance which the farm families receive. (It makes no difference in costing the labor for the economic analysis if part of this allowance is a grant and part is a loan.) In the case of land reform settlement in Chile, the Inter-American Development Bank considered the cost of the settlers' labor during the development period to be equal to the family allowance they received. Of course, if the labor of the settlers could be used elsewhere, then the going hourly or daily wage would be the proper price to use.

Although agricultural labor in a country or project area is presently unemployed or underemployed, this may not be the case ten years hence when development has had a chance to proceed. In this case, you may wish to use all three positions I have suggested: from the first to the tenth years your shadow price would be zero; from the eleventh through the twentieth years labor would be thought to be fully employed at the peak season so you shadow price agricultural labor at, say, one-half the annual money wage; and from the twenty-first year to the end of the project analysis period you use the going wage rate as the best indicator of the value of agricultural labor.

While the value of unskilled agricultural labor may reasonably be shadow priced below the going wage rate, skilled labor probably should not be. In most cases skilled labor is quite scarce, and, indeed, a case may even be made for saying certain kinds of skilled labor should be shadow priced at a level above its wage to reflect its scarcity.

Capital. Shadow pricing capital is so common in project analysis that it is frequently not recognized for what it is. Comparing proposed projects to the opportunity cost of capital instead of the actual borrowing rate, for example, amounts to using a shadow price for capital.

The Little-Mirrlees valuation method. Little and Mirrlees in their Social Cost Benefit Analysis, volume 2 of the Manual of Industrial Project Analysis in Developing Countries (17), have proposed a considerable modification of the system of shadow prices outlined in this book which they feel more adequately reflects true social costs and benefits and, thus, will lead to better project investment decisions. Their valuation system essentially prices every input and output in terms of foreign exchange or a foreign exchange based "accounting price" (the term they prefer to shadow price). They explicitly allow for planners as they determine their shadow prices to make a value judgment that a dollar's worth of savings may be worth more than a dollar's worth of consumption. Implicitly the method allows for the value judgment that consumption by lower income people has a greater social worth than consumption by those whose incomes are higher. Although their proposals are directed primarily toward industrial projects, they feel their valuation system to be equally applicable to agriculture and have illustrated its application in several unpublished case studies. (They consider it applicable, too, to power, transportation, and communications projects, but suggest it may have less usefulness in sectors such as education and health where measurement of benefits is especially difficult.) The Little-Mirrlees proposals are basically new only in the valuation system they propose to reach the shadow or accounting prices to be employed in the economic analysis. Once the appropriate accounting prices have been determined, the methodology they recommend to compare projects and to decide whether they are worthwhile implementing is the same as that discussed in connection with the net present worth criterion in the next chapter (pages 70 and 71) and could equally well be used in any social benefit-cost computation.

In the Little-Mirrlees system, all inputs and outputs are classified as either traded goods and services, nontraded goods and services, or unskilled labor. Traded goods are those which are imported or exported– or would be if the country followed policies which would result in optimum industrial development. Nontraded goods and services--of which the most important (apart from unskilled labor which is treated separately) are power, internal transportation, construction, and land--are valued by breaking the nonlabor costs down into traded goods or other nontraded goods which are, in turn, broken down until "following the chain of production around, one must eventually end at commodities that are exported or are substituted for imports" (17, Vol. 2, p. 91). Ultimately, one comes out with tradables and unskilled labor.

Valuing unskilled labor involves determining a shadow wage rate which lies somewhere between the marginal value product of agricultural labor and the amount an industrial worker will consume when employed in the proposed project. Just where this shadow wage rate lies is determined by a formula which allows for the choice a government wants to make between present and future consumption, the length of time a government feels national savings are likely to be inadequate, and the amount of extra savings generated by new investments. In practice, for industrial wages the shadow rate comes close to being set at the market wage less taxes--that is, at the consumption level. Also in practice, Little and Mirrlees imply (although they do not say so) that the shadow wage rate for agricultural labor would be established close to its marginal value product. In both cases the shadow wage would have to be revalued at international prices of those tradable goods which compose the "market basket" of goods which each class of workers consumes.

When dealing with projects in the private sector, because consumption of those who provide the funds is considered to have relatively little social value, the proportion of private profits which is consumed is treated as a social cost to the project. (The authors imply that profits going to smallholder farmers should not be treated in this manner but rather as a benefit.)

Once all inputs and outputs have been revalued in terms of their accounting price or foreign exchange, the net "social profit" for each year can be determined. This, in turn, permits judging a project using the present worth criterion outlined in the next chapter (pages 70 and 71). This involves determining the "accounting rate of interest" - analogous to the opportunity cost of capital taken up in the next chapter (pages 90 and 91) - "the rate of interest such that there is just a sufficient number of projects, with positive present social value, to add up to the total amount of investment which available savings (domestic and foreign) permit" (17, Vol. 2, p. 95).

Since the appearance of Little and Mirrlees' second volume in 1969, their valuation proposals have aroused a continuing exchange among planners in developing countries and among professional development economists. Comments about the system have centered around its complexity and whether, in fact, it leads to better investment decisions. There is little doubt that their system of determining accounting prices is difficult both to understand and to apply. Even highly trained economists admit to ambiguities in the system as Little and Mirrlees expound it and question its practical applicability. To suggest that it could be used broadly within a government appears to presuppose a supply of highly trained manpower able to devote its time to determining accounting prices which is questionable in any developing country. Little and Mirrlees themselves recognize the complexity of their proposals but have suggested that a rather small group of economists in a central planning agency could compute the most critical accounting prices for a country which all development agencies could then employ in their project analyses. A number of other accounting prices could be determined using a "standard conversion factor," a shortcut method to price items which are less important to the project. Finally, market prices could be used when the amounts involved would be too small to affect the outcome of the project investment decision.

Many have questioned whether, in fact, the Little-Mirrlees valuation system will lead to such different investment priorities as to justify the extra analytical effort it entails over, say, the method outlined in this book. After all, it is pointed out, much–perhaps even most–of the benefit from economic analysis of projects comes simply from the discipline of preparing a project in sufficient detail to undertake the economic analysis. If so, a sophisticated requirement in valuation of inputs and outputs may contribute only marginally to the usefulness of the analysis.

Few tests have been made to determine whether the Little-Mirrlees methodology would lead to a significantly different investment pattern from the valuation methodology for economic analysis outlined in this book–and even fewer to determine what effect their proposed valuation procedures might have on agricultural projects. Some preliminary tests by the World Bank staff have led to the conclusion that there would be very few, if any, changes in investment decisions were the Little-Mirrlees system adopted. (A more thorough test.is now being conducted.)

Economists in developing countries, on the whole, seem to be taking the attitude that the Little-Mirrlees method is too complex in comparison to other methods of shadow pricing to justify the additional improvement in the quality of investment decisions it might bring. Few planning agencies are attempting to introduce the method, although they are watching others' efforts to use it with considerable interest. The United Kingdom Overseas Development Administration has announced it will adopt a modified Little-Mirrlees valuation methodology in evaluating projects proposed for its assistance and has incorporated the method it proposes to use in its new Manual for Project Appraisal (24). The German bilateral assistance agency has also announced its intention to use a modified Little-Mirrlees valuation method and has prepared a manual (10). Several other bilateral agencies·have also indicated they would like to try to adopt the method in their aid efforts. Among international agencies, although there has been considerable interest in the Little-Mirrlees proposal, there has been no attempt to introduce it, even in modified form, on a broad scale. In the World Bank, for instance, the system is not being used and, for the moment at least, it is not proposed to do so.

4. COMPARING COSTS AND BENEFITS

The basic concept underlying economic and financial analysis of projects is simple: for alternative projects we compare the costs with the benefits to determine which alternative gives us a greater return for our money.

We are, however, immediately up against a problem if our project lasts more than one year, as most do. We must find some way to compare projects which have differently shaped future cost and benefit streams. The usual method of comparison is through discounting. We will focus on three discounted measures commonly applied to agricultural projects: benefit-cost ratio, net present worth, and internal rate of return.

There is an extensive and occasionally esoteric literature devoted to discounted measures of project worth. It is not my purpose here to review that literature or even to suggest that I will deal with all the issues it raises. Rather, I would like to point out a few practical considerations about using discounted measures to evaluate the worth of agricultural projects and to touch upon some of the more common criticisms of the three discounted measures. If you would like to proceed from our discussion, a good place to begin is with the review article by Prest and Turvey (22) and the text by Merrett and Sykes (19).

First of all, let me make clear two most important points:

-- There is no one best technique for estimating project worth (although some are better than others and some are especially deficient).

-- Don't forget that these economic and financial measures of investment worth are only a tool of decision making. There are many nonquantitative and noneconomic criteria for making project decisions. The usefulness of the analytical techniques we will discuss is to improve the decision making process (and to give some idea of the economic cost of noneconomic decisions), not to substitute for judgment.

Undiscounted measures of project worth

Before taking up discounting, it may be of interest to illustrate just how some common undiscounted measures of project worth can lead to misleading choices among projects.[1]

_____
1   This section owes much to Bierman and Smidt (2).

47

Let's take four hypothetical pump irrigation investments to illustrate some of the problems associated with using undiscounted measures to choose among projects. All may be thought of as being more or less alternatives for each other. Since these are illustrative only, I will be making some highly unrealistic irrigation assumptions in the hope of illustrating more clearly and quickly some points about project analysis. Later, we will try to make the analysis as realistic as worthwhile in practice.

For these pump irrigation investments, I have invented a new kind of pump: one that completely evaporates (or, perhaps to say it more technically, has no salvage value) after three years. We might say that this is an area where the water is so sandy the pump wears out in three years. I will assume for purposes of convenience that there is no uncertainty about either costs or returns.

To emphasize that both what are generally called "operation and maintenance" costs and what are called "production costs" must be included in estimating project worth, I have given each a separate column. For illustrative purposes, of course, I could just as well have combined them into one cost column called "operation, maintenance, and production costs."

Table 4-1 then, gives the four pump irrigation project alternatives.

Ranking by inspection. In some cases, we can tell by simply looking at the investment costs and the shape of the cash flow stream that one project is better than another. In general, there are two such instances: (1) with the same investment, two projects produce the same net value of production for a period but one continues to earn longer than the other; in these examples, we know project II is better than project I; (2) in other instances, for the same investment, the total net value of production may be the same but one has more of the flow earlier in the time sequence. Thus, we can tell that project IV is better than III. We cannot, however, tell by inspection if project IV is better than project II. More elaborate analysis is necessary.

In many cases, projects can, indeed, be examined and rejected on the basis of inspection. A clear-cut case might be two alternative investments in irrigation where one will cost more but yield no more return. Most people probably would not even consider that project analysis; they would simply look for the cheapest means to realize a given end.

Payback period. The payback period is the length of time from the beginning of the project before the net benefits return the cost of the capital investment. The payback period is a common rough means of choosing between investments in business

Table 4-1. Four Hypothetical Pump Irrigation Schemes
(Thousand United States Dollars)

Project	Year	Project Costs			Gross Costs	Gross Value of Production	Net Value of Production[b]
		Capital Items	O & M[a] Costs	Production Costs			
I	1	$20,000	$2,000	$3,000	$25,000	$15,000	$10,000
	2	–	2,000	3,000	5,000	15,000	10,000
	3	–	–	–	–	–	–
	Total	$20,000	$4,000	$6,000	$30,000	$30,000	$20,000
II	1	$20,000	$2,000	$3,000	$25,000	$15,000	$10,000
	2	–	2,000	3,000	5,000	15,000	10,000
	3	–	2,000	3,000	5,000	5,972	972
	Total	$20,000	$6,000	$9,000	$35,000	$35,972	$20,972
III	1	$20,000	$2,000	$3,000	$25,000	$10,000	$ 5,000
	2	–	2,000	3,000	5,000	11,500	6,500
	3	–	2,000	3,000	5,000	17,000	12,000
	Total	$20,000	$6,000	$9,000	$35,000	$38,500	$23,500
IV	1	$20,000	$2,000	$3,000	$25,000	$10,000	$ 5,000
	2	–	2,000	3,000	5,000	17,000	12,000
	3	–	2,000	3,000	5,000	11,500	6,500
	Total	$20,000	$6,000	$9,000	$35,000	$38,500	$23,500

a. Operation and maintenance.

b. Net value of production is the gross value of production less operation and maintenance and production costs.

enterprises, especially where there is a high degree of risk. In agricultural projects, however, it is not a common measure.

Looking at the four hypothetical irrigation projects, we can rank them according to payback period:

Table 4-2. Payback Period

Project	Payback Period (Years)	Ranking
I	2.0	1
II	2.0	1
III	2.8	4
IV	2.7	3

In this case, project I and project II both have the same payback period, but we know by inspection that project II will continue to return benefits in the second year. Hence, the payback period is an inadequate criterion to choose between these two alternatives, one of which we know by inspection to be better than another.

If we were to modify projects III and IV so that the capital cost of each were $23,500 then they would each have equal payback periods of three years. Yet we know by inspection that project IV is better because the time sequence of the cash flow means that the project will repay more of the returns earlier in the sequence, obviously desirable since the earlier benefits are received the earlier they can be reinvested (or consumed), and, hence, the more valuable they are. Thus, payback period has two major weaknesses as a measure of investment worth: (1) the payback period fails to consider earnings after the payback period; and (2) it fails to take into consideration differences in the timing of proceeds.

Proceeds per dollar of outlay. Sometimes, investments can be ranked by the total proceeds divided by the total amount of the investment:

Table 4-3.   Total Proceeds per Dollar of Outlay
(Thousand United States Dollars)

Project	Project Costs Capital Items	Net Value of Production	Proceeds per Dollar of Outlay	Ranking
I	$20,000	$20,000	1.00	4
II	$20,000	$20,972	1.05	3
III	$20,000	$23,500	1.18	1
IV	$20,000	$23,500	1.18	1

By this criterion, we find that projects III and IV receive equal ranking, although we know by simple inspection that IV is a better project because the returns are received earlier. Here, again, the proceeds per dollar of outlay criterion fails to consider timing; a dollar to be received in the future weighs as heavily as a dollar in hand today.

Average annual proceeds per dollar of outlay. To compute this investment choice criterion, obviously closely related to proceeds per dollar of outlay, the total proceeds are first divided by the number of years and this average of the proceeds per year is divided by the original outlay.

Table 4-4. Average Annual Proceeds Per Dollar of Outlay
(Thousand United States Dollars)

Project	Project Costs Capital Items	Total Net Value of Production	Average Net Value of Production	Average Annual Proceeds per Dollar of Outlay	Ranking
I	$20,000	$20,000	$10,000	0.50	1
II	$20,000	$20,972	$ 6,991	0.35	4
III	$20,000	$23,500	$ 7,833	0.39	2
IV	$20,000	$23,500	$ 7,833	0.39	2

This investment criterion has a very serious flaw: by failing to take into consideration the length of time of the benefit stream, it automatically introduces a serious bias toward short-lived investments with high cash proceeds. We can see this operate: project I ranks much better than project II, although we know by simple inspection that project II is the better project. Similarly, the criterion cannot choose between projects III and IV although, again by inspection, we know project IV is superior because it returns its benefits earlier. This criterion, however, can be misleading because it seems to allow for time by introducing "annual" into the terminology.

(This, incidentally, is the criterion used to evaluate savings accounts. That is, we are interested in the annual return per dollar of outlay in the case where interest is not compounded. The weakness of the criterion is avoided by assuming all savings accounts will yield their benefits indefinitely.)

Average income on book value of the investment. In this measure of investment worth, the ratio of annual benefits to the

Table 4-5. Average Income on Book Value
(Thousand United States Dollars)

Project	Average Net Value of Production	Average Depreciation	Average Income (Proceeds less Depreciation)	Average Book Value	Income on Book Value (Percent)	Rank
I	$10,000	$10,000	$ 0	$10,000	0	4
II	$ 6,991	$ 6,667	$ 324	$10,000	3	3
III	$ 7,833	$ 6,667	$1,166	$10,000	12	1
IV	$ 7,833	$ 6,667	$1,166	$10,000	12	1

book value of the assets (that is, after subtracting depreciation) is the criterion. This is a useful and a commonly used measure of the performance of an individual firm. Since it is widely known as a measure of performance, it is sometimes also used as an investment criterion.

For purposes of illustration, we will assume straight line depreciation on our irrigation projects and thus will compute the average book value by dividing the investment by two.

Although this procedure correctly ranks projects I and II, it fails to rank projects III and IV because it fails to take adequate account of the timing of the benefit stream.

Looking at these measures of investment worth, we can see that they share a common weakness: they fail to take into account adequately the timing of benefits. In the case of ordinary inspection, there was no way of choosing between projects II and IV, and, in any event, if the projects were much more complex than these oversimplified illustrative examples, the projects would be too complicated to rank by inspection. As for the other measures, they all founder on the problem of timing.

To overcome this weakness, we may turn to the use of discounting. Basically, this is a technique by which one can "reduce" future benefit and cost streams to their "present worth." Then we may compare these present worth estimates with each other either to derive a ratio of the present worths of the benefits with the costs--the benefit-cost ratio--or to consider the difference between their present worths--the net present worth measure--or to see what discount rate would be necessary to make the net present worth equal zero – a measure of the earning capacity of the project known as internal rate of return. It is this last measure which can give us a reliable ranking, and we shall return to the question of ranking these hypothetical pump irrigation schemes once we have discussed it.

Time value of money

"A bird in hand is worth two in the bush."
"Un tiens vaut mieux que deux tu l'auras."
"Más vale pájaro en mano que cien volando."

The folk wisdom of people down through the ages--with all its real sophistication and genius of simplicity--lies at the heart of economic and financial analysis of projects lasting more than one year. When we get right down to it, all we are trying to do in the more formal analysis is to compare the present worth to us of two alternative forms of investment. At first glance, the technique may seem complicated and abstract; in practice it is not.

Interest. If we lend our money to someone to use, we can normally expect to be paid interest for the use of that money. In the same manner, banks, cooperatives, and credit unions will pay interest on savings deposits. How much interest will be paid varies from time to time and also with the chances that the borrowed money may not be repaid either at all or on time. But the principle is well known and simple.

Economists generally explain interest as arising from one of two reasons, although many others are sometimes suggested. The simplest explanation is that if we lend money to someone else, we are deferring until the future the possibility of using that money for present pleasures. If we do this we are entitled to a reward--and interest is that reward. Another, closely related but rather better explanation is that interest is related to current income foregone. If a farmer lends money to his neighbor, the farmer is passing by the opportunity to use that money for some productive purpose--say, to increase his own fertilizer use. On the other hand, his neighbor is gaining the use of the money to put to a productive purpose, perhaps to increase the amount of fertilizer he applies. It is only reasonable that the lender be compensated for the income foregone and that the borrower pay something for his use of the lender's money.

If the money is lent at 5 percent a year, then $1,000.00 lent on January 1 will be repaid on the following December 31 with $50.00 interest, or a total of $1,050.00 is repaid the lender. Hence, $1,000.00 x 1.05 = $1,050.00.

Now if the borrower wants to keep the money for two years, he must pay 5 percent for the use of the money for the first year, and then an additional 5 percent for the money for the second year. In addition, of course, he must pay interest on the amount he would have paid the lender at the end of the first year--that is, he must pay "compound" interest. Thus:

1973 $1,000.00 x 1.05 = $1,050.00
1974 $1,050.00 x 1.05 = $1,102.50

The borrower would then repay $1,102.50 to the lender at the end of the second year (assuming he had not made any interest payment in the meantime).

The same thing holds true for however long the money may be held:

1975 $1,102.50 x 1.05 = $1,157.62[1]
1976 $1,157.62 x 1.05 = $1,215.50
1977 $1,215.50 x 1.05 = $1,276.28

Now, let's note two accounting conventions. The first is that interest is generally stated on an annual basis. Hence, if we say a loan is made at 5 percent, it is implied that we mean 5 percent a year. The second accounting convention is that the money is borrowed at the beginning of the period (say, January 1, 1973) and returned on the last day of the period (say, December 31, 1973). It is easy, of course, to adjust this for other conventions. Interest is sometimes compounded monthly or quarterly. But in project analysis we generally assume that the period we are talking about is a year.

There is another accounting convention which is widely used and will be used in this book, but which is not as universal as the ones about the period for which interest is paid and the assumed dates. That is that the present (or the day just before the beginning of the project period) will be noted as t_0 and the end of the first year noted as t_1, so that money is lent today, or t_0, and interest is paid at the end of the first year, or t_1. (This gives some difficulty later when we talk about investment, but is clear enough for the present.)

Now, if we take another series for illustration, suppose we were to lend out $650 for five years, at 9 percent interest:

Year		Amount Loaned		Interest Rate	Amount Due at End of Year
t_1	1973	$650	x	1.09	$ 708
t_2	1974	708	x	1.09	772
t_3	1975	772	x	1.09	841
t_4	1976	841	x	1.09	917
t_5	1977	917	x	1.09	1,000

---

[1]   In the illustrative computations in this book, the following rule is used for rounding:

1. When a value of 4 or less is to be dropped, the digit to the left is unchanged.
2. When a value of 6 or more is to be dropped, the digit to the left is increased by 1.
3. When a value of exactly 5 is to be dropped, the digit to the left if even is left unchanged; if odd, it is raised by 1. Under this rule, all numbers which have been rounded by dropping an exact 5 will be reported as even numbers. Thus,

1975 $1,102.50 x 1.05 = $1,157.625 = $1,157.62
1976 $1,157.62 x 1.05 = $1,215.501 = $1,215.50
1977 $1,215.50 x 1.05 = $1,276.275 = $1,276.28

Hence, if we were to lend out $650 for five years at 9 percent annual interest, compounded, at the end of the fifth year the total of exactly $1,000 would be due for repayment.

In practice it is cumbersome to calculate compound interest in the manner we have been using here. Normally a table is used which does this for us. A convenient set is Compounding and Discounting Tables for Project Evaluation published by the Economic Development Institute of the World Bank (8), but there are many other, equivalent sets of tables.

To illustrate how the compounding tables are used, we may consider the table for 9 percent. For our purposes, each line refers to a year, but it can also be interpreted as referring to any other compounding period. At the head of each column is stated what that column indicates. For this purpose we are interested in the first column on the left hand page entitled "Compounding Factor for 1--What an initial amount becomes when growing at compound interest." Now if we are interested in what will be due if we lend $650 for five years at 9 percent interest, we look down the first column opposite the fifth period to find the compounding factor (often termed the compound interest factor) which is 1.539 rounding to three decimals. To find out how much is due, we multiply the amount of the initial loan by the compounding factor for the proper number of years:

$$\$650 \times 1.539 = \$1,000$$

Obviously, the short cut using tables is a great convenience.

(For most project purposes, if we carry our factors to no more than three decimal places it will be quite accurate enough, given the nature of the underlying data.)

If, for instance, we wanted to lend the same $650 at 9 percent interest for fifteen years, we can find out how much will be due at the end of that period of time very quickly:

$$\$650 \times 3.642 = \$2,367$$

Present worth (discounting). Now, suppose we turn to a somewhat different question. If a borrower promised to pay us $1,000 at the end of five years assuming an interest rate of 9 percent, how much is that promise worth to us today? Put another way, what is the present worth of $1,000 five years in the future assuming

the interest rate is 9 percent? To determine that, we must divide
the amount due by 1.09 each year, as follows:

Year	Amount Promised at End of Year		Interest Rate		Worth at Beginning of Year
t_5 1977	$1,000	:	1.09	=	$917
t_4 1976	917	:	1.09	=	814
t_3 1975	841	:	1.09	=	772
t_2 1974	772	:	1.09	=	708
t_1 1973	708	:	1.09	=	650
t_0 1972	650				

Or, the present worth of a future income of $1,000 five years
hence is $650.

Now, note that the calculation we have just so laboriously
gone through is exactly upside down from what we had done earlier
when we were talking about compound interest. Then we asked
what would be the amount to be repaid five years in the future
if we loaned $650 today at 9 percent compound interest, and found
the amount repayable would be $1,000. Turning the question upside
down, we asked what would be the present worth of $1,000 paid
five years in the future assuming an interest rate of 9 percent, and
computed that value to be $650.

This process of finding the present worth of a future income
is called "discounting." The interest rate assumed for discounting
is the "discount rate." There is no difference between the interest
rate and the discount rate. The only variation is the point of view:
the interest rate assumes looking from here to the future, while
discounting looks backward from the future to the present.

Again, it is laborious to calculate this in the manner illustrated
so "discount tables" normally are used. If you turn to your
Compounding and Discounting Tables for Project Evaluation for 9
percent, on the right hand page you will find the first column
entitled "Discount factor--How much 1 at a future date is worth
today" assuming a 9 percent discount rate, (which is the same as
saying a 9 percent interest rate). This column gives the discount
factors (often termed the present worth factors) for 9 percent. To
find what is the present worth to us of $1,000 received five years
in the future, multiply the discount factor for the fifth year by
the amount due in the future:

$$\$1,000 \times .650 = \$650$$

Or, to illustrate again, what is the present worth to us of
$6,438 received nine years in the future if the discount rate is 15

percent? Turning to the 15 percent tables, opposite the ninth period we find .284, so:

$$\$6,438 \times .284 = \$1,828$$

<u>Present worth of a stream of future income.</u> Now, instead of someone proposing to pay a single amount in some future year, suppose we are to receive a stream of income for a period of years. What would be the present worth to us today of that stream of future income? You will recognize this is a common question, since an investment in a development project often will return the same benefit in each of several years, and we need to know what the present worth of that future stream of income is in order to know how much we are justified in investing today to receive that stream of income. In order to resolve this question, we will again need to know the interest rate, the period of time we are talking about, and, of course, the amount of the income stream.

Suppose we take the $6,438 noted above and assume we are to receive that amount each year for nine years. We can discount that income stream back to the present for each year using our table for 15 percent.

Year		Income to be Recieved		Discount Factor (= Present Worth Factor) at 15 Percent		Present Worth
t_1	1973	$6,438	x	.870	=	$5,601
t_2	1974	6,438	x	.756	=	4,867
t_3	1975	6,438	x	.658	=	4,236
t_4	1976	6,438	x	.572	=	3,683
t_5	1977	6,438	x	.497	=	3,200
t_6	1978	6,438	x	.432	=	2,781
t_7	1979	6,438	x	.376	=	2,421
t_8	1980	6,438	x	.327	=	2,105
t_9	1981	6,438	x	.284	=	1,828
Total		$57,942		4.772		$30,722

Thus, the present worth of a stream of income of $6,438 received each year for nine years assuming a discount rate (which is, of course, a rate of interest) of 15 percent is $30,722. That is, the present worth is the sum of all the present worths for all the years added together. (Note that although the total undiscounted dollar value of the income stream is $57,942, the present worth is <u>not</u> that amount. Clearly, $6,438 received nine years in the future is not worth $6,438 to us today; that is what discounting is all about.)

Working out the present worth of a future stream of income by this means is awkward and time consuming. It is much faster if we just take the sum of the discount factors (that is, present worth factors) and multiply by the annual income to be received:

$$\$6,438 \ \times \ 4.772 \ = \ \$30,722$$

Conveniently, we can use discounting tables directly to find the present worth of a future stream of income. If you will look at the 15 percent tables in <u>Compounding and Discounting Tables for Project Evaluation</u> you will note the second column on the right hand page is entitled "Present worth of an annuity -- How much 1 received or paid annually for X years is worth today." This column gives us the present worth of a future income stream of one per year. Note this second column is simply the running subtotal of the first column. Thus, the first year both columns read .870. The second year, however, the first column giving us the present worth factor for the income received in the second year reads .756, so that if we received the same income in both the first year and the second year, the present worth of that two-year income stream would be multiplied by the sum of the two present worth factors .870 + .756 = 1.626. Looking across at the second column we find the present worth of 1 per period is, indeed, 1.626, saving us the trouble of adding up the first column as we go along.

We can try some other examples. What is the present worth of $12,869 received annually for fourteen years if the discount rate is 8 percent? Turning to the table for 8 percent we can find the present worth of an annuity factor for the fourteenth year giving us:

$$\$12,869 \ \times \ 8.244 \ = \ \$106,092$$

so the present worth of $12,869 received annually for fourteen years at a discount rate of 8 percent is $106,092. Put another way, if the going rate of interest is 8 percent, then we could afford to invest $106,092 in an enterprise that would yield us an annual return of $12,869 for each of fourteen years.

Many investments, of course, do not begin to repay us the first year. Suppose we are thinking of oil palm which comes into bearing about the fifth year and continues to produce commercially for about twenty years. Obviously, we are concerned only with the present worth of a future income stream beginning with the fifth year and continuing through the twenty-fourth year.

To illustrate this, let us return to the example above. Suppose our hypothetical investment instead of repaying us $6,438 each year from the first year through the ninth year would only repay us $6,438 each year beginning with the fifth year and continuing through the ninth. What would be the present worth of that income stream assuming the same 15 percent discount rate?

	Year	Income to be Received		Discount Factor (= Present Worth Factor) at 15 Percent		Present Worth
t_5	1977	$6,438	x	.497	=	$3,200
t_6	1978	6,438	x	.432	=	2,781
t_7	1979	6,438	x	.376	=	2,421
t_8	1980	6,438	x	.327	=	2,105
t_9	1981	6,438	x	.284	=	1,828
	Total	$32,190		1.916		$12,335

Or, an income stream of $6,438 received from the fifth through the ninth years at a discount rate of 15 percent has a present worth to us of $12,335 today.

Note we could have calculated the present worth of our income stream by multiplying the $6,438 by the sum of the discount factors for the fifth through the ninth years:

$$\$6,438 \text{ x } 1.916 = \$12,335$$

For just five years, it is easy enough simply to add the discount factors, but when we are working with longer periods it is easier to use a shortcut: we can simply subtract from the present worth of an annuity factor for a stream of income received for the whole period the present worth of an annuity factor for a stream of income for the period before the income begins. That is:

Present worth of an annuity factor
for 9 years at 15 percent   4.772
LESS present worth of an annuity factor
for 4 years at 15 percent   -2.855

Present worth of an annuity factor
for 5th through 9th years at
15 percent   1.917

In this case, we would have been off by one point because of rounding.

Don't overlook that if we want the fifth through the ninth years, we subtract the figure for the fourth year from the figure for the ninth year, not the figure for the fifth year, since we want a factor which represents the years from five through nine inclusive.

If you always total the discount factors when you lay out your computation, you provide yourself with an internal check that you have correctly listed them without an error in computation or an error in subtracting the wrong year. When you total your discount factors the sum will equal the present worth of an annuity factor for the number of years in the computation. It is quite uncommon for rounding errors to be more than .001.

(Although I have chosen to refer to the more complete set of compounding and discounting tables for illustrative purposes in this discussion, for most project evaluation uses the three place tables found on pages 212 to 215 are sufficient and may be more convenient.)

Benefit-cost ratio

Recalling our earlier comment that anyone interested in comparing alternative investments would naturally compare costs and benefits, and recognizing the need to take account of the differing time streams of alternative projects by means of discounting, we may turn to the first of the discounted measures of project worth in common use: the benefit-cost ratio.

That is to say,

$$\frac{\text{Present worth of benefits}}{\text{Present worth of costs}} = \text{Benefit-cost ratio}[1]$$

(Incidentally, economists are quite inconsistent in their use of "benefit-cost ratio." About half the time they say "cost-benefit ratio." Here, however, I will stick to "benefit-cost ratio" to emphasize the computation by which the measure is worked out: that is, to take the benefits and divide them by the costs.)

The benefit-cost ratio is used almost exclusively as a measure of social benefit--that is, for economic analysis as we have defined it--and most commonly for water resource projects. It is almost never used for private investment analysis.

We may illustrate computation of the benefit-cost ratio with the simple irrigation example set out in table 4-6. We will assume a small earth fill dam is to be built over the period of two years for a total cost of $13,500,000. After that, there is an annual operation and maintenance cost. To keep this illustration from becoming cumbersome, we will only carry through the analysis for seven years. At the end of seven years, of course, the dam will not be used up. To allow for this, we will consider that the dam at that point has a "salvage value" of $331,000. This introduces something we have not touched on before, but it is very simple: the salvage value is treated as a "benefit" in the last year of the project (see page 106).

---

1 For a more formal mathematical statement see page 98.

To compute the benefit-cost ratio, we must decide upon the discount rate to be used. In general, there are two discount rates which might be chosen and a third which is sometimes proposed. Probably the best discount rate to use is the "opportunity cost of capital"--that is, the profitability of the last possible investment in an economy given the total available capital. Although good as a theoretical definition, this is difficult to apply as a practical working tool: no one knows what the opportunity cost of capital really is. In most developing countries it is assumed to be somewhere between 8 and 15 percent, although I refuse to be drawn into an argument as to how defensible these figures are. For our illustrative example we will assume the opportunity cost of capital to be 12 percent. Another discount rate which often is chosen for the benefit-cost ratio calculation is the borrowing rate for the project which is to be financed. This has the undesirable result, however, that the selection of projects will be influenced by the financing terms available rather than being based solely upon their relative economic impact. A third rate sometimes suggested is the social rate of return, a rate which, it is suggested, more adequately reflects the time preference of the society as a whole than does the opportunity cost of capital. Although interesting in theory, it is too difficult to identify in practice to be commonly used for agricultural project analysis.

Before we go on, let me inject another accounting convention. Although there may be questions about how reasonable this actually is, the important thing is that as long as the accounting convention is consistently observed, it will not introduce a bias or consistent error into the ranking of projects compared on the basis of discounted measures of project worth. The accounting convention is that all costs and all benefits are discounted for the first year and for each year thereafter. To many people, this seems inconsistent. Investments must be made before the first year is ended, they say, so how can you assume that they be discounted--that is, that their present worth is something less than their actual face value? The answer is somewhat arbitrary: first, in projects lasting over several years, it makes no difference in the relative rankings; second, costs in actual practice are paid out during the course of each year and not all on January 1 and to allow for this on something like a day-to-day basis is just too complicated to be worth the effort. In any event, let me note that World Bank usage is to discount both costs and benefits beginning with the first year but that some international lending agencies discount costs beginning with the second year. In this book we will adopt the World Bank convention and let it go with that.

Now if we want to use discounting to help us compare the cost and benefit streams of our small dam project, we must first

Table 4-6. Analysis of Earth Fill Dam Small-Scale Irrigation Project
Illustrating Computation of Benefit-Cost Ratio
(Thousand United States Dollars)

I. COMPARING GROSS BENEFITS TO GROSS COSTS

Year	Project Costs Capital Items	O & Mª Costs	Production Costs	Gross Costs	D.F.^b 12%	Present Worth 12%	Total Value of Production (= Gross Benefits)	D.F.^b 12%	Present Worth 12%
1	$ 7,500	$ 0	$ 0	$ 7,500	.893	$ 6,698	$ 0	.893	$ 0
2	6,000	0	0	6,000	.797	4,782	0	.797	0
3	0	600	700	1,300	.712	926	6,000	.712	4,272
4	0	600	700	1,300	.636	827	6,000	.636	3,816
5	0	600	700	1,300	.567	737	6,000	.567	3,402
6	0	600	700	1,300	.507	659	6,000	.507	3,042
7	0	600	700	1,300	.452	588	6,000	.452	2,712
							331^c	(.452)	150
Total	$13,500	$3,000	$3,500	$20,000	4.564	$15,217	$30,331	4.564^d	$17,394

Benefit-cost ratio at 12% = $\dfrac{\$17{,}394{,}000}{\$15{,}217{,}000}$ = 1.1; Net present worth at 12% = $17,394,000 - $15,217,000 = $2,177,000

II. COMPARING NET BENEFITS TO INVESTMENT PLUS OPERATION AND MAINTENANCE COSTS

Year	Project Costs Capital Items	O & Mª Costs	Total Costs	D.F.^b 12%	Present Worth 12%	Total Value of Production (= Gross Benefits)	Production Costs	Net Benefits	D.F.^b 12%	Present Worth 12%
1	$ 7,500	$ 0	$ 7,500	.893	$ 6,698	$ 0	$ 0	$ 0	.893	$ 0
2	6,000	0	6,000	.797	4,782	0	0	0	.797	0
3-7	0	600^e	600^e	2.874^f	1,724	6,000^e	700^e	5,300^e	2.874^f	15,232
						331^c		331^c	(.452)	150
Total	$13,500	$3,000	$16,500	4.564	$13,204	$30,331	$3,500	$26,831	4.564^d	$15,382

Benefit-cost ratio at 12% = $\dfrac{\$15{,}382{,}000}{\$13{,}204{,}000}$ = 1.2; Net present worth at 12% = $15,382,000 - $13,204,000 = $2,178,000^g.

(For notes see following page.)

discount each stream in order to find its present worth. You will see that this has been done for the gross costs and the gross benefits in the first part of table 4-6. Dividing the present worth of the gross benefits by the present worth of the gross costs we find the benefit-cost ratio. Thus,

$$\frac{\text{Present worth of gross benefits}}{\text{Present worth of gross costs}} = \frac{\$17,394,000}{\$15,217,000} = 1.1$$

One point about the computation: note you cannot take the total of the discount factors and multiply it by the total of the cost or benefit stream to come out with the present worth. Taking the gross cost stream in table 4-6 as an example, you cannot reach the present worth of $15,217,000 by multiplying the undiscounted total of the gross costs, $20,000,000, by the total of the discount factors, 4.564. You must follow the year-by-year procedure.

Suppose the benefit-cost ratio worked out to be less than one? Well, then, we would have a case where <u>at the discount rate assumed</u> the present worth of the benefits is less than the present worth of the costs and one is not recovering his investment. It would be better to put the money in a bank at the assumed interest rate than to invest it in the project.

Note that the absolute value of the benefit-cost ratio will vary depending on the interest rate chosen. The higher the interest rate, the smaller the resulting benefit-cost ratio, and if a high enough rate is chosen the benefit-cost ratio will be driven down to less than one.

In practice, it is probably more common not to compute the benefit-cost ratio using gross costs and gross benefits, but rather to compare the present worth of the net benefits with the present worth of the investment cost plus operation and maintenance costs. This reflects United States government practice where the benefit-cost ratio has been a common measure applied to assess the

---

Table 4-6. (Continued)

   a. Operation and maintenance.

   b. Discount factor.

   c. Salvage value.

   d. The sum is the discount factor for each year totaled; hence, the value of .452 for the seventh year is included only once.

   e. Since this is an annual amount, it is included five times to reach the total.

   f. Factor for the third through the seventh years (see pages 58 and 59 for method of calculation).

   g. The net present worth varies slightly between the two methods of computing the benefit-cost ratio because of rounding.

"national economic development" effect of water resources projects. More specifically, the ratio is computed by taking the present worth of the gross benefits less "associated" costs and comparing it to the present worth of the "project economic costs." Associated costs are "the value of goods and services over and above those included in project costs needed to make the immediate products or services of the project available for use or sale." Project economic costs are "the sum of installation costs; operation, maintenance, and replacement costs; and induced costs. . ." Induced costs are "uncompensated adverse effects caused by the construction and operation" of the project. The second half of table 4-6 illustrates how the benefit-cost ratio may be computed using this convention. (It is assumed there are no induced effects.) You will note one result of computing the benefit-cost ratio using this convention of netting out is to make it larger than when gross costs are compared to gross benefits. (Further details of United States government practice will be found in Senate Document No. 97 (26) which also gives definitions for how costs and benefits are computed by United States agencies.)

In United States practice it is common to evaluate a project on the basis of its "average annual net benefit." This is a measure equivalent to the net present worth criterion taken up in more detail in the next section. First, both the present worth of the benefits and the present worth of the costs are multiplied by the capital recovery factor to find their average annual equivalents. (The capital recovery factor may be found in many discounting table sources; in Compounding and Discounting Tables for Project Evaluation (8), for example, it is the column to the far right in the two page spread devoted to each percentage interval.) Then, applying this procedure to the second part of table 4-6 and rounding, we find:

$\begin{bmatrix} \text{Present} \\ \text{worth of} \\ \text{benefits} \\ \text{at } 12\% \end{bmatrix}$	X	$\begin{bmatrix} \text{Capital} \\ \text{recovery} \\ \text{factor at} \\ 12\% \text{ for} \\ 7 \text{ years} \end{bmatrix}$	−	$\begin{bmatrix} \text{Present} \\ \text{worth of} \\ \text{costs} \\ \text{at } 12\% \end{bmatrix}$	X	$\begin{bmatrix} \text{Capital} \\ \text{recovery} \\ \text{factor at} \\ 12\% \text{ for} \\ 7 \text{ years} \end{bmatrix}$	=	$\begin{matrix} \text{Average} \\ \text{annual} \\ \text{net} \\ \text{benefit} \end{matrix}$
($15,382,000 x		.219)	−	($13,204,000 x		.219)	=	$477,000

(As this is being written, the United States government is embarking on hearings for a comprehensive revision of its criteria for evaluating water resources projects. It is proposed all projects be evaluated from three distinct viewpoints, each with its own account: effects on national economic development, effects on environmental quality, and effects on regional development. Reliance on a favorable benefit-cost ratio as an indicator of the merits of a plan would be reduced, although benefit-cost ratios would continue to be computed. "Beneficial effects" contributing to the several objectives of a plan or program (and discounted where appropriate) would be compared with the "adverse effects" (also discounted if appropriate). If the beneficial effects, both quantifiable and nonquantifiable, were judged to exceed the adverse effects, again considering both quantifiable and nonquantifiable factors, a plan or program would be considered to be justified. Details of the new evaluation proposals have been published by the United States Water Resources Council (27) in anticipation of its hearings.)

When the benefit-cost ratio is used to evaluate projects, the formal decision criterion is to accept all projects with a ratio of one or greater (except in the case of mutually exclusive projects, a topic to which we will return later on pages 110 to 128).

Although in practice projects with higher benefit-cost ratios are often regarded as being preferable (other things being equal), ranking by benefit-cost ratio can lead to an erroneous investment choice. The benefit-cost ratio discriminates against projects with relatively high gross returns and operating costs even though these may be shown to have a greater wealth generating capacity than alternatives which have a higher benefit-cost ratio. McKean (18, pp. 107-116) discusses this point with illustrative examples.

Although different conventions for netting out costs and benefits may have been used for different projects, no matter how the netting out is done the same group of projects will be accepted using the benefit-cost ratio criterion strictly construed--that is, the same group of projects will have benefit-cost ratios of one or greater. However, a different netting out convention can change the value of the ratio as we saw when two alternative conventions were applied to the same project in table 4-6. These points can be seen to be true by observation. If the present worth of the benefits exceeds the present worth of the costs, then the benefit-cost ratio, obviously, will be greater than one. However, moving costs from the numerator to the denominator or vice versa--as we did when we took production costs away from the gross cost stream and instead deducted them from the gross benefit stream--will change the ratio value (and perhaps the rank of a project compared to alternatives) although the ratio will, of course, remain greater than one.

When the benefit-cost ratio is used as a criterion for evaluating projects in a country, it is desirable that all analysts follow a common netting out convention to derive their cost and benefit streams. If they do, they can greatly reduce the chances of a misleading choice indication should administrators rank projects by their ratio values--as they almost always tend to do despite the restrictions of the formal choice criterion. Only in the most extreme cases of differences in relationships between gross returns and operating costs will the benefit-cost ratio criterion computed using the same netting out convention fail to rank project alternatives correctly.

Discounted cash flow measures

Another way to estimate the worth of a project is to subtract the costs from the benefits on a year-to-year basis to arrive at the incremental net benefit stream--the so-called "cash flow"--and then to discount that. This approach will give either the net present worth of the project or the internal rate of return. (It is possible to derive either the net present worth or the internal rate of return by discounting the cost and benefit streams separately. By subtracting the present worth of the cost stream from the present worth of the benefit stream the net present worth can be determined. This was illustrated in table 4-6. The discount rate which will make the present worths of the cost and benefit streams equal is the internal rate of return. However, discounting the cash flow directly as outlined in the following sections is computationally more convenient.)

Derivation of the cash flow. When we look at a project we can see it as earning a stream of gross benefits from which we must deduct the capital investment and pay the other input costs--the machinery, fertilizer, pesticides, labor, management, consultants, and the like. What is left over is a residual (which will be negative in the early years of the project) and which is available (1) to recover the investment made in the project--the return of capital; and (2) to compensate for the use of the money involved in the project--the return to capital (or on capital). This residual is termed the cash flow.

This definition of cash flow applies specifically to investment analysis. When carrying out the analysis from the standpoint of the economy as a whole, it comes essentially to being the same as the net incremental benefit from the project. In financial analysis, the cash flow amounts to the net incremental benefit accruing to the entity from whose standpoint the analysis is being undertaken. Accountants, however, normally have a different definition in mind when they use the term "cash flow." In accounting terminology, the cash flow is essentially the sum of the profits plus the depreciation allowances, usually after payment of taxes. (Project analysts sometimes term this concept as the "cash throw off" to distinguish it from the definition of cash flow used for project analysis.)

The major characteristic of the cash flow is that it includes undifferentiated both the return of capital and the return to capital.

Specifically, to compute the cash flow we do not deduct from the gross returns any allowance for depreciation (that is, return of capital) nor any allowance for interest on the capital employed which has been supplied by the entity for which we are doing the analysis. You will recall that in economic analysis our point of view is that of the society as a whole and it is assumed that all capital is supplied by someone somewhere in the society. Hence, in economic analysis we do not subtract any allowance for depreciation nor for interest on any of the capital employed in the project. (As for depreciation, we do not subtract it because our analytical technique automatically takes care of the return of capital in determining the worth of a project. How this works is illustrated in more detail on pages 85 to 87).

Perhaps the tabulation in figure 4-1 can make the definition of cash flow clearer.

There are two important differences in the manner in which we derive the cash flow when we are carrying out an economic as opposed to a financial analysis. In economic analysis, you will recall from pages 4 to 8, income taxes, sales taxes, and other taxes, and customs duties are transfer payments within the society, not payments for resources used in production. Hence, taxes and duties are not deducted from the benefit stream when deriving the cash flow as the basis on which to compute the productivity of capital. To the whole economy, taxes are a "benefit" available to repay the society for the use of its capital invested in the project and may be used for whatever purpose the society decides best. In financial analysis, on the other hand, taxes are a cost which the individual entity must pay before arriving at the amount available for recovering its capital and compensating it for the use of its capital--that is, its cash flow. Hence, taxes are a cost just like any other expenditure.

The second important difference is that in financial analysis we generally must account for outside capital borrowed by the entity which is undertaking the project--whether the entity be a farmer, an individual businessman, or the shareholders of a corporation taken as a group. In financial analysis when borrowed capital is received it is normally entered into the receipts stream as a kind of "benefit" received. Then, when a payment of interest or a repayment of principal is made to the outside supplier of capital it is deducted from the gross return as a cost in deriving the cash flow. An example may be seen in table 6-1, pages 134 and 135. Note, however, that sometimes a financial analysis will be undertaken to estimate the return to all resources employed in the enterprise regardless of ownership as a test of financial viability. This question does not arise in economic analysis in the manner in which we treat it because

Figure 4-1. Derivation of the Cash Flow in Project Analysis

From the viewpoint of ECONOMIC analysis (some prices may be shadow prices):

GROSS RETURN	less	CAPITAL ITEMS AND INPUTS	less	LABOR AND MANAGEMENT COSTS	= CASH FLOW
Gross benefit:		Goods and services (not labor):		Remuneration for labor and management:	Remuneration for all the society's capital used:
Cash payment from buyers less value of subsidies Value of subsistence production Value of unsold output		Capital equipment Fertilizer Electricity Machinery Maintenance supplies Etc. (Above excluding sales taxes) Add: value of input subsidies		Wages Salaries Bonuses Manager's salary Consultants' fees Social security In kind payment Home-consumed production $= MVP_L$	Return of capital Depreciation Amortization Return to capital Interest Dividends Reinvested earnings Home-consumed production $> MVP_L$ Income taxes Customs duties Sales taxes

From the viewpoint of FINANCIAL analysis (all prices are market prices including taxes and subsidies):

GROSS RETURN	less	CAPITAL ITEMS, INPUTS, AND TAXES	less	LABOR AND MANAGEMENT COSTS	= CASH FLOW
Gross benefit:		Goods and services (not labor):		Remuneration for labor and management:	Remuneration for the entity's own capital used
Cash payment from buyers including value of subsidies Value of subsistence production Value of unsold output Receipts of borrowed capital		Capital equipment Fertilizer Electricity Machinery Maintenance supplies Etc. Income taxes Sales taxes Customs duties Payment to outside capital suppliers Interest Principal		Wages Salaries Bonuses Manager's salary Consultant's fees Social security In kind payment Home-consumed production $= $ wage equivalent	Return of entity's own capital: Depreciation Amortization Return to entity's own capital Interest Dividends Reinvested earnings Home-consumed production $> MVP_L$

of our assumption that all resources employed in the project belong to someone within the society and hence there are no "outside" suppliers of capital.

There may be occasions, however, when you would like to look at the returns to the society from a project for which foreign capital is borrowed. In this case, the kind of economic analysis outlined in this book is a valid indicator of project worth and will give the correct ranking of projects if the money borrowed from abroad may be used for any of a wide range of projects (or, at least, if the lender agreed to supply a stipulated amount of money subject to agreement that it would be spent on a particular project selected by joint agreement from a wide range of alternatives). If, however, a foreign lender is only prepared to lend for one particular project which he has stipulated in advance, then the project analyst may want to determine what will be the returns to the society's own capital if it participates in the project. He can do this by treating the society as a kind of corporate entity in which the citizens are the shareholders and run the equivalent of a financial analysis to determine the return to the society's own capital.

The "cash" flow as it is derived for project analysis may include some noncash elements and hence it may be more convenient to think of it as an "accounting benefits stream" rather than as "cash." In economic analysis of agricultural projects, the most important of these is the value of home consumed production over and above the marginal value product of agricultural labor. This might appear in a settlement project, for example, where unemployed agricultural laborers are established on small holdings. Because the settlers can now earn a good living, their income is considerably above the shadow wage which we would impute as a cost. If this is so, the excess of the value of the home consumed production over and above the shadow wage represents not a cost of production but an incremental benefit available for remunerating capital and is included in the cash flow. (This is true even though the settler's family eats the subsistence production; we say nothing in computing the economic analysis about who actually receives the cash flow. This point was taken up in more detail on pages 5 and 6). Hence, part of our "cash" flow is home consumed production. To try to account for this in our terminology is cumbersome; we simply define cash flow as including the residual benefits available for remuneration of capital whether or not it is in money form.

Another noncash value which may increase the cash flow is the value of unsold output. If this output is simply being held in the normal inventory and will be sold soon, it is often treated as a benefit in the year it is produced rather than in the year it is sold.

One thing you should note. As was pointed out earlier, if you subtract costs, including investment costs, from benefits then during the early years of the project you will have a negative figure--that is, investment costs and initial operating and maintenance and production costs will be larger than the benefits. You will then have a negative cash flow. Stated another way, in the early years of the project you will have "negative benefits." The jargon may take a bit of getting used to, but really causes no trouble.

Net present worth. The most straightforward discounted cash flow measure of project worth is the net present worth (often abbreviated as NPW). This is simply the present worth of the cash flow stream.[1] (As noted before, the net present worth may also be computed by finding the difference between the present worth of the benefit stream less the present worth of the cost stream, both costs and benefits defined as we did for deriving the cash flow in the previous section.)

Economists are also somewhat inconsistent in their terminology for this measure. It is often referred to as the net present value or NPV. In this book we will refer to it as the net present worth to emphasize the parallel with the discounting technique.

The same problem of choice of discount rate mentioned in connection with the benefit-cost ratio arises also in connection with the net present worth criterion. Most analysts recommend using the opportunity cost of capital in the society, although there is an admittedly arbitrary element in deciding just what that rate is. As noted, many underdeveloped countries seem to feel the opportunity cost of capital is in the neighborhood of about 8 to 15 percent.

Returning to the small dam irrigation scheme analyzed in table 4-6, we can see how the net present worth is computed. The discounted gross benefit has a present worth of $17,394,000; the discounted gross cost has a present worth of $15,217,000; and the difference between the two--the net present worth at a 12 percent discount rate--is $2,177,000.

Although the net present worth may be computed by subtracting the total discounted present worth of the costs from that of the benefits, it is easier and normal practice to compute it by discounting the cash flow. Table 4-7 illustrates how this works in the case of the small dam irrigation example.

An incidental advantage of the net present worth measure as compared with the benefit-cost ratio is that it makes no difference at all at what point in the computation process the netting out takes place. Perhaps you noted that in table 4-6 where both

---

[1]   For a more formal mathematical statement see page 98.

conventions of netting out gave the same net present worth although they changed the benefit-cost ratio. To get the cash flow, you may subtract gross costs from gross benefits, the investment costs from the net benefits, or any other computation pattern that suits your analytical needs providing only that you avoid double counting. (Internal rate of return has a similar netting out advantage.)

The formal selection criterion for the net present worth measure of project worth is to accept all projects with a positive net present worth when discounted at the opportunity cost of capital. An obvious problem of the net present worth measure is that the selection criterion cannot be applied unless there is a relatively satisfactory estimate of the opportunity cost of capital.

No ranking of acceptable alternative projects is possible with the net present worth criterion, a serious drawback to its use in practice. Net present worth, of course, is an absolute, not a relative measure. A small, highly attractive project may have a smaller net present worth than a large, marginally acceptable project. As long as both have a positive net present worth and the administrative capacity exists to implement both, this is not important. Our selection criterion tells us to do both (there will be enough money if the opportunity costs of capital has been correctly estimated). But if for any reason we must choose between acceptable projects, then the net present worth is an unreliable indicator. Since, in practice, what often happens is that individual projects as they are prepared are subjected to economic analysis for some kind of general idea of whether they are suitable for implementation, it would be desirable to have a ranking as well as the "go-no-go" criterion provided by net present worth.

Internal rate of return. Another way of using discounted cash flow for measuring the worth of a project is to find that discount rate which just makes the net present worth of the cash flow equal zero.[1] This discount rate is termed the internal rate of return and, in a sense, represents the average earning power of the money used in the project over the project life.

Internal rate of return turns out to be a very useful measure of project worth. It is the measure which the World Bank uses for practically all its economic and financial analyses of projects, as do most other international financing agencies.

In order to avoid confusion between the use of internal rate of return in economic analysis and the use of the same technique in financial analysis, the World Bank has adopted a distinguishing terminology. When the internal rate of return is used in economic analysis, the result is termed the internal economic return; in

---

[1] For a more formal mathematical statement see page 98.

Table 4-7.   Analysis of Earth Fill Dam Small-Scale Irrigation Project
Illustrating Computation of Net Present Worth
(Thousand United States Dollars)

| Year | Project Costs | | | | Total Value of Production (= Gross Benefits) | Incremental Benefit (= Cash Flow) | D.F. 12% | Present Worth 12% |
	Capital Items	Operation & Maintenance Costs	Production Costs	Gross Costs				
1	$ 7,500	$ 0	$ 0	$ 7,500	$ 0	$− 7,500	.893	$− 6,698
2	6,000	0	0	6,000	0	− 6,000	.797	− 4,782
3	0	600	700	1,300	6,000	+ 4,700	.712	+ 3,346
4	0	600	700	1,300	6,000	+ 4,700	.636	+ 2,989
5	0	600	700	1,300	6,000	+ 4,700	.567	+ 2,665
6	0	600	700	1,300	6,000	+ 4,700	.507	+ 2,383
7	0	600	700	1,300	6,000	+ 4,700	.452	+ 2,124
−	−	−	−	−	331[a]	+ 331	(.452)[b]	+ 150
Total	$13,500	$3,000	$3,500	$20,000	$30,331	$+10,331	4.564	$+ 2,177

a. Salvage value.
b. Omitted from total to avoid double counting.

Net present worth at 12% = $2,177,000

financial analysis it is called the internal financial return. In this
book we will follow the Bank terminology.   When the emphasis
of our discussion is on methodology we will refer to internal rate
of return, but when we are talking of economic analysis we will
refer to the internal economic return and when discussing financial
analysis, the internal financial return.

To see how the internal rate of return is calculated, we may
look again at the small scale irrigation project for which we derived
the cash flow in table 4-7. This time, however, instead of discounting
at 12 percent, let's discount at 18 percent as in table 4-8, column
11. By selecting the 18 percent discount rate we have driven the
net present worth of the project down to zero. Put another way,
at a discount rate of 18 percent, this project just breaks even--that
is, it will earn back all the capital and operating costs expended
upon it and pay us 18 percent for the use of our money in the
meantime.

To take yet another vantage point, we could have asked
ourselves what interest rate will this project earn?   What is the
earning power of the money invested in this project? This earning
power of a project is the internal rate of return.

To illustrate how the internal rate of return measure can be
applied to help choose among project alternatives, we may return
to the four hypothetical pump irrigation schemes set out in table
4-1 which we discussed in connection with undiscounted measures
of project worth. In the analysis laid out in table 4-9,the internal
rate of return of each project has been determined by finding that
discount rate which most nearly makes the present worth of the

Table 4-8.   Analysis of Earth Fill Dam Small-Scale Irrigation Project
Illustrating Computation of Internal Rate of Return
(Thousand United States Dollars)

(1)	(2)	(3)	(4)	(5)	(6)	(7)	(8)	(9)	(10)	(11)
		Project Costs								
		Operation &				Present	Total Value	Present	Incremental	Present
	Capital	Maintenance	Production	Gross	D.F.	Worth	of Production	Worth	Benefit	Worth
Year	Items	Costs	Costs	Costs	18%	18%	(= Gross Benefits)	18%	(Cash Flow)	18%
1	$ 7,500	$ 0	$ 0	$ 7,500	.847	$ 6,352	$ 0	$ 0	$− 7,500	$− 6,352
2	6,000	0	0	6,000	.718	4,308	0	0	− 6,000	− 4,308
3	0	600	700	1,300	.609	792	6,000	3,654	+ 4,700	+ 2,862
4	0	600	700	1,300	.516	671	6,000	3,096	+ 4,700	+ 2,425
5	0	600	700	1,300	.437	568	6,000	2,622	+ 4,700	+ 2,054
6	0	600	700	1,300	.370	481	6,000	2,220	+ 4,700	+ 1,739
7	0	600	700	1,300	.314	408	6,000	1,884	+ 4,700	+ 1,476
−	−	−	−	−	(.314)[a]	−	331[b]	104	+ 331	+ 104
Total $13,500	$3,000	$3,500	$20,000	3.811	$13,580	$30,331	$13,580	$+10,331	$ 0

a. Omitted from total to avoid double counting.
b. Salvage value.

$$\text{Benefit-cost ratio at } 18\% = \frac{\$13,580,000}{\$13,580,000} = 1.0$$

Net present worth at 18% = $13,580,000 - $13,580,000 = $0

Internal rate of return (internal economic return) = 18%

project equal to zero. We can see that the internal rate of return does, in fact, separate out the projects unambiguously. We note that project II has an internal rate of return of 9 percent while project I has an internal rate of return of zero--confirming our choice between them on the basis of our observation that the project which continues longer with the same investment will be superior. Likewise, project IV has an internal rate of return of 17 percent while project III has an internal rate of return of 14 percent, confirming our observation that a project with earlier returns is preferable to one with later. Finally, the internal rate of return measure clearly shows project IV to be preferable to project II which we could not do by observation nor with confidence with any other measure. (For purposes of comparison, the benefit-cost ratios and the net present worths of our hypothetical pump projects are also shown. You will note the benefit-cost ratio correctly ranks the projects--although we must carry the measure out to two decimals to do so--since the relationship between the gross returns and the operating costs is not greatly different among the projects. The net present worths of the projects also ranks them correctly since all have costs of a similar order of magnitude.)

The formal selection criterion for the internal rate of return measure of project worth is to accept all projects having an internal rate of return above the opportunity cost of capital.

Projects are ranked in order of the value of the internal rate of return. (The lowest acceptable internal rate of return is often

Table 4-9. Rankings of Hypothetical Pump Irrigation Schemes by Internal Rate of Return
(Thousand United States Dollars)

Project	Year	Gross Costs	Gross Value of Production (= Gross Benefit)	Incremental Benefit (= Cash Flow)	D.F. 12%	Present Worth 12%	Present Worth Calculation at Internal Rate of Return D.F. 0%	Present Worth 0%	Rank
I	1	$25,000	$15,000	$-10,000	.893	$-8,930	1.000	$-10,000	4
	2	5,000	15,000	+10,000	.797	+7,970	1.000	+10,000	
	3	–	–	–	–	–	–	–	
	Total	$30,000	$30,000	$ 0	1.690	$- 960	2.000	$ 0	

Benefit-cost ratio at 12% = $\dfrac{\$25,350}{\$26,310}$ = 0.96[a] ; Net present worth at 12% = $-960,000; Internal rate of return = 0%

Project	Year	Gross Costs	Gross Value of Production (= Gross Benefit)	Incremental Benefit (= Cash Flow)	D.F. 12%	Present Worth 12%	Present Worth Calculation at Internal Rate of Return D.F. 9%	Present Worth 9%	Rank
II	1	$25,000	$15,000	$-10,000	.893	$-8,930	.917	$-9,170	3
	2	5,000	15,000	+10,000	.797	+7,970	.842	+8,420	
	3	5,000	5,972	+ 972	.712	+ 692	.772	+ 750	
	Total	$35,000	$35,972	$+ 972	2.402	$- 268	2.531	$ 0	

Benefit-cost ratio at 12% = $\dfrac{\$29,602}{\$29,870}$ = 0.99; Net present worth at 12% = $-268,000; Internal rate of return = 9%

(For note see following page.)

Table 4-9. Rankings of Hypothetical Pump Irrigation Schemes by Internal Rate of Return (Thousand United States Dollars)
(Continued)

Project	Year	Gross Costs	Gross Value of Production (= Gross Benefit)	Incremental Benefit (= Cash Flow)	D.F. 12%	Present Worth 12%	Present Worth Calculation at Internal Rate of Return D.F.	Present Worth Calculation at Internal Rate of Return Present Worth	Rank
III	1	$25,000	$10,000	$-15,000	.893	$-13,395	14% .877	14% $-13,155	2
	2	5,000	11,500	+ 6,500	.797	+ 5,180	.769	+ 4,998	
	3	5,000	17,000	+12,000	.712	+ 8,544	.675	8,100	
	Total	$35,000	$38,500	$+ 3,500	2.402	$+ 329	2.321	$- 57	

Benefit-cost ratio at 12% = $\frac{\$30,200}{\$29,000}$ = 1.01; Net present worth at 12% = $+329,000; Internal rate or return = 14%

Project	Year	Gross Costs	Gross Value of Production (= Gross Benefit)	Incremental Benefit (= Cash Flow)	D.F. 12%	Present Worth 12%	Present Worth Calculation at Internal Rate of Return D.F.	Present Worth Calculation at Internal Rate of Return Present Worth	Rank
IV	1	$25,000	$10,000	$-15,000	.893	$-13,395	17% .855	17% $-12,825	1
	2	5,000	17,000	+12,000	.797	+ 9,564	.731	+ 8,772	
	3	5,000	11,500	+ 6,500	.712	+ 4,628	.624	+ 4,056	
	Total	$35,000	$38,500	$ 3,500	2.402	$+ 797	2.210	$+ 3	

Benefit-cost ratio at 12% = $\frac{\$30,667}{\$29,870}$ = 1.03; Net present worth at 12% = $+797,000; Internal rate of return = 17%

a. The derivation of the benefit-cost ratio is not given in this table.

termed the "cutoff rate," and normally is set slightly above the opportunity cost of capital.)

One word of caution. In the case of mutually exclusive projects, direct comparison of internal rates of return can lead to an erroneous investment choice. This danger can be avoided either by discounting the differences in the cash flows of alternative projects or by using the net present worth criterion (see pages 110 to 128).

Relationships of discounted measures of project worth. We can now see the interrelationships between the three discounted measures of project worth we have been discussing. The internal rate of return is that rate which just makes the net present worth of the project equal zero and the benefit-cost ratio equal one. Tables 4-8 and 4-9 illustrate these interrelationships.

Computing the internal rate of return. In real life one cannot, except by a lucky accident, just choose out of thin air that discount rate which will make the cash flow equal to zero as we did for illustrative purposes in tables 4-8 and 4-9. Unhappily, there is no formula for finding the internal rate of return; we are forced to resort to trial and error.

To begin, a discount rate is chosen which a quick guess indicates might be in the right neighborhood. One way to make a quick approximation from which to begin is outlined in table 4-10. A bit of practice using this table and your first estimate will go quickly and with fair accuracy. It can be a great time saver. We can see how this works by applying it to the irrigation project in table 4-8.

Step 1. Start with the cash flow and take the early years when it is negative--in this case two. If there is a period when a heavy investment has been followed by a lapse of more or less maintenance while a project is maturing, take only the period of heavy investment. Such a situation might arise in an orchard project, for instance. Then the planting and other establishment investments would be the "initial costs" and the period while only weeding and care was given to the trees while they were maturing and before they come into bearing would be considered the "lapse" which is dealt with in step 4.

So now we have

$$\frac{\text{Average annual benefits}}{\text{Total initial costs}} = \frac{\$4,700}{\$13,500} = .35$$

Step 2. We reduce the step 1 estimate taking the five year

Table 4-10. Initial Estimate of the Internal Rate of Return
(Assumes internal rate of return
less than 100% and investment-type activity.)

Using the cash flow, following the step below:

STEP 1
Determine:

$$\frac{\text{Average annual benefits}}{\text{Total initial costs}} = \begin{array}{l} \text{Estimated internal rate of return in} \\ \text{decimal terms (i.e., not percent)} \end{array}$$

STEP 2
Reduce the estimate in step 1 by subtracting the amount indicated:

Duration of the Benefit Stream (Years)	Estimated value in step 1			
	Less than 0.1	0.1-0.2	0.2-0.3	More than 0.3
5	-	-	0.18	0.13
10	0.08	0.07	0.05	0.02
15	0.05	0.03	0.02	0.0
20	0.02	0.01	0.0	0.0
25	0.02	0.01	0.0	0.0
More than 25	0.0	0.0	0.0	0.0

STEP 3
Reduce the step 2 estimate by the amount indicated for the number of years in the investment period:

STEP 4
Reduce the step 3 estimate by the amount indicated for the lapse between the end of the investment period and the time of the first benefits:

Investment Period	Subtract from Step 2 Estimate	Lapse (Years)	Subtract from Step 3 Estimate
1	0	1	(Step 3 Estimate)2
2	1/2(Step 2 Estimate)2	2	2(Step 3 Estimate)2
3	(Step 2 Estimate)2	3	3(Step 3 Estimate)2
4	1.5(Step 2 Estimate)2	4	4(Step 3 Estimate)2
5	2(Step 2 Estimate)2	5	5(Step 3 Estimate)2

STEP 5
   a.   If benefits are larger in early years than later years, increase the step 4 estimate somewhat.

   b.   If benefits are greater in later years than in early years, decrease the step 4 estimate somewhat.

STEP 6
Shift the decimal point two places to the right to obtain the estimated internal rate of return in percentage terms (i.e., step 5 estimate x 100)

Source: Economic Development Institute teaching materials prepared by Frank H. Lamson-Scribner.

length of the benefit stream and the value in step 1 as more than 0.3.

$$.35 - .13 = .22$$

Step 3.   We reduce the step 2 estimate as indicated.

$$\frac{.22 \ \text{x} \ .22}{2} = .02$$

$$.22 - .02 = .20$$

Step 4.   In this project there is no lapse between the end of the investment period and the beginning of the benefit period, so no reduction is made.

Step 5.   The benefit stream is uniform (except for the salvage value which is small enough to ignore for purposes of approximation).   As a result, no adjustment need be made for step 5.

Step 6.

$$.20 \ \text{x} \ 100 = 20\%$$

which is our initial estimate of the internal rate of return of the project (and slightly higher than the true value, as we know from table 4-8).

Next, we proceed as laid out in table 4-11. First, we discount the cash flow by 20 percent.   The present worth of the cash flow is found to be $-560.   When the discounted present worth of the cash flow is negative, we know that the present worth of the costs is greater than the present worth of the benefits. The project cannot pay such a high rate of interest and still recover the capital investment.   Hence, we know the discount rate we have chosen is too high.   Now we need a discount rate which is on the low side. In this case, we chose 15 percent.   Discounting our cash flow, we find it to have a value of $+977 at this rate.   The positive value shows that the present worth of the project benefits is greater than the present worth of the costs.   The project could pay a higher rate of interest and still recover the capital invested.   Hence, we know 15 percent is too low a discount rate for this project.

Table 4-11. Analysis of Earth Fill Dam Small-Scale Irrigation Project Illustrating Interpolation to Estimate Internal Rate of Return (Thousand United States Dollars)

Year	Project Costs			Gross Costs	Total Value of Production (= Gross Benefits)	Incremental Benefit (= Cash Flow)	D.F. 15%	Present Worth 15%	D.F. 20%	Present Worth 20%
	Capital Items	Operation & Maintenance Costs	Production							
1	$ 7,500	$ 0	$ 0	$ 7,500	$ 0	$ − 7,500	.870	$−6,525	.833	$−6,248
2	6,000	0	0	6,000	0	− 6,000	.756	−4,536	.694	−4,164
3	0	600	700	1,300	6,000	+ 4,700	.658	+3,093	.579	+2,721
4	0	600	700	1,300	6,000	+ 4,700	.572	+2,688	.482	+2,265
5	0	600	700	1,300	6,000	+ 4,700	.497	+2,336	.402	+1,889
6	0	600	700	1,300	6,000	+ 4,700	.432	+2,030	.335	+1,574
7	0	600	700	1,300	6,000	+ 4,700	.376	+1,767	.279	+1,311
−	−	−	−	−	331[a]	+ 331	(.376)[b]	+ 124	(.279)[b]	+ 92
Total	$13,500	$3,000	$3,500	$20,000	$30,331	$+10,331	4.161	$+ 977	3.604	$− 560

a. Salvage value.

b. Omitted from total to avoid double counting.

Internal rate of return (internal economic return) = $15 + 5 \left(\frac{977}{1,537}\right) = 15 + 5 \ (.64) = 15 + 3.2 = 18\%$

Just where does the real internal rate of return lie? We could find this by successively narrowing down our limits until finally we find that discount rate which will make the sum exactly zero, but this requires a lot of repetitive computation and fractional discount tables which do not exist. Instead, we use interpolation to estimate the true value. (Interpolation is simply finding the intermediate value between the two discount rates we have chosen. Perhaps you learned to interpolate when you studied trigonometry in secondary school; the process used here is exactly the same.)

The rule for interpolating the value of the internal rate of return lying between discount rates too high on the one side and too low on the other is

| Internal rate of return | = | Lower discount rate | + | Difference between the discount | $\times$ | $\left(\dfrac{\text{Present worth of cash flow at the lower discount rate}}{\text{Absolute difference between the present worths of the cash flow at the two discount rates}} \right)$ |

This procedure has been applied at the bottom of table 4-11. The lower discount rate is 15 percent. The difference between the two discount rates is the difference between 15 percent and 20 percent which is 5 percent. The present worth of the cash flow stream at the lower discount rate of 15 percent is $+977. The absolute difference between the present worths of the cash flow at the two discount rates is $977 + $560 = $1,537. (Recall that the absolute difference is simply the sum of the two values ignoring the sign which is attached to them). Hence:

$$\text{Internal rate of return} = 15 + \left(\frac{977}{1,537} \right) = 15 + 5 \,(.64) = 15 + 3.2 = 18\%$$

In practice, it is better not to try to interpolate between a spread wider than about five percentage points. The internal economic or financial return should always be rounded to the nearest whole percentage point since the underlying projections never can justify the implication of greater precision.

Interpolation between discount rates which bracket the true internal rate of return always somewhat overstates the true return.

This is so because our linear interpolation technique makes the implicit assumption that as we move from one discount rate to another the internal rate of return will change following a straight line, whereas in fact the true value of the internal rate of return follows a concave curvilinear function as indicated in figure 4-2. The error introduced by interpolation normally is slight and disappears when you round the result to the nearest whole percentage point, but a final rate of return figure should always be verified. This can be done most easily by taking advantage of the fact that the interpolation error becomes less and less as we approach one of the discount rates between which we are interpolating. Thus, a verification procedure which reduces the computational burden is to use the internal rate of return estimated by interpolation to discount the cash flow once again. Depending on whether the resulting present worth of the cash flow is positive or negative, you can then interpolate between your estimated internal rate of return and either the higher or the lower of the discount rates you previously used. This procedure is illustrated in table 4-12. Interpolating between 15 percent and 20 percent gives us an estimated internal rate of return of 19 percent. Discounting the cash flow at 19 percent shows the present worth to have a negative value of Rp.-.21 thousand million. Interpolating again this time between 15 percent and 19 percent we find the estimate to be 18.48 percent which would be rounded to the nearest whole percentage point of 18 percent. Because we know that the interpolation process introduces very little error at this point but nonetheless does slightly overestimate the true rate of return and since we have rounded to the lower whole percentage value, we could confidently stop at this point. However, in table 4-12, for purposes of illustration, one further verification is made by interpolating between 18 and 19 percent. At 18 percent we have a positive present worth and at 19 percent a negative present worth so we know the internal rate of return rounded to the nearest whole percentage point must be either one or the other value. Since the interpolated value between 18 and 19 percent is 18.36 percent and we know that to be above the true rate by some small amount, we now know for certain that the internal rate of return rounded to the nearest whole percentage point must be 18 percent.

Another example may be seen in Table 5-2, page 105. If we interpolate between 20 and 25 percent, our estimated internal economic return is 22.52 percent which would be rounded to 23 percent. But knowing that linear interpolation overestimates the true internal rate of return we would want to verify this estimate. The present worth at 23 percent is $-25,000. Interpolating between 20 and 23 percent we find an estimated internal economic return

Figure 4–2. INDONESIA: Djatiluhur Irrigation Project
Illustrating Interpolation Error

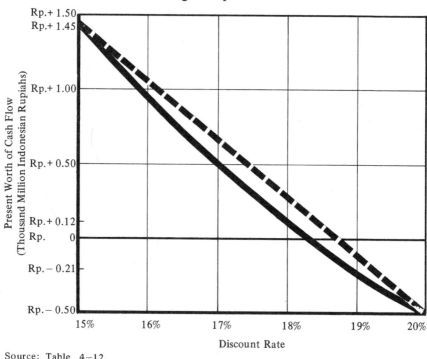

Source: Table 4–12.

of 22.25 percent which we can round with confidence to 22 percent.
(Further verification will show the present worth at 22 percent is
$+4,000.)

Reinvestment of returns. A criticism of the internal rate of
return method often heard is that there is an implicit assumption
that all returns from the project will be reinvested at the internal
rate of return. This is not, in fact, the case. Instead, the internal
rate of return is correctly interpreted as being "the rate of return
on capital outstanding per period while it is invested in the project"
(19, p. 38). Returns withdrawn from a project may be reinvested
at any other rate or consumed without affecting the internal rate
of return of the project.

More   than   one   possible   solution.   Under   certain
circumstances--extremely uncommon in agricultural projects--it is
possible that more than one discount rate will make the present
worth of the cash flow equal zero. This possibility has been the
source of considerable (and generally exaggerated) criticism of the
internal rate of return as a discounted measure of project worth.

Table 4-12. INDONESIA: Djatiluhur Irrigation Project
Computation of Internal Rate of Return Illustrating Interpolation
(Thousand Million Indonesian Rupiahs)

Year	Costs	Benefits[a]	Incremental Benefit (= Cash Flow)	D.F. 15%	Present Worth 15%	D.F. 18%	Present Worth 18%	D.F. 19%	Present Worth 19%	D.F. 20%	Present Worth 20%
1	Rp. .5	Rp. —	Rp. — .5	.870	Rp. — .44	.847	Rp. — .42	.840	Rp. — .42	.833	Rp. — .42
2	2.1	.4	— 1.7	.756	—1.29	.718	—1.22	.706	—1.20	.694	—1.18
3	3.7	.7	— 3.0	.658	—1.97	.609	—1.83	.593	—1.78	.579	—1.74
4	3.7	1.3	— 2.4	.572	—1.37	.516	—1.24	.499	—1.20	.482	—1.16
5	2.0	1.9	— .1	.497	— .05	.437	— .04	.419	— .04	.402	— .04
6	.5	2.2	+ 1.7	.432	+ .73	.370	+ .63	.352	+ .60	.335	+ .57
7-30	.5[b]	2.6[b]	+ 2.1[b]	2.782	+5.84	2.019	+4.24	1.825	+3.83	1.653	+3.47
Total	Rp. 24.5	Rp. 68.9	Rp. +44.4	6.567	Rp. +1.45	5.516	Rp. + .12	5.234	Rp. — .21	4.978	Rp. — .50

Source: IBRD. Djatiluhur Irrigation Project — Indonesia. Report No. PA-37. Washington: IBRD, 1970. p. 26; annex 10, p. 1.

a. Assumes only an improvement in water control; this is, no accompanying increase in the use of modern inputs.

b. Since this is the annual amount, it is included 24 times in calculating the undiscounted total.

Internal rate of return
interpolating between 15% and 20%: $15 + 5 \left(\frac{1.45}{1.95}\right) = 15 + 5 \, (.74) = 15 + 3.70 = 18.70 = 19\%$

Internal rate of return
interpolating between 15% and 19%: $15 + 4 \left(\frac{1.45}{1.66}\right) = 15 + 4 \, (.87) = 15 + 3.48 = 18.48 = 18\%$

Internal rate of return
interpolating between 18% and 19%: $18 + \frac{.12}{.33} = 18 + .36 = 18.36 = 18\%$

More than one solution can exist <u>only</u> when, following a period of positive cash flows sizeable enough that the cumulative present worth up to that point is positive, there then occur negative cash flows such that the present worth at t_0 of the cash flow from a given year onward (discounted in the normal way) is negative. Under such circumstances there <u>may</u> be more than one discount rate which will bring the present worth of the cash flow down to zero, although this will not necessarily be the case.

Negative cash flows for particular years are quite often found in agricultural projects. They can arise, for instance, when pumps must be replaced in an irrigation scheme or at the beginning of a replanting cycle in a crops project. Usually, however, the negative cash flows late in the project will have to be quite large for there to be multiple solutions; an occasional negative year or a final year or two of negative cash flows will generally not give rise to multiple solutions.

The kinds of situations where there are large negative cash flows late in the life of the project, although rare in agriculture, can be found in natural resource projects. In mining, they might occur, for example, if a bauxite firm were required as a part of its concession to restore the landscape after digging out the ore deposit. To illustrate a multiple solution we may turn to a natural resource example given by Grant and Ireson (9, 4th ed., p. 509-510). Take the case of an oil company offered a lease on a group of oil wells on which the primary reserves are close to exhaustion. The major condition of the purchase is that the oil company must agree to undertake the injection of water into the underground reservoir in order to make possible a secondary recovery at such time as the primary reserves are exhausted. The lessor will receive a standard royalty from all oil produced from the property whether from the primary or secondary reserves. No immediate payment from the oil company is required. The company estimates it will realize $50,000 a year for five years before exhausting the primary reserves. Then it must expend $800,000 for the water flooding project, after which it will realize $100,000 a year for the following fifteen years. The internal rate of return calculation is shown in table 4-13.

From the standpoint of agricultural project analysis, this is a curiosity of internal rate of return theory of virtually no practical importance. Should you happen to meet it, the analytical problem can be resolved by using either the extended yield method or the auxillary interest rate method. A discussion of these methods will be found in Merrett and Sykes (19, pp. 158-165) and Grant and Ireson (9, pp. 546-565).

<u>Point in time for internal rate of return calculations.</u> Internal rate of return calculations can be done from any point in time and

**Table 4-13. Internal Rate of Return Calculation for an Oil Well Project
Illustrating Two Solutions
(Thousand United States Dollars)**

Year	Net Benefit (= Cash Flow)	D.F. 20%	Present Worth 20%	D.F. 25%	Present Worth 25%	D.F. 40%	Present Worth 40%	D.F. 45%	Present Worth 45%
1-4	$+ 50	2.589	$+129	2.362	$+118	1.849	$+ 92	1.720	$+ 86
5	−750	.402	−302	.328	−246	.186	−140	.156	−117
6-20	+100	1.879	+188	1.265	+126	.462	+ 46	.345	+ 34
Total	$+950	4.870	$+ 15	3.955	$− 2	2.497	$− 2	2.221	$+ 3

Source: Grant and Ireson (9, 4th ed., p. 509).

all points will give the same return. In our illustrations we always calculate from t_0 into the future because that simplifies the calculation and emphasizes our concern with internal rate of return as a measure of investment worth. But if we chose the end of the project, for example, we could increase by compound interest factors all values in the cash flow and find that interest rate which just made the stream equal zero. If we were to choose a point midway through the project period as t_0 we could increase all values before the time from which we choose to work (say from t_{-5} to t_{-1}) by compound interest factors and draw down all future values (say from t_{+1} to t_{+14}) by using discount factors. Again, we would be looking for that interest rate which makes the value of the cash flow stream at t_0 equal zero.

What happened to depreciation? We can return now to look at a question which sometimes vexes people who are trying to use discounted measures of project worth.

In determining the gross cost stream for calculating our discounted measures of project worth we have not included depreciation as a "cost." It does not appear in the gross cost computation for the benefit-cost ratio. When we discussed cash flow, we noted that it was an undifferentiated combination of: (1) depreciation or amortization--return of capital, and (2) returns paid for the use of capital such as dividends, profits, and the like--returns to capital. We did not subtract out depreciation as a cost. Yet the internal rate of return is a measure of the earning capacity of a project--that is, the return to capital--while net present worth determines if a project can earn more than some stated amount of return to capital. What happened to depreciation?

The easiest way to go about illustrating what happens to depreciation is to compute the benefit-cost ratio, the net present worth, and the internal rate of return of a hypothetical example such as that shown in table 4-14. In this case, we are analyzing a project which doesn't exactly lose money, but on the other hand doesn't make money, either. In other words, its internal rate of return is zero, its net present worth at zero discount rate is zero, and its benefit-cost ratio at zero rate of interest is just exactly one.

The important question here is: did we get our money back? The answer, obviously, is yes. We spent $1,200,000 over the five years of the project and by the end of the fifth year we have received just exactly $1,200,000 back. So we didn't lose any of our capital and we recovered all of our other costs.

Did we earn anything on this project? Clearly no. Both the internal rate of return and the net present worth of this project were simply zero, and the benefit-cost ratio had to be computed at a zero rate of interest in order for it to come out to be one.

Therefore, return of capital is realized (that is, depreciation is covered and fully accounted for) when the project earns an internal rate of return of zero or greater, when the net present worth at zero discount rate is zero or greater, or when the benefit-cost

**Table 4-14. Discounted Measures of Project Worth
Illustrating Treatment of Depreciation
(Thousand United States Dollars)**

Year	Project Costs — Capital Items	Project Costs — Production Costs	Project Costs — Gross Costs	Total Value of Production (= Gross Benefit)	Incremental Benefit (= Cash Flow)	D.F. 0%	Present Worth 0%
1	$1,000	$ 0	$1,000	$ 0	$−1,000	1.000	$−1,000
2	−	50	50	300	+ 250	1.000	+ 250
3	−	50	50	300	+ 250	1.000	+ 250
4	−	50	50	300	+ 250	1.000	+ 250
5	−	50	50	300	+ 250	1.000	+ 250
Total	$1,000	$200	$1,200	$1,200	$ 0	5.000	$ 0

Benefit-cost ratio at 0% $= \dfrac{1,200}{1,200} = 1.0$

Net present worth at 0% $= \$0$

Internal rate of return $= 0\%$

ratio is one at a zero or greater rate of interest. We do not need to include depreciation separately as a "cost" in analyzing our project. It is automatically taken care of in the computation process. (There is another convenience: we do not need to make any decision as to what depreciation schedule to use, a notoriously difficult and arbitrary choice which is essentially an accounting, not an economic, problem.)

Of course, if the internal rate of return is less than zero, if the net present worth at zero discount rate is less than zero, or if the benefit-cost ratio at zero rate of interest is less than one, then we would not only have earned nothing, but actually would not even have recovered all our costs.

Length of the project period

For how long a period should you carry out your economic analysis? The general rule is to choose a period of time which will be roughly comparable to the economic life of the project.

Where the project turns on a fairly sizable initial capital investment, such as a tubewell or an orchard, a convenient starting point for establishing the period of the analysis is the technical life of the major investment item. In some projects, however, you may find that although the technical life of the major investment is quite long, the economic life is expected to be much shorter because of obsolescence. This is common in industrial projects and in transportation projects but is rather uncommon in agricultural projects. Even so, you might expect the economic life of a processing plant producing frozen foods to be shorter than the technical life of the equipment, or even that equipment for producing chicken broilers might become obsolete before it is completely worn out. In most agricultural projects, however, we do not anticipate rapidly changing technology will make a major investment obsolete over a medium-term period of twenty to twenty-five years.

Where the economic life of your project is not limited by considerations of obsolescence and the technical life of the major investment asset extends beyond about twenty-five years, there is another consideration which comes into play which helps establish a reasonable economic life for the project and, hence, for your analysis. At the kinds of discount rates we are talking about and the kinds of opportunity costs for capital we think exist in developing countries, any returns to an investment beyond about twenty-five years probably will make no difference in your ranking of alternative projects. As a result, few agricultural project analyses need be carried out beyond twenty-five years. But if the technicians with whom you are working feel you should carry the project out for a longer period because coconuts will bear for forty years or because a dam can reasonably be expected to last fifty years, it may be easier just to run the analysis through to a period which satisfies them rather than to discuss the matter further. Save the discussion for the difficult problems of project design and implementation.

To illustrate, we can make two approaches: looking at the discount factors themselves and running an illustrative internal rate of return.

First, the discount factors. Suppose you have a large dam. Reasonably, we can expect the dam to last well over fifty years, even though its effectiveness after fifty years may be greatly reduced because of silting. Yet look at the impact on the present worth (and hence, on present decision making) of those far distant benefits. At 14 percent, any benefit received in the fiftieth year is worth to us today only one-thousandth of its face value--a thousand dollars of return in fifty years is worth only one dollar today. Beyond fifty years this dwindles to such a minor amount that it is hard even to find a table to give the present worth factor.

Even if we are talking about extending the period of analysis from twenty-five to fifty years, the difference this additional twenty-five years makes is rather minor. Again, looking at the discount factors:

Present worth of an annuity factor for 50 years at 14 percent	7.133
LESS present worth of an annuity factor for 25 years at 14 percent	-6.873
Present worth of an annuity factor for 26th through 50th years at 14 percent	0.260

So doubling the life of the project by adding twenty-five years to the analysis is only to increase the total present worth of the project to us by about one-fourth of one year's annual return. Put another way, the return from the twenty-sixth to the fiftieth year is worth to us today only about three months' worth of the same return during the first year.

We can see the effect on the internal economic return in the calculation shown in table 4-15 drawn from the Lilongwe

Table 4-15. MALAWI: Lilongwe Development Program Illustrating Effect on Internal Economic Return of Doubling Project Life from 25 to 50 Years (Thousand Malawi Pounds)

Year	Incremental Benefit (= Cash Flow)	D.F. 10%	Present Worth 10%	D.F. 15%	Present Worth 15%
	Assuming Project Life of 25 Years				
1	M£ – 920	.909	M£ – 836	.870	M£ – 800
2	– 569	.826	– 470	.756	– 430
3	– 556	.751	– 418	.658	– 366
4	– 492	.683	– 336	.572	– 281
5	– 360	.621	– 224	.497	– 179
6	– 164	.564	– 92	.432	– 71
7	+ 30	.513	+ 15	.376	+ 11
8	+ 372	.467	+ 174	.327	+ 122
9	+ 563	.424	+ 239	.284	+ 160
10	+ 650	.386	+ 251	.247	+ 161
11	+ 710	.350	+ 248	.215	+ 153
12	+ 751	.319	+ 240	.187	+ 140
13	+ 781	.290	+ 226	.163	+ 127
14-25	+ 884	1.974	+ 1,745	.881	+ 779
Total	M£ + 11,404	9.077	M£ + 762	6.465	M£ – 474

Internal economic return = $10 + 5 \left(\dfrac{762}{1,236}\right) = 13\%$

Year	Incremental Benefit (= Cash Flow)	D.F. 10%	Present Worth 10%	D.F. 15%	Present Worth 15%
	Assuming Project Life of 50 Years				
1-25[a]	M£ + 11,404	9.077	M£ + 762	6.465	M£ – 474
26-50	884	0.838	+ 741	.197	+ 174
	M£ + 33,504	9.915	M£ + 1,503	6.662	M£ – 300

Internal economic return = $10 + 5 \left(\dfrac{1,503}{1,803}\right) = 14\%$

Source: Lilongwe Development Program. Report No. TO-610a. Washington: IBRD, 1968. Annex 4.

a. From total line in first section of the table.

Development Program in Malawi. Doubling the assumed life of the project (and assuming no more investment) increases the internal economic return by only 1 percent from 13 percent to 14 percent. Given the probable error in estimating yields, prices, and rates of acceptance by farmers, this difference is meaningless.

How far to carry out computations of discounted measures

In agricultural projects, it is misleading to carry out the computations of discounted measures very far. The underlying estimates of the data are so inaccurate at best that carrying out the computations to a number of places implies a precision which is spurious.

Internal economic return and internal financial return are best rounded to the nearest whole percentage point. Since extremely high internal rates of return are difficult to interpret on theoretical grounds, it is better to report them simply as being very high. As a practical limit, I would suggest not giving internal rates of return greater than 50 percent. Above that value, internal economic or internal financial returns may be reported as "over 50 percent."

For net present worth, it is normal to report the result to the nearest thousand or million units of currency, although in smaller projects the result may sometimes be given to the nearest unit.

Benefit-cost ratios are generally best rounded to the nearest tenth of a ratio value. A benefit-cost ratio for which the computation results in a value of 1.434 would be reported as 1.4.

To determine discounted measures of project worth at these levels of accuracy, discount factors of three decimal places are sufficient.

Choosing the discount rate

We have touched over and over on the problem of choosing the discount rate. For benefit-cost ratios or net present worth calculations the most appropriate rate is the opportunity cost of capital--that rate which will just result in all the capital in the economy being invested if all possible projects were undertaken which yielded that much or more return. If set perfectly, the rate would just reflect the choice made by the society as a whole between present and future returns, and, hence, the amount of total income the society is willing to save. As indicated, there are practical problems of establishing this rate. Many meetings supposedly to be devoted to a discussion of proposed projects have become sidetracked into a discussion of the opportunity cost of capital. In practice, the rate chosen is simply a rule of thumb: 12 percent seems to be a popular choice and almost all countries seem to think it lies somewhere between 8 percent and 15 percent. If you analyze a project and find an internal rate of return several percentage points higher than what some compromise has agreed to be the opportunity cost of capital then you stand a good chance of avoiding becoming bogged down in an argument about the "true" opportunity cost of capital.

Considerable attention is devoted in the professional literature to the question of the "social time preference rate." It is suggested that the discount attached to future returns by the society as a whole is different from that which individuals would use. Normally, it is felt that the society has a longer time horizon, so that its discount rate would be lower. This implies a different (generally lower) rate of interest should be used for public projects than for private projects, giving rise to some awkward allocation problems both in theory and in application. And, of course, just what is the social time preference rate is almost impossible to resolve.

It should be emphasized that financial rates of interest such as the government borrowing rate or the prime lending rate are almost always too low to justify their use in economic analysis.

Comparability of ranking among measures

Taking our opportunity cost of capital as the discount or cutoff rate, from any array of possible project alternatives all three discounted measures of project worth we have discussed will identify exactly the same group of projects for implementation, although mutually exclusive projects will have to be subjected to further tests if the benefit-cost ratio or the internal rate of return criterion is used (see pages 110 to 128). Neither the benefit-cost ratio nor the net present worth criterion can be relied upon to rank the projects accepted; the formal choice criterion simply tells us to accept the whole group. Internal rate of return, however, can be used to rank the projects within the group.

Some of the contrasts among the benefit-cost ratio, the net present worth, and the internal rate of return are compared in tabular form in table 4-16.

Limitations of partial analysis

It should be noted that all three of our discounted measures of project worth are what economists call "partial" analysis. That is, we assume that the projects themselves are too small in relation to the whole economy to have a significant impact on prices. If, however, the project proposed is a very large one in relation to the economy (or, perhaps, even to the region) no partial measure of project worth is appropriate and much more elaborate analytical procedures must be called into play. Neither benefit-cost ratio, net present worth, nor internal rate of return would be an appropriate analytical tool to apply to such projects as the Indus Basin development, the Mekong river development scheme, nor, perhaps, to a very large integrated regional agricultural development program.

Table 4-16. Comparison of Discounted Measures of Investment Worth

Item	Benefit-cost Ratio	Net Present Worth	Internal Rate of Return
1. Decision criterion	Accept all projects where b/c ratio 1 or more when discounted at opportunity cost of capital.	Accept all project where n.p.w. positive when discounted at opportunity cost of capital.	Accept all project with i.r.r. greater than opportunity cost of capital beginning with project having largest i.r.r.
2. Ranking.	May give incorrect ranking among project not mutually exclusive if have substantially different relationships between gross returns and operating costs (page 65).	Gives no ranking for order of implementation.	Will give correct ranking among project not mutually exclusive.
3. Mutually exclusive alternatives	May give erroneous choice.	Will normally give correct choice if accept projects with largest net present worth at opportunity cost of capital.	May give erroneous choice since small project may have higher i.r.r. than a larger project with still yields more than the opportunity cost of capital. Must discount differences between cash flows of alternatives (pages 113 to 123).
4. Choosing discount rate.	Must agree on suitable discount rate for all projects. If use opportunity cost of capital, it must be determined.	Must determine opportunity cost of capital.	Determined internally. Opportunity cost of capital problem arises only in determining cutoff rate.

Project analysis and national income growth

In developing countries where increasing national income rapidly is a major economic objective, analytical techniques should enable us to rank project alternatives correctly in terms of their relative contribution to income growth. Economic analysis using discounted cash flow as discussed in this chapter makes a major contribution to this objective. (Financial analysis rankings, obviously, do not). The project with the highest internal economic return will in general be that project which contributes most to national income. If all projects with a benefit-cost ratio greater than one or a positive net present worth at the opportunity cost of capital are identified, that will be the pattern of projects which will make the greatest contribution to income growth. A simple diagrammatic model can be used to indicate the relationship between discounted cash flow project analysis and national income accounting.[1]

Measures of national income. The most common measure of national income is either the gross domestic product (GDP) or the gross national product (GNP). Most national plans define the economic objective of development in terms of growth of GDP or GNP.

The gross domestic product is defined as the value of the gross output of goods and services produced in the country less the value of the intermediate goods and services--that is, those used in the process of producing other goods or services. Gross national product is the same as GDP except it includes income earned abroad and excludes income transferred out of the country by foreign owners.

The gross domestic product can be measured in three ways, all of which are equivalent and will give the same result:

1. The value of all expenditure on final goods and services produced (plus an allowance for home consumed production), less imports. In practice this is the means most commonly used because the data are most readily available.

2. The sum of all factor income payments including capital consumption allowances, and (for a market price measure) all indirect taxes net of subsidies.

3. The sum of the value added from every producing unit.

It is this third measure which is of most interest to us in the present context because it is through value added that we link project analysis theory with national income theory.

Value added. The value added of any enterprise is the market price of the goods and services completed less the cost of materials and services purchased from others -- the difference between gross output and the value of intermediate consumption. Value added may be gross or net. Gross value added includes payments for taxes, interest, rent, profits, reserves for depreciation, and compensation to management and other employees, including social security. Net

---

1 This model was originally developed by George B. Baldwin.

value added excludes depreciation. For present purposes we are interested in gross value added because it is the gross value added by all the productive enterprises in the economy which adds up to the gross domestic product.

The Baldwin project model. Starting from this view of national income as the sum of the value added of all productive enterprises (including, of course, projects), we may lay out a schematic "picture" or diagrammatic model of a project. (The way we will present the model is most directly applicable to internal economic return. With minor modifications it is equally applicable to benefit-cost or net present worth criteria).

We can picture a project in its simplest form as in figure 4-3.

Figure 4–3. Simple Model of a Project

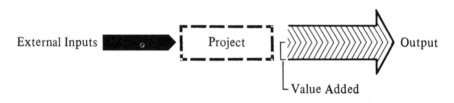

Here we see clearly that the difference between what the external inputs are worth and what the final output is worth is the value added created by the project. (We are assuming all costs and benefits are brought into the project accounts so that they are attributed directly to the project and that there are thus no secondary costs or benefits.)

How does the project create this added value? Obviously, through the use of its own, internal resources. We may conveniently divide these into just two major classes: labor and capital. Thus, our project now looks like figure 4-4.

Here we have an arrow representing the flow of output from a project--say, rice from a new irrigation scheme. The total output is made up of the contributions to the stream of output as a result of the external inputs (say, fertilizer, pesticides, and so forth) and the contribution of the project's own internal inputs of labor and capital. The value added is that amount of the total output stream which is attributable to the contribution of the internal inputs of labor and capital.

So far, we have been talking of "real" resource flows. That is, we have been talking of rice or coconuts or wheat or beef cattle.

**Figure 4—4. General Model of a Project Primarily from
the Standpoint of Economic Analysis Showing Real Resource Flows**

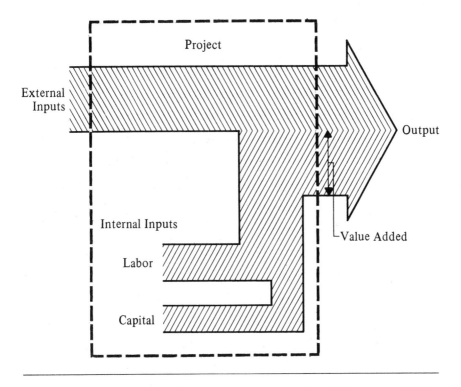

(Or automobiles or gasoline or consumer services if you would like
to be more general.)

Flowing in the other direction is the money stream--the money
paid for each of the real goods or services or their value stated
at shadow prices. The project receives payment from its customers
and, in turn, pays its suppliers for the external inputs it uses. What
is left over is available to remunerate the internal factors of
production. This, of course, is divided between remuneration to
the labor in the project and to the capital in the project. This
more complicated pattern is indicated in figure 4-5, the general
model of the project seen primarily from the standpoint of economic
analysis showing money flows.

We may examine the model in some detail. First, note that
figure 4-5 which shows money flows is the mirror image of figure
4-4 which shows real resource flows.

In figure 4-5, within the dotted rectangle which is the
"boundary" of the project, we represent the money flows which

Figure 4–5. General Model of a Project Primarly from
the Standpoint of Economic Analysis Showing Money Flows

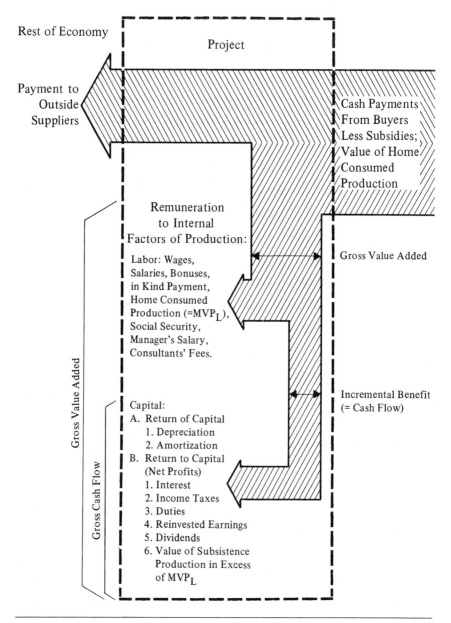

are the remuneration to internal factors of production. The first
point of interest is that the value added is identical to the total
of the remuneration to the internal factors of production (given

that we are assuming all effects are brought into the project accounts and that there are no secondary costs or benefits). The value added amounts, of course, to the difference between the value of goods and services provided by outside suppliers and the value of what is supplied by the project to customers plus the value of unsold output including home consumed production. (It may be stretching things a little to list home consumed production as a "money flow," but the only alternative is to adopt some very awkward terminology such as "money flows and imputed in kind payments." It seems better just to keep in mind that in kind payments may be valued at market prices for shadow prices and thought of as part of the money flow.)

The value added, in turn, is divided between remuneration to labor and remuneration to capital.

Labor payments include all kinds of remuneration for all kinds of labor--wages, salaries, bonuses, in kind payments, subsistence production up to the shadow price of labor, manager's salary, consultants' fees, and social security contributions. In kind payments and subsistence production greater than the shadow price of labor--which, you will recall, is an estimate of the marginal value product of labor (MVP_L)-- are properly attributable to capital remuneration, not to the wage component.

There is also a conceptual difficulty in the treatment of the manager's remuneration. Is an entrepreneur's compensation a return for his management skill or a return to his capital? We resolve this, sometimes rather arbitrarily, by assuming that the manager's salary is whatever we would have to pay to attract a manager of equal competence but who contributes none of the capital. In agricultural project analysis, we are inclined to simplify even further: in the case of farmers who own their own farms and supply most of both the labor and management skills, we are likely to attribute to the farmer only the equivalent of his wage as a laborer and nothing at all for his management skill. Anything over wage is considered return to capital.

Since we value labor at its going wage or at its marginal value product--its shadow price--it receives the same remuneration per unit regardless of which project alternative it is employed for. The residual which is left is the incremental benefit which we generally term the cash flow. If we can now choose that project alternative which will maximize the cash flow relative to the capital resources used, then we will know that we are at the same time maximizing the value added and, in turn, maximizing the contribution of capital to the national income. That is our macroeconomic investment objective and that is what the internal economic return enables us to do (as do the benefit-cost ratio and net present worth criteria given that we accept all project alternatives indicated by our formal decision criteria).

Appendix. Mathematical formulations

The formal mathematical statements of the most important discounted measures of project worth are given below.

$$\text{Benefit-cost ratio} = \frac{\sum_{t=1}^{n} \frac{B_n}{(1+i)^n}}{\sum_{t=1}^{n} \frac{C_n}{(1+i)^n}}$$

$$\text{Net present worth} = \sum_{t=1}^{n} \frac{B_n - C_n}{(1+i)^n}$$

Internal rate of return is that discount rate i such that

$$\sum_{t=1}^{n} \frac{B_n - C_n}{(1+i)^n} = 0$$

where

B_n = benefits in each year.

C_n = costs in each year.

n = number of years.

i = interest (discount) rate.

5. APPLYING DISCOUNTED MEASURES OF PROJECT WORTH

When you turn to applying discounted measures of project worth for economic and financial analysis of proposed projects you may run into some practical questions about their use. There are several of these which I would like to address in this chapter.

Sensitivity analysis (treatment of uncertainty)

One of the real advantages of careful economic and financial analysis of a project is that it may be used to test what happens to earning capacity if something goes wrong. How sensitive is a project's internal economic or financial return to increased construction costs? To a stretch-out in the implementation period? To a fall in prices? Reworking an analysis to see what happens under these changed circumstances is termed sensitivity analysis. It is one means of trying to deal with a key reality of project analysis: the fact that projections are subject to a high degree of uncertainty about what will happen.

All projects should be subjected to sensitivity analysis. In agriculture there are four main general kinds of sensitivity analyses which should be considered.

Prices. Probably every agricultural project should be examined to see what happens to its profitability if the price assumptions prove wrong. For this you can make alternative assumptions about future prices and see how these affect the internal economic and financial returns.

Testing a project to see what will happen to the internal economic return when you assume different shadow prices is also a kind of sensitivity analysis. You could examine a project to see what would be the impact on the internal economic return if you use the going wage for labor or a shadow price, the foreign exchange rate or a shadow price for foreign exchange, and so forth. Because of the difficulties of establishing shadow prices, if your project turns out to be relatively insensitive to shadow pricing, it is probably better to present your analysis in terms of the money prices and to note that the internal economic return is relatively insensitive to shadow prices.

Delays in implementation. Most agricultural projects are very subject to delays in implementation. Farmers may fail to adopt new practices as rapidly as we anticipate, they may find it harder to master new techniques than we had thought, or other technical difficulties may be underestimated. Testing to determine the impact of delay on the internal economic and financial returns from a proposed agricultural investment is an important part of the sensitivity analysis.

Cost overrun.   In those agricultural projects which involve significant construction costs, the project should be tested for its sensitivity to a cost overrun.

Yields.   You may wish to test a proposed project for its sensitivity to errors in yield estimates.   There is a tendency in agricultural projects to be optimistic about potential yields, especially when a new cropping pattern is being proposed and the agronomic information is based mainly on experimental trials.   A test to determine how sensitive the project's internal economic and financial returns are to lower yields may not only provide information useful in deciding whether to implement the project, but may also emphasize the need to assure proper extension services if the project is to yield as high a rate of return as could reasonably be expected.

The technique of sensitivity analysis is not complicated: you just do the calculation of the measure of project worth over again using the new estimates for one or another element of cost or return. To illustrate, consider table 5-1 for the Djatiluhur Irrigation Project in Indonesia.   In this case the project was tested for its sensitivity to a 30 percent cost overrun and to a 10 percent fall in the price of rice.   You will note what happened to the internal economic return.   The 30 percent cost overrun caused the return to fall by about 29 percent, while the 10 percent fall in the price of rice caused the internal economic return to fall by about 14 percent.   Whoever must make the project decision may now ask himself, "am I willing to run the risk of that large a drop in the internal economic return given how likely I think the cost overrun or the lower price is?"

Sensitivity analysis is really a straightforward (but often quite sufficient) means to deal with the question of risk and uncertainty in project analysis.   A much more elaborate risk analysis technique using probability theory and requiring use of a computer is outlined by Reutlinger (23). That approach is generally termed probability analysis.   By contrast, the techniques we have been discussing (including testing them through sensitivity analysis) are normally termed most probable outcome analysis.

Contingency allowances

Cost estimates for the investment period of a project generally are prepared on the assumption that there will be no modifications

Table 5-1. INDONESIA: Djatiluhur Irrigation Project Sensitivity Analysis (Thousand Million Indonesian Rupiahs)

Most Probable Outcome							
Year	Costs	Benefits [a]	Incremental Benefit (=Cash Flow)	D.F. 20%	Present Worth 20%	D.F. 25%	Present Worth 25%
1	Rp. .5	Rp. —	Rp. - .5	.833	Rp.- .42	.800	Rp.- .40
2	2.1	.4	- 1.7	.694	- 1.18	.640	- 1.09
3	3.7	.8	- 2.9	.579	- 1.68	.512	- 1.48
4	3.7	1.4	- 2.3	.482	- 1.11	.410	- .94
5	2.0	2.1	+ 0.1	.402	+ .04	.328	+ .03
6	0.5	2.5	+ 2.0	.335	+ .67	.262	+ .52
7-30	0.5	2.9	+ 2.4	1.653	+ 3.97	1.044	+ 2.51
Total	Rp. 24.5	Rp. 76.8	Rp. + 52.3	4.978	Rp.+ .29	3.996	Rp.- .85

$$\text{Internal economic return} = 20 + 5\left(\frac{.29}{1.14}\right) = 21\%$$

Assuming 30% Overrun							
Year	Costs	Benefits [a]	Incremental Benefit (=Cash Flow)	D.F. 15%	Present Worth 15%	D.F. 20%	Present Worth 20%
1	Rp. 0.6	Rp. -	Rp. - 0.6	.870	Rp.- .52	.833	Rp.- .50
2	2.7	0.4	- 2.3	.756	- 1.74	.694	- 1.60
3	4.8	0.8	- 4.0	.658	- 2.63	.579	- 2.32
4	4.8	1.4	- 3.4	.572	- 1.94	.482	- 1.64
5	2.6	2.1	- 0.5	.497	- .25	.402	- .20
6	0.6	2.5	+ 1.9	.432	+ .82	.335	+ .64
7-30	0.6	2.9	+ 2.3	2.782	+ 6.40	1.653	+ 3.80
Total	Rp. 30.5	Rp. 76.8	Rp. + 46.3	6.567	Rp.+ .14	4.978	Rp.- 1.82

$$\text{Internal economic return} = 15 + 5\left(\frac{.14}{1.96}\right) = 15\%$$

Assuming 10% Lower Rice Price							
Year	Costs	Benefits [a]	Incremental Benefit (=Cash Flow)	D.F. 15%	Present Worth 15%	D.F. 19% [b]	Present Worth 19%
1	Rp. .5	Rp. -	Rp. - .5	.870	Rp.- .44	.840	Rp.- .42
2	2.1	.4	- 1.7	.756	- 1.29	.706	- 1.20
3	3.7	.7	- 3.0	.658	- 1.97	.593	- 1.78
4	3.7	1.3	- 2.4	.572	- 1.37	.499	- 1.20
5	2.0	1.9	- .1	.497	- .05	.419	- .04
6	.5	2.2	+ 1.7	.432	+ .73	.352	+ .60
7-30	.5	2.6	+ 2.1	2.782	+ 5.84	1.825	+ 3.83
Total	Rp. 24.5	Rp. 68.9	Rp. + 44.4	6.567	Rp.+ 1.45	5.235	Rp.- .21

$$\text{Internal economic return} = 15 + 4\left(\frac{1.45}{1.66}\right) = 18\%$$

Source: IBRD. Djatiluhur Irrigation Project — Indonesia. Report No. PA-37.
Washington: IBRD, 1970. p. 26; annex 10, p. 1.
a. Assumes only an improvement in water control; that is, no accompanying increase in the use of modern inputs.
b. For a discussion of the interpolation interval see page 81.

in design which will lead to changes in the physical work required; that there will be no exceptional conditions such as an unanticipated underground geology; and that there will be no adverse phenomena such as floods, landslides, or unusually bad weather. Normally, too, project cost estimates assume there will be no relative changes in domestic or international prices during the investment period, and that the general price level will not rise. Clearly, it would be unrealistic to rest project cost estimates simply on these assumptions of perfect knowledge and complete price stability. Sound project planning requires provision be made in advance for possible adverse physical or price changes that are likely to add to the base line costs by including contingency allowances as a regular part of the project cost estimates.

Contingency allowances may be conveniently divided between those which provide for physical contingencies and those which provide for price contingencies. In turn, price contingency allowances may be divided between those which are intended to provide for relative changes in prices and those which are intended to allow for general inflation. Physical contingencies and price contingencies intended to provide for increases in the relative costs of project items during the investment period are a means of allowing for the fact that physical changes and relative price shifts are expected to occur even though it cannot be forecast with any confidence just how their influence will be felt. These contingency allowances, then, are expected, if unidentified, project costs and properly form part of the cost base when computing the internal financial and economic rates of return or other measures of project worth.

Inflation, however, poses a different problem. We have noted earlier that the most common means to deal with inflation when computing measures of project worth is to assume that all prices will be affected equally by any rise in the general price level and that the internal financial or economic return or other measure of project worth normally is calculated on the assumption of constant prices. Sound project preparation, however, must take into account that there may well be inflation and that cost estimates based on current prices may lead to a financial squeeze on the project as investment proceeds. If inflation is expected to be significant, provision needs to be made in preparing the project financing plan for the effects of a general price rise on project costs so that adequate budget funds can be anticipated and the project will not be subject to delay. Inflation contingency allowances which would then be included in the financing plan would not, however, be included among the costs when estimating the internal financial or economic rate of return. In some projects, especially those involving large initial investments, an alternative approach may be easier for decision makers to use. Both project costs and project returns may be increased by the amount of an anticipated general price rise. This will eliminate the need for a separate inflation contingency allowance or for excluding these contingencies from the financial and economic rate of return calculations. It does, however, require a defensible year-by-year estimate of the rate at which inflation is expected to proceed. Since future price increases can affect costs only until work is completed, the overall inflation contingency allowance is built up by applying the appropriate year end price increase factors to the unexpended costs at each year end. For example, assuming prices are rising by 10 percent a year, the inflation contingency allowance on a project involving expenditures spread equally over three years would be about 16 percent of its basic cost, not 30 percent.

Contingency allowances are normally not included for the operating costs of a project once the initial investment stage is passed. Rather, such problems as higher than anticipated production expenditures are normally dealt with by the use of sensitivity analysis.

In agricultural credit projects, it is generally not necessary to include contingency allowances. Changes in unit costs for this type of project primarily will affect the number of loans which can be made with the funds available rather than the economic justification of the project itself. However, contingencies in agricultural credit projects normally will be treated in the discussion of the economic justification of the project, perhaps in conjunction with the sensitivity analysis.

Contingency allowances are best shown separately in project tables with appropriate explanations of how they were arrived at in the accompanying text and notes. To avoid double counting, any contingency allowances already included in the basic material used to prepare the project analysis should be eliminated. The amount of a contingency provision will vary with the nature of the project and its general components. Contingency allowances should be determined item by item in each project, not based on some notional standard allowance. In general, contingency allowances should not be so large that they can cover any conceivable cost overrun since the possibility of this occurring is small. Such excessive prudence will reduce the pressure for careful cost estimating, relax pressure for tight cost control during project execution, and lead to misleading low estimates of the financial and economic return.

Physical contingency allowances are normally estimated separately for each major category of cost and separately for local and foreign exchange costs. Projects which include large civil engineering works require higher contingency allowances than projects which cover only the supply and erection of equipment. The cost of engineering works will be influenced by such factors as the topography and geology of the project area, the amount of field work necessary to prepare the detailed designs, unforeseen technical difficulties (especially if the project involves subsurface work), the risk of underestimating the amount of work which will actually be required, changes in design during construction, and unusually bad weather which may interrupt work. If large amounts of equipment are involved, contingencies may be appropriate to allow for errors in estimating the exact amount of equipment and the quantity of spare parts which will be needed.

Contingency allowances for relative price changes during the early investment phase of a project may reflect anticipated influences arising from domestic price increases, the expected trend of prices in leading supplier countries, price trends for particular kinds of work or kinds of equipment which are to be used, and the effect of the project on local prices where implementation of the project may exert a strong upward pull on prices of locally supplied labor and raw materials.

Replacement costs

Many agricultural projects require investments which have different lives. A good example is found in the case of a pump irrigation scheme where the earthworks and pump platforms may be expected to last thirty to fifty years but where the pumps themselves may have a life of only ten to fifteen years. In preparing the analysis, allowance must be made for the replacement costs of the pumps during the life of the project.

Treatment of replacement costs is simple. You include them in the capital items column for the appropriate year in your project analysis. In net present worth and internal rate of return analysis you then net them out when you compute the cash flow. This may make the cash flow for that particular year negative, but only rarely in an agricultural project could that introduce analytical complications (see pages 82 to 85).

The treatment of replacement costs is illustrated in table 5-2. The project is a pump irrigation scheme in the lower Mekong delta which would permit growing a second crop during the dry season. Canal construction and earthworks which take two years to construct would be necessary. Once the project is in operation, the earthworks are assumed to have a life of fifty years. The pumps, on the other hand, are postulated to have a life of only fifteen years.

Table 5-2. VIET NAM: Pump Irrigation Scheme to Permit Second Cropping
Illustrating Treatment of Replacements Costs
(Thousand United States Dollars)

Year	Project Year	Investment Costs Capital Items	O&M	Value of Production	Incremental Benefit (=Cash Flow)	D.F. 20% a/	Present Worth 20%	D.F. 23% a/	Present Worth 23%
1968	1	$ 323	$ –	$ –	$ – 323	.833	$ – 269	.813	$ – 263
1969	2	560	–	–	– 560	.694	– 389	.661	– 370
1970-83	3-16	–	46	259	+ 213	3.202	+ 682	2.715	+ 578
1984	17	125 b/	46	259	+ 88	.045	+ 4	.030	+ 3
1985-98	18-31	–	46	259	+ 213	.207	+ 44	.122	+ 26
1999	32	125 b/	46	259	+ 88	.003	–	.001	–
2000-13	33-46	–	46	259	+ 213	.014	+ 3	.006	+ 1
2014	47	125 b/	46	259	+ 88	.000	–	.006	–
2015-18	48-51	–	46	259	+ 213	.000	–	.000	–
2019	52	–	46	342 c/	+ 296 c/	.001	–	.000	–
						.000		.000	
Total		$1,258	$2,300	$13,033	$ + 9,475	4.999	$ + 75	4.348	$ – 25

Source: Personal communication from Mr. James Meitus, December 1967.

a. For a discussion of the interpolation interval see page 81.

b. Pump replacement.

c. Includes $83,000 salvage value allowance for pumps; earthworks are assumed to have no salvage value.

Internal economic return = $20 + 3(\frac{75}{100}) = 22\%$

Salvage values

Often at the end of a project there may reasonably be expected to be some salvage value--that is, the capital asset will not have been all used up in the course of the project period and there will be a "residual asset." The way to cope with this is to treat the salvage value of any capital item (say a dam or a stand of trees) as a "benefit" received by the project during the last year of the project analysis period. You will recall this is the way we treated the salvage values in the illustrative example given in table 4-6, page 62. Another example is found in table 5-2.

On the whole, salvage values will not change the internal economic or financial return estimate unless the analysis period is short or unless the value of the capital items is quite large in relation to the value of the benefit stream. For agricultural projects carried out to twenty-five years or so, the salvage value will rarely change the rate of return by as much as a percentage point. The reasons are just the same as we noted when discussing the length of the project period: at the earning capacities for the kinds of projects we are talking about, the present worth of future benefits (and, hence, the present worth of salvage values) is just not very great. A practical result of this is that projects are quite insensitive to errors in estimating salvage values. A rather gross estimate in a twenty-five year project is adequate. Note that in table 5-2, no error in estimating the salvage value could affect the internal economic return. Including salvage values in the project analysis will forestall criticisms of your analysis or attempts to discredit a project with a low initial investment in favor of another with a high initial investment on the grounds that you ignored the salvage value. This may be important when discussing irrigation projects or livestock projects because the technicians' concern and attention may be largely focused upon the problems associated with the capital investment in the dam or in the buildup of the breeding herd.

Sunk costs

Sunk costs are those which have been expended in the past on a project. There is an important point to be kept in mind here: when we consider a project expenditure it is only future returns for future costs which are the basis for our decision. Expenditures in the past, the sunk costs, do not affect our choice.

The purpose of economic and financial analysis is to help determine which among the alternatives open to us provides the best use of resources. Our decision starts from today; what is past is past and cannot be changed. The argument that much has already been spent on a project and therefore the project must be continued is not a valid decision criterion. In practice, of course, if you have already spent a considerable amount on a project, you probably will find the future returns to the future costs of finishing the project will be quite attractive. The ridiculous extreme is where only one dollar is needed to complete a project but where no benefit can be realized until it is complete. The "return" to the last dollar is extremely high, and it is clearly worthwhile to finish the project. But there may well be cases where a project is midway toward completion and it would be better simply to stop the project or else draw it to an early conclusion and then to use the available future resource expenditures freed from the project for higher yielding alternatives. For this kind of situation, discounted measures of project worth are a useful tool and provide valid guides to project decisions.

(On occasion you may wish to determine what actually was the rate of return on a completed project. For this you can compare the return from all expenditures over the past life of the project with all the returns. But note that this kind of analysis is useful only for working out some kind of a comparison of what past projects have yielded as a help to improve judgments about future projects. It is not an analysis of alternatives which permits us to make a decision about what to do at the present time. The money spent in the past on the project is already gone; we do not have as one of the alternatives not to do a completed project.)

Working capital

Confusion sometimes arises about how to treat capital used for short-term purposes and revolving within a single year. This might be the case, for example, for production credit lent to farmers but recovered at the end of the growing season. Such capital is sometimes overlooked because it may not show up as a net expenditure in a year-by-year buildup of project costs and benefits. It is not, however, available for other purposes in the society and is properly considered a project cost. It should be entered as a cost in the cash flow buildup the year it is first used. It then becomes a part of the salvage value at the end of the project.

Interest during construction

Treatment of interest during construction may also give rise to confusion. For the purposes of estimating the internal economic return, the net present worth, or the benefit-cost ratio, interest during construction--like all other remuneration to capital--is not treated as a cost to the project. The reason is that the economic analysis estimates a kind of average return to the project over its entire lifetime from the beginning through the construction period and on as implementation proceeds to the end of the project life.

The confusion about interest during construction arises in part because many lending institutions add the value of interest due during construction to the principal of the loan and do not require borrowing countries to pay any interest until the project begins to operate and new wealth is flowing into the economy. In effect, we may think of the financing institution as lending to the borrower to cover the costs of the interest through relending the interest payments immediately back to the borrower. In practice, there is not even this formality. The accounts simply note the increase in the loan necessary to cover the interest payments and add that to the principal of the loan which is due and on which interest is payable. This is sometimes known as "capitalizing" the interest during construction. Then the borrower pays back during the lifetime of the loan the principal and the entire interest due, including interest on the amount lent to cover the interest cost.

In financial analysis, of course, interest paid for money borrowed from outside lenders whether during construction or during the operation of the project is treated as a cost in the analysis.

Internal foreign exchange rate

In countries where there are balance of payments problems and where import substitution or export promotion are important objectives, it is useful to estimate how much it costs in terms of domestic currency to earn a unit of foreign exchange through a proposed project. This might arise, for instance, in preparing an oil palm planting project where export is the objective or in evaluating a fertilizer plant intended to reduce imports. It is not enough just to earn or save foreign exchange; some idea must be formed of its cost and a judgment made about whether that cost is too high. By expressing the cost of earning or saving a unit of foreign exchange in terms of the internal foreign exchange rate, a direct comparison may be made with the official exchange rate and various shadow prices for foreign exchange as one basis for evaluating a project.

There are many approaches to estimating the internal foreign exchange rate and numerous theoretical problems to be resolved. These have been discussed at length by Bruno (see, for example, (3) whose name is so closely identified with this topic that the internal foreign exchange rate is often termed the Bruno test.

Table 5-3 illustrates a straightforward approach to estimating the internal foreign exchange rate. This approach is suitable for most project purposes. Its major limitations are the tendency for some "domestic" costs in fact to involve imports--the import consumption of workers, for example--and the partial analysis problem which is common to all discounted measures of project worth. Its advantages are its simplicity and the ease with which the result can be interpreted.

In order to calculate the internal foreign exchange rate by this method it is necessary to know four items:

1. The foreign exchange value of the product to be produced.
2. The foreign exchange cost incurred to produce the product (that is, such things as imported fuels, imported raw materials, and the like).
3. The domestic currency cost of producing the output.
4. The opportunity cost of capital.

The present worth of the net foreign exchange saving (discounted at the opportunity cost of capital) is compared with the present worth of the domestic cost of realizing these savings. The ratio between the two present worths is the internal foreign exchange rate and may be directly compared with the official exchange rate or with shadow exchange rates.

The calculations are laid out in table 5-3. The Indian Farmers Fertilizer Cooperative, Ltd., proposed to build a modern petrochemical fertilizer facility in the state of Gujarat, India. The economic analysis gives the costs and benefits broken down into their foreign exchange components as listed in the table. The internal foreign exchange rate assuming a 12 percent opportunity cost of capital is Rp. 8.92 = US$1.

Since the official exchange rate at the time of the analysis was Rp. 7.50 = US$1, if the official exchange rate is accepted as a true measure of the value of the rupee (and 12 percent is accepted as the opportunity cost of capital), then it would cost more to manufacture a dollar's worth of fertilizer through the project for import substitution than it would to buy the fertilizer from abroad. However, at the time the analysis was undertaken, it was widely considered in India that a shadow price of at least 25 percent less than the official exchange rate would better reflect the true value of the rupee. This would make the shadow exchange rate Rp. 9.375 = US$1. If this rate is accepted (and still accepting 12 percent as the opportunity cost of capital), then it would cost less to produce a dollar's worth of fertilizer than to import it since the internal exchange rate of Rp. 8.92 = US$1 is a more favorable exchange rate than the shadow rate of Rp. 9.375 = US$1.

Table 5-3. INDIA: Indian Farmers Fertilizer Cooperative Fertilizer Project
Internal Foreign Exchange Rate

Foreign Exchange (Million United States Dollars)

Year	Value of Production	Investment Costs	Production Costs	Other Costs or Savings[a]	Incremental Savings	D.F. 12%	Present Worth 12%
1970	$ –	$ 7	$ –	$ –	$– 7	.893	$– 6
1971	–	15	–	–	– 15	.797	–12
1972	–	15	–	–	– 15	.712	–11
1973	12	–	12	–	0	.636	0
1974	38	–	18	–	+ 20	.567	+11
1975	43	–	20	–	+ 23	.507	+12
1976	56	–	26	–	+ 30	.452	+14
1977	56	–	25	–	+ 31	.404	+13
1978	56	–	25	–	+ 31	.361	+11
1979-84	56	–	25	–	+ 31	1.483	+46
Total	$597	$37	$276	$ –	$ +284	6.812	+78

Source: Computed from United States. Department of State. Agency for International
Development. *India: IFFCO Fertilizer Project Proposal and Recommendations for the
Review of the Development Loan Committee.* AID-DLC/P-851. Washington: Department of
State, 1969. Annexes 4A and 4B.

a. Includes such differences in cost or savings as foreign exchange for insurance, domestic
currency savings in distribution from avoiding port charges and locating production
closer to the point of use, and the like.

Discounting differences between cash flows to choose among mutually exclusive alternatives

Direct comparison of the internal economic or financial
returns or the benefit-cost ratios either of mutually exclusive
alternative projects or of mutually exclusive forms of the same
project can lead to an incorrect investment decision. This is so
because undertaking a small, high paying project may preclude
generating more wealth through a moderately remunerative but

Domestic Currency (Million Indian Rupees)

Year	Investment Costs	Production Costs	Other Costs or Savings a/	Incremental Costs	D.F. 12%	Present Worth 12%
1970	Rp. 107	Rp. –	Rp. –	Rp. 107	.893	Rp. 96
1971	172	–	–	172	.797	137
1972	56	–	–	56	.712	40
1973	24	38	–	62	.636	39
1974	–	81	–	81	.567	46
1975	–	90	–	90	.507	46
1976	–	109	–	109	.452	49
1977	–	109	–	109	.404	44
1978	–	109	–	109	.361	39
1979-84	–	108	–	108	1.483	160
Total	Rp. 359	Rp. 1,184	Rp. –	Rp. 1,543	6.812	Rp. 696

$$\text{Internal foreign exchange rate} = \frac{\text{Present worth of domestic currency cost of realizing foreign exchange saving}}{\text{Present worth of net foreign exchange saving}} = \frac{\text{Rp. } 696}{\text{US\$ } 78} = 8.92$$

larger alternative. When we are faced with choosing between mutually exclusive alternatives discounting the differences between the cash flows provides a convenient analytical tool for making the investment decision and in many situations a simple comparison of net present worths will suffice.

It should be emphasized that the analytical problem of choosing among mutually exclusive alternatives arises only when it is not possible, or at least not desirable, to implement more than one of the alternatives. If we can do more than one alternative, then the problem is exactly the same as we have been treating all along and we need only apply the straightforward decision criteria we have been discussing. Similarly, when a small project can be expanded by phases to become a larger alternative no analytical problem is posed. Implementing a small first phase project does not preempt a larger two phase project; we can implement both the first phase and the second phase judging each phase by its internal economic return in comparison to other project opportunities open to us.

We will take up five instances of mutually exclusive alternatives:

1.   The most general case is where we have entirely different alternative projects which are mutually exclusive–say, a choice between a small irrigation project which preempts a site and a larger one using the same site.

2.   As a variation of mutually exclusive alternatives we will discuss the scale of a project, viewing a large project as a mutually exclusive alternative to a small version of the same project.

3.   A third instance is the special case of timing where we wish to assess whether it would be better to begin a project now or later. In effect, postponing a project is a mutually exclusive alternative to undertaking it immediately.

4.   Another special case is when we have alternative technologies where the choice of one technology means we do not choose its alternative.

5.   The final case is that of additional purposes in multipurpose projects--the river basin project with an irrigation purpose included is a mutually exclusive alternative to the same project omitting irrigation.

In all these instances we will apply the same analytical technique to make the investment decision: we will find the differences between the cash flows year by year of the alternatives and find the internal rate of return of the stream of the differences. This internal rate of return can generally be interpreted as being the internal economic or financial return to the additional resources necessary to do a larger alternative as opposed to a smaller one, although in each instance exactly how we phrase this interpretation will vary with the circumstances. (Students of economics will recognize that we are, in effect, finding the marginal return for the marginal cost incurred.)

In several instances we will also discuss using the net present worths of mutually exclusive alternatives to choose between them. When the opportunity cost of capital is known, this is a simpler analytical technique.

Discounting differences between cash flows can be used for choosing among any number of mutually exclusive alternatives but it must be applied successively to every possible pair of alternatives. In practice, it is primarily used when the choice has already been narrowed down on other grounds to between two or perhaps three rather clear-cut alternatives.

Mutually exclusive projects.   Occasionally in agriculture we may be faced with the choice between two mutually exclusive alternative projects of an entirely different nature, one small and high yielding and the other large but low yielding.   At a given location we may have a choice either of constructing a small irrigation project limited to the best land utilizing rather simple equipment, or else building a considerably larger project involving a more extensive area and more costly, complicated engineering works.   If the small scheme is built it preempts the site so that the larger project cannot be built.

Mutually exclusive alternatives of this nature are uncommon in agriculture because it is usually possible to expand an agricultural project by successive phases.

When mutually exclusive alternatives are met, to choose between them by discounting the differences in the cash flows we first subtract year by year the cash flow of the cheaper alternative from the cash flow of the more expensive. We then discount the stream of differences to find its internal rate of return. This gives us the internal economic or financial return to the incremental investment necessary to undertake the larger, less remunerative alternative. We can then compare this return with that from other project opportunities, with a cutoff rate, or with the opportunity cost of capital.

Tables 5-4 through 5-6 illustrate how this works.   In table 5-4, we have a highly remunerative small-scale irrigation scheme costing $500,000 which preempts the site available.   A less remunerative alternative large-scale project costing $2,500,000 is presented in table 5-5. On the basis of a direct comparison between the internal economic returns of the two projects, we would choose the smaller scheme with its internal economic return of 27 percent as compared to 16 percent for the larger. However, in table 5-6 we note that the internal economic return of the differences between the cash flows of the two projects is 14 percent. The proper choice criterion, then, is whether we have alternative projects yielding

Table 5-4. Benefit-Cost Ratio, Net Present Worth, and Internal Economic Return of a Small Scale Irrigation Scheme Alternative
(Thousand United States Dollars)

Year	Gross Costs	D.F. 12%	Present Worth 12%	Gross Benefits	Present Worth 12%	Incremental Benefits (= Cash Flow)	Present Worth 12%	D.F. 25%	Present Worth 25%	D.F. 30%	Present Worth 30%
1	$500.0	.893	$446.5	$ —	$ —	$- 500.0	$-446.5	.800	$-400.0	.769	$-384.5
2	5.0	.797	4.0	140.0	111.6	+ 135.0	+107.6	.640	+ 86.4	.592	+ 79.9
3	5.0	.712	3.6	140.0	99.7	+ 135.0	+ 96.1	.512	+ 69.1	.455	+ 61.4
4	5.0	.636	3.2	140.0	89.0	+ 135.0	+ 85.9	.410	+ 55.4	.350	+ 47.2
5	5.0	.567	2.8	140.0	79.4	+ 135.0	+ 76.5	.328	+ 44.3	.269	+ 36.3
6-20	5.0	3.864	19.3	140.0	541.0	+ 135.0	+521.6	1.265	+170.8	.880	+118.8
Total	$595.0	7.469	$479.4	$2,660.0	$920.7	$+2,065.0	$+441.2	3.955	$+ 26.0	3.315	$- 40.9

Benefit-cost ratio at 12% $= \dfrac{920.7}{479.4} =$ 1.9

Net present worth at 12% = $441,200

Internal economic return $= 25 + 5 \left(\dfrac{26.0}{66.9} \right) = 27\%$

Table 5-5. Benefit-cost Ratio, Net Present Worth, and Internal Economic Return of a Large Scale Irrigation Scheme Alternative (Thousand United States Dollars)

Year	Gross Costs	D.F. 12%	Present Worth 12%	Gross Benefits	Present Worth 12%	Incremental Benefits (= Cash Flow)	Present Worth 12%	D.F. 15%	Present Worth 15%	D.F. 20%	Present Worth 20%
1	$1,500.0	.893	$1,339.5	$ —	$ —	$-1,500.0	$-1,339.5	.870	$-1,305.0	.833	$-1,249.5
2	1,000.0	.797	797.0	—	—	-1,000.0	- 797.0	.756	- 756.0	.694	- 694.0
3	100.0	.712	71.2	350.0	249.2	+ 250.0	+ 178.0	.658	+ 164.5	.579	+ 144.8
4	100.0	.636	63.6	450.0	286.2	+ 350.0	+ 222.6	.572	+ 200.2	.482	+ 168.7
5	100.0	.567	56.7	550.0	311.8	+ 450.0	+ 255.2	.497	+ 223.6	.402	+ 180.9
6-20	100.0	3.864	386.4	660.0	2,550.2	+ 560.0	+2,163.8	2.907	+1,627.9	1.879	+1,052.2
	$4,300.0	4.469	$2,714.4	$11,250.0	$3,397.4	$+6,950.0	$+ 683.1	6.260	$+ 155.2	4.869	$- 396.9

Benefit-cost ratio at 12% = $\frac{3,397.4}{2,714.4}$ = 1.3

Net present worth at 12% = $683,100

Internal economic return = $15 + 5(\frac{155.2}{552.1})$ = 16%

higher than the 14 percent we could realize from the incremental investment necessary to implement the larger project. If we do, then we accept the smaller project; if we do not, then we accept the larger.

An alternative technique to choose between mutually exclusive alternatives is to compare directly their net present worths at the opportunity cost of capital. In the case of the two projects in tables 5-4 and 5-5, let us assume an opportunity cost of capital of 12 percent. We can then see that although the smaller project has the higher internal economic return it has the smaller net present worth. If we choose the smaller scheme we forego a net present worth of $241,900 which otherwise would be available to the society. (Recall that if the opportunity cost of capital is set correctly we would be able to implement all projects having a positive net present worth at that opportunity cost.) This approach shares the weakness of all net present worth applications that an accurate estimate of the opportunity cost of capital must be available. It also gives us no ranking to tell whether to proceed with the larger project or to choose an entirely different investment.

Scale of a project. Sometimes we may wish to choose between a small form of a project and a larger version of the same project. We might think of a land settlement project which we could confine to a rather small area of high fertility soil or else undertake on a larger basis using poorer soils. Simply comparing directly the internal economic returns (although not the net present worths) could lead to an erroneous investment choice.

One analytical approach would be to find the cash flow of the smaller version, subtract it from the cash flow of the larger, and discount the stream of the differences. The result would be the internal economic return to the additional resources needed to undertake the larger project which we could then compare with a cutoff rate or the opportunity cost of capital. This would be parallel to the analysis illustrated in the previous section for mutually exclusive alternatives.

But note that in this case doing the small project does not preempt the site. We can choose, if we wish, to undertake the small project and then proceed to expand it. Under these circumstances, we do our analysis not of the small version versus the large version, but of the small version as the first phase of a two phase program. In that case, the internal economic return of the second phase of the program is the internal economic return of the differences between the cash flows of the two versions. This is a more direct approach and one which is more easily understandable. Trying to cast the analysis in the form of

Table 5-6. Internal Economic Return of Differences Between Cash Flows of Mutually Exclusive Alternative Projects
(Thousand United States Dollars)

Year	Cash Flow of Large Scheme	Cash Flow of Small Scheme	Differences Between Cash Flows	D.F. 12%	Present Worth 12%	D.F. 15%	Present Worth 15%
1	$ - 1,500.0	$ - 500.0	$ - 1,000.0	.893	$ - 893.0	.870	$ - 870.0
2	- 1,000.0	+ 135.0	- 1,135.0	.797	- 904.6	.756	- 858.1
3	+ 250.0	+ 135.0	+ 115.0	.712	+ 81.9	.658	+ 75.7
4	+ 350.0	+ 135.0	+ 215.0	.636	+ 136.7	.572	+ 123.0
5	+ 450.0	+ 135.0	+ 315.0	.567	+ 178.6	.497	+ 156.6
6-20	+ 560.0	+ 135.0	+ 425.0	3.864	+1,642.2	2.907	+1,235.5
Total	$ + 6,950.0	$ + 2,065.0	$ + 4,885.0	7.469	$ + 241.8	6.260	$ - 137.3

Internal economic return of the differences between cash flows $= 12 + 3\left(\dfrac{241.8}{379.1}\right) = 14\%$

discounting the differences between cash flows of mutually exclusive alternatives is a needless scholastic refinement.

Of course, if we have sufficient administrative and other resources, we may quite well implement two phases–or even more–simultaneously.   By analyzing each phase separately, our analysis can tell us directly how large we can make the project before we reach a phase which has an internal economic return below our cutoff rate.

Timing.   A special case of the choice between mutually exclusive projects is the question of whether to begin a project immediately or to postpone it.   The same project begun today or at some future time may be considered, from an analytical standpoint, to be two different, mutually exclusive projects.

Postponing a project can be advantageous only in circumstances where the potential benefit or cost stream will increase independently of when a project is begun.   In most agricultural projects this is not the case.   Rather, it is assumed that costs and benefits will come at some given period of time after the start of the project.   If the project is postponed, both costs and benefits will also be postponed and for the same period of time.

However, questions of when is the best time to begin implementation can arise in agricultural projects when there is a processing facility to be constructed.   We may want to establish sugar beets in a new area.   We have an idea of the maximum rate at which we can expand sugar beet acreage given the limitations imposed by extension work, rates at which farmers will adopt new practices, and the like.   We have a choice between shipping the beets to another area for processing -- incurring both a transportation cost and a loss in sucrose -- or building a new factory of a minimum economic size.   Here we have a case where timing should be assessed. The potential benefit of the project grows independently of the beet factory up to its capacity since it is dependent upon the rate at which farmers increase their output of beets.   In the first years of the project it might be too expensive to provide for local processing, but at some point the savings in transport costs and sucrose losses will make it economic to build the factory. The problem is when is it most economic to begin.

There are two general approaches to determining the optimum time to begin a project. The simplest is to compute the present worth of the project assuming it to be begun in different years and discounting by either the cutoff rate for project investment or the opportunity cost of capital if a good estimate is available. (The same year is taken as t_0 for all of the alternative present worth computations.) The project should be begun in that year when the present worth is the greatest. Prior to that time, postponing the project will increase its present worth at the given cutoff rate or opportunity cost of capital; after that time the present worth of the project will be less than it need be.

Discounting the differences between cash flows in successive years can also be used to determine the optimum time to begin a project. This method is more complicated to compute and still requires use of either the cutoff rate or an estimate of the opportunity cost of capital. General practice is to use the present worth method, since in any event a discount rate must be chosen and the present worth method is both simpler to compute and easier to interpret.

If discounting the differences between cash flows is to be used, the general rule for choosing the optimum time to begin is to start in that year when the internal rate of return of the difference between the cash flows of the earlier year and the next year just equals or slightly exceeds the cutoff rate for project investment or the opportunity cost of capital. In effect, this rule tells us to begin the project in the year when the incremental return for making the investment as opposed to postponing it just equals the cutoff rate or the opportunity cost of capital. (Economists will recognize that this states that the optimum time to begin the project is when the marginal cost equals the marginal return.)

The application of both methods can be illustrated by examining the Kenya feeder road example laid out in table 5-7. The road is estimated to cost £760,000 to construct divided equally between two years. It is assumed to have an economic life of thirty years. The earliest the project could be begun was in 1970. Once the road is complete, there is a two-year period while the traffic builds up rapidly as people learn about the new road and new traffic is generated. After that, the traffic level is determined by the general economic conditions of the area and is assumed to grow by 9 percent per year to 1991 and thereafter to be constant for the balance of the economic life of the road. The cash flows given in table 5-7 are based on the benefit stream derived from the traffic estimates. (The traffic estimates were made on the basis of growth over 20 years on the assumption the road was begun in 1970. It will be seen that even if traffic were assumed to continue to grow after 1991 the optimum time to begin the project would not change.) A salvage value is assumed based on linear depreciation in those cases where the benefit stream does not last a full thirty years.

To determine the optimum time to begin the project using the present worth method, an opportunity cost of capital in Kenya of 12 percent was assumed. The present worth of the road for each timing alternative from 1970 through 1977 was computed using

Table 5-7 KENYA: Third Highway Loan Project Feeder Road No. 10 Illustrating Optimum Timing (Thousand Kenya Pounds)

(1)	(2)	(3)	(4)	(5)	(6)	(7)	(8)	(9)
				Cash Flow Assuming Construction to Begin in:				
Year	1970	1971	1972	1973	1974	1975	1976	1977
1970	−380.0	−	−	−	−	−	−	−
1971	−380.0	−380.0	−	−	−	−	−	−
1972	+ 61.0	−380.0	−380.0	−	−	−	−	−
1973	+ 69.1	+ 67.0	−380.0	−380.0	−	−	−	−
1974	+ 77.7	+ 75.3	+ 73.0	−380.0	−380.0	−	−	−
1975	+ 84.7	+ 84.7	+ 82.7	+ 79.7	−380.0	−380.0	−	−
1976	+ 92.3	+ 92.3	+ 92.3	+ 89.7	+ 86.4	−380.0	−380.0	−
1977	+100.6	+100.6	+100.6	+100.6	+ 97.8	+ 94.5	−380.0	−380.0
1978	+109.7	+109.7	+109.7	+109.7	+109.7	+106.9	+102.6	−380.0
1979	+119.6	+119.6	+119.6	+119.6	+119.6	+119.6	+116.0	+111.8
1980	+130.3	+130.3	+130.3	+130.3	+130.3	+130.3	+130.3	+126.4
1981	+142.0	+142.0	+142.0	+142.0	+142.0	+142.0	+142.0	+142.0
1982	+154.8	+154.8	+154.8	+154.8	+154.8	+154.8	+154.8	+154.8
1983	+168.8	+168.8	+168.8	+168.8	+168.8	+168.8	+168.8	+168.8
1984	+183.9	+183.9	+183.9	+183.9	+183.9	+183.9	+183.9	+183.9
1985	+200.5	+200.5	+200.5	+200.5	+200.5	+200.5	+200.5	+200.5
1986	+218.5	+218.5	+218.5	+218.5	+218.5	+218.5	+218.5	+218.5
1987	+238.2	+238.2	+238.2	+238.2	+238.2	+238.2	+238.2	+238.2
1988	+259.7	+259.7	+259.7	+259.7	+259.7	+259.7	+259.7	+259.7
1989	+283.0	+283.0	+283.0	+283.0	+283.0	+283.0	+283.0	+283.0
1990	+308.5	+308.5	+308.5	+308.5	+308.5	+308.5	+308.5	+308.5
1991- 2000	+336.3	+336.3	+336.3	+336.3	+336.3	+336.3	+336.3	+336.3
2001	+336.3	+361.6 [a/]	+386.9 [b/]	+412.2 [c/]	+437.5 [d/]	+462.8 [e/]	+488.1 [f/]	+513.4 [g/]
Present Worth at 12%	+238.9	+262.2	+279.1	+290.8	+297.6	+300.6	+299.6	+295.4
Internal Economic Return	15%	16%	16%	17%	18%	19%	20%	21%

1969 as t_0 (that is, 1970 = t_1). The present worth is greatest if the road is postponed five years and construction is begun in 1975. This, then, is the optimum timing alternative. Beginning the road either before or after 1975 results in a lower present worth of the project at a 12 percent opportunity cost of capital.

The same optimum timing is indicated if we use the method of discounting the differences between the cash flows of successive years as is done in columns 10 through 16 of table 5-7. Subtracting the cash flow for the road begun in 1970 from the cash flow if

(1)	(10)	(11)	(12)	(13)	(14)	(15)	(16)
	Differences between Cash Flows Assuming Construction to Begin in Alternative Years Indicated						
Year	1971 less 1970 (3) - (2)	1972 less 1971 (4) - (3)	1973 less 1972 (5) - (4)	1974 less 1973 (6) - (5)	1975 less 1974 (7) - (6)	1976 less 1975 (8) - (7)	1977 less 1976 (9) - (8)
1970	+380.0	0	0	0	0	0	0
1971	0	+380.0	0	0	0	0	0
1972	−441.0	0	+380.0	0	0	0	0
1973	− 2.1	−447.0	0	+380.0	0	0	0
1974	− 2.4	− 2.3	−453.0	0	+380.0	0	0
1975	0	− 2.0	− 3.0	−459.7	0	+380.0	0
1976	0	0	− 2.6	− 3.3	−466.4	0	+380.0
1977	0	0	0	− 2.8	− 3.3	−474.5	0
1978	0	0	0	0	− 2.8	− 4.3	−482.6
1979	0	0	0	0	0	− 3.6	− 4.2
1980	0	0	0	0	0	0	− 3.9
1981-2000	0	0	0	0	0	0	0
2001	+ 25.3	+ 25.3	+ 25.3	+ 25.3	+ 25.3	+ 25.3	+ 25.3
Present Worth at 12%	+ 23.3	+ 17.0[h]	+ 11.7	+ 6.7[h]	+ 3.1[h]	− 1.1[h]	− 4.2
Internal Economic Return to Investment Made During the Year	8%	9%	10%	10%	11%	12%	13%

Source: Adapted from IBRD. *Appraisal of a Third Highway Project − Kenya.* Report No. PTR-24a. Washington: IBRD, 1969.

a. Includes salvage value of £25,300.
b. Includes salvage value of £50,600.
c. Includes salvage value of £75,900.
d. Includes salvage value of £101,200.
e. Includes salvage value of £126,500.
f. Includes salvage value of £151,800.
g. Includes salvage value of £177,100.
h. Does not total due to rounding.

the road were begun in 1971 gives the differences shown in column 10. The net present worth of the differences at a 12 percent opportunity cost of capital is +23.3 which is the difference between the present worths of columns 2 and 3. The internal rate of return of column 10 is 8 percent. We can interpret this to mean that the incremental return to the capital used in the whole project if we begin in 1970 as opposed to beginning in 1971 is 8 percent. Since our opportunity cost of capital is 12 percent, it would pay us to postpone the project and to use our capital elsewhere in the meantime. The same analysis applies for every column up to and including column 14. In column 15, the difference between the cash flows assuming the project is begun in 1976 instead of 1975 shows an internal rate of return of 12 percent. This means that if we undertake the project in 1975 instead of postponing it to 1976, the incremental return on our capital will be 12 percent for the capital used in the whole project. Since this is just our opportunity cost of capital, it will pay us to begin the project in 1975 which is, thus, our optimum timing. This, of course, is the same result as we obtained using the present worth method. We can carry the analysis one step further for illustrative purposes. If we were to postpone our project from 1976 to 1977, the incremental return to our capital would be 13 percent. But there is no point in postponing the project longer because our opportunity cost of capital is 12 percent and by definition we are able to undertake all projects yielding over 12 percent. If we postpone the project, we will be foregoing a possible return on our money which would not all be productively employed. Again, of course, this is the same result as the present worth method gives.

(In some timing analyses the layout in table 5-7 where the earlier year is subtracted from the later year could give more than one internal rate of return solution since the difference stream begins with positive numbers which are followed by large negative numbers (see pages 82 to 85). Should this anomaly occur. It can be avoided by using the present worth method.)

Note how in this Kenya feeder road example of mutually exclusive timing alternatives an investment decision based on a simple internal economic return computation alone would lead to an erroneous choice. Beginning the project in 1970 would yield an overall economic return from the project as a whole of 15 percent. Since this is well above the opportunity cost of capital, at first glance it might seem justified to proceed with the project although we know, of course, that the incremental return to our capital would be below its opportunity cost and that postponing the project will increase its present worth. Choosing the optimum starting year of 1975 means the project will have an internal economic return of 19 percent. If we postpone the project still further, we know the present worth at the opportunity cost of capital falls and the incremental economic return rises above the opportunity cost of capital, but note that the simple internal economic return to the project as a whole continues to rise and might be misleading to the unwary project analyst. (Under our assumptions--and carrying out the project to the end of its economic life to avoid distortions due to a large salvage value--the internal economic return will rise until we reach the timing alternative which assumes construction to begin in 1987. From that point onward the cash flow of each timing alternative is the same and the internal economic return will remain constant at 35 percent.)

Choice between technologies (crossover discount rate). Discounting the differences between total cost streams (not cash flows as we have defined them for project analysis), can be used to supplement an economic or financial analysis to be certain a project's technology, design standards, and construction phasing have been correctly chosen. It may also be used to choose the minimum cost alternative when it is difficult to quantify the benefits of a project.

The method is used when there is a choice between two alternative techniques performing essentially the same function but which have different cost streams. We may want to choose between a grain storage system which involves a high initial investment for silos but low upkeep, or one which has much lower construction costs but which will entail substantial annual maintenance. In such a case, we will prefer the alternative with the lower present worth. However, if the cost streams have different shapes, the lower present worth may be different between a low discount rate and a high discount rate, so that our choice of alternatives will depend upon what the opportunity cost of capital or the cutoff rate is. At some discount rate a pair of alternatives may have the same present worth and we may be indifferent which we choose. This is known as the crossover or equalizing discount rate and can be found either by discounting the differences between the cost streams or graphically. If our cost of capital or cutoff rate is below the crossover rate, we will prefer the alternative entailing the higher initial capital outlay but lower expenditures in the future; above the crossover discount rate we will prefer the technological alternative with the lower initial cost even though this involves higher continuing costs later.

We may illustrate this with a forestry project in Tunisia for which the analysis is laid out in table 5-8 and figure 5-1. It is proposed to clear an area covered with maquis, a scrubby underbrush found in the Mediterranean region, at the rate of 400 hectares a year for five years in order to prepare the ground for reforestation. Two technological alternatives are available. The land can be cleared manually at a cost of $47,850 a year spread evenly over the five-year period for an undiscounted total cost of $239,250. Alternatively, tractors and clearing equipment could be purchased and the area cleared mechanically at a lower undiscounted total cost of $215,008. The mechanical clearing alternative involves a large initial capital expenditure of $90,700; after that, however, operation and maintenance costs are only some $25,000 a year.

Table 5-8. TUNISIA: Choice between Mechanical and Manual Land Clearing Alternatives Illustrating Crossover Discount Rate[a] (United States Dollars)

Manual Clearing Alternative

Year	Wages	Other Costs	Total Costs	Present Worth 10%	Present Worth 15%
1	$ 44,050	$ 3,800	$ 47,850		
2	44,050	3,800	47,850		
3	44,050	3,800	47,850	$181,399	$160,393
4	44,050	3,800	47,850		
5	44,050	3,800	47,850		
Total	$220,250	$ 19,000	$239,250	$181,399	$160,393

Mechanical Clearing Alternative

Year	Equipment Cost–	Operation and Maintenance	Total Costs	Present Worth 10%	Present Worth 15%
1	$ 90,700[b]	$ 21,586	$112,286	$102,068	$ 97,689
2	–	25,134	25,134	20,761	19,001
3	–	25,134	25,134	18,876	16,538
4	–	26,227	26,227	17,913	15,002
5	–	26,227	26,227	16,287	13,035
Total	$ 90,700	$124,308	$215,008	$175,905	$161,265

Crossover Discount Rate

Year	Difference between Cost Streams	Present Worth 10%	Present Worth 15%
1	$−64,436	$−58,572	$−56,059
2	+22,716	+18,763	+17,173
3	+22,716	+17,060	+14,947
4	+21,623	+14,769	+12,368
5	+21,623	+13,428	+10,747
Total	$+24,242	$+ 5,448	$− 824

$$\text{Crossover discount rate} = 10 + 5(\frac{5,448}{6,272}) = 14\%$$

Source: Adapted from personal communication from Mr. Hans Warfvinge, Swedish International Development Authority, December 1971.

a. All prices at market prices.
b. Tractor and clearer CIF Tunis taxes included.

The proper choice between these two alternatives must allow for the time value of money. If a discount rate of 10 percent is assumed, we find the mechanical alternative continues to be cheaper and has the lower present worth. At 15 percent, however, we find the manual method has the lower present worth and, hence, costs less. If we subtract year by year the cost stream of the cheaper undiscounted alternative--in this case the mechanical clearing--from the more expensive undiscounted alternative--the manual clearing--and then find the discount rate which brings the stream of the differences between the cost streams to zero we will find that discount rate at which the present worths of the two alternatives

Figure 5–1. TUNISIA: Choice between Mechanical and Manual Land Clearing Alternatives Illustrating Graphical Derivation of Crossover Discount Rate

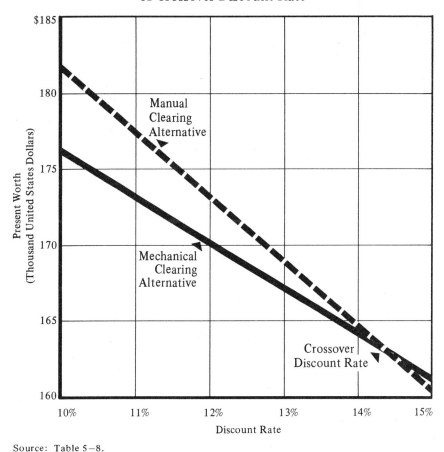

Source: Table 5–8.

are equal (hence, the term equalizing discount rate). From an economic standpoint, at this rate we are indifferent between the alternatives. (This discount rate may also be derived graphically as illustrated in figure 5-1.) In the Tunisian example, this crossover or equalizing discount rate is 14 percent. If our opportunity cost of capital were 10 percent, we would prefer the mechanical clearing alternative assuming our criteria were based strictly on cost grounds. If the opportunity cost of capital were 15 percent, we would prefer the manual clearing alternative even though it is the more expensive in absolute (undiscounted) terms. If the opportunity cost of capital were 14 percent, we would be essentially indifferent between the alternatives.

In Tunisia, where the opportunity cost of capital is probably very little if any less than 14 percent, the manual alternative would doubtlessly be chosen if for no other reason than the employment effect it would have. Note, too, that the example uses market prices. If we were to shadow price labor at 50 percent of its wage the undiscounted cost of the manual clearing alternative falls to $129,125 which makes it well below the undiscounted cost of the mechanical alternative even if we reduce the cost of the tractor and clearing equipment by the amount of duties and taxes. At the shadow wage, there would be no case for the mechanical alternative in this example. In other projects, however, the effect of the shadow wage would be to reduce the crossover discount rate, possibly moving it below a cutoff rate so that a labor intensive alternative which would not be attractive at market prices might prove to be more desirable if we use shadow prices in the economic analysis.

Additional purposes in multipurpose projects. A variation of the mutually exclusive alternatives problem arises in multipurpose projects, of which the classic example is a river basin development. The reason we are interested in multipurpose projects, of course, is that often it is possible to provide a group of related goods and services more cheaply from a single project than it is to provide the same benefits from the most economic alternative single purpose projects. But there is a danger that a very beneficial purpose (flood control, perhaps) may drive up the overall internal economic return and so hide the fact that another purpose (irrigation perhaps) should be omitted.

Discounting the differences between cash flows to test projects for additional purposes may be illustrated by the multipurpose river basin development project for which the relevant information is given in table 5-9.

The differences between the cash flows of the project with and without irrigation is determined. The internal economic return

Table 5-9. UNITED STATES: Multipurpose River Basin Project
(Thousand United States Dollars)

Year	Costs	Benefits Flood Control	Benefits Irrigation	Benefits Power	Cash Flow	Cash Flow without Irrigation	Difference between Cash Flows with and without Irrigation	Present Worth 2.5%	Present Worth 5%
1	$- 3,588	$ —	$ —	—	$-3,588	$-2,456	$- 1,132	$-1,105	$-1,078
2	- 8,188	—	—	—	-8,188	-6,218	- 1,970	-1,875	-1,787
3	- 4,848	—	—	—	-4,848 a/	-1,983 a/	- 2,865	-2,662	-2,475
4-100	- 206	+ 271	+ 380	a/	a/	a/	+ 246 b/	+8,304	+4,213
Total	$-36,606	$+26,287	$+36,860				$+17,895	$+2,662	$-1,127

	Separable Costs			Alternative Costs		
Year	Flood Control	Irrigation	Power	Flood Control	Irrigation	Power
1	$ 84	$ 1,132	$ 600	$ 2,380	$ 1,880	$ 715
2	1,244	1,970	1,530	4,740	5,270	2,100
3	907	2,865	2,085	1,370	2,565	1,495
4-100	5	134	61	22	220	226
Total	$2,700	$18,965	$10,132	$10,624	$31,055	$26,232

Source: Adapted from United States. Department of the Interior. Bureau of Reclamation. *Reclamation Instructions Series 110. Project Planning.* Washington: Department of the Interior, 1959. p. 116.5.19.

a. The benefit from power is taken to be the present worth of the most economic alternative for providing that power. Hence, the contribution to cash flow cannot be computed — only the contribution to total present worth at a given discount rate. See text for fuller explanation.

b. Since the power benefit is the same between the alternatives with and without the irrigation component, although the undiscounted cash flows cannot be computed (as noted in footnote a), the difference between the two cash flows can be determined. Let us represent the value of the power benefit by 'e.' Then, the difference between the cash flows for the fourth through the hundredth years is computed as $(-206 + 271 + 380 + e) - [-(206 - 134) + 271 + e] = 246$.

$$\text{Internal economic return of irrigation component} = 2.5 + 2.5\left(\frac{2662}{3789}\right) = 4\%$$

of that difference is then computed using the normal internal rate
of return technique. In this case, the result shows the additional
investment necessary to include the irrigation component has an
internal economic return of 4 percent. This is then compared with
a cutoff rate or an opportunity cost of capital. In the case of
this project, the United States government at the time the project
was analyzed used a discount rate of 2.5 percent. At that rate,
the 4 percent internal economic return on the additional investment
necessary to include the irrigation component was above the cutoff
rate and the additional cash flow generated by the irrigation
component had a positive net present worth of $2,662,000, so the
irrigation purpose was considered economically justified. If,
however, the cutoff rate had been 5 percent, then the cutoff would
have been above the internal economic return for the irrigation
component, the net present value of the additional investment
necessary to include the irrigation component would have been
$-1,127,000, and including the irrigation purpose in the project
would not have been economically justified.

(A particular complication arises in regard to the benefit of
the power component. The economic benefits of electricity are
generally considered not possible to estimate. What is the benefit
of electricity, especially if much of it goes for household use? In
economic analysis, this is usually resolved by assuming alternative
projects generating the same amount of electricity have equivalent
benefits and simply choosing the one for which the present worth
of the costs is lowest. In comparing projects such as this
multipurpose project, the problem of valuing the power benefits is
avoided because although the absolute amounts of the cash flows
cannot be calculated, the differences between them can be. This
is so because the benefits from electricity remain the same whether
or not the project includes an irrigation component. A fuller
discussion will be found in van der Tak (28).

Presenting results of discounted project analyses

Once you have completed your project analysis, you will want
to present the results in a manner which others can use and follow.
Every project will, of course, require its own form of presentation.

Something on the order of the format used in the Ivory Coast
Cocoa Project case study in chapter 7 may be a convenient pattern.
This has the advantage of laying out the summary analysis to show
clearly the costs and the benefits. It makes it easy to show the
treatment of the "without" the project situation and were there
a net value of production foregone item not dealt with by land
purchase or by including rent as a cost, it could easily be

incorporated. Separating out the costs borne at the project level from those borne at the farm level is convenient for administrators.

It is unnecessary to include the details of the discounting computation in your summary presentation (although you may want to include them in an annex to your report). A notation in the main text and at the bottom of the summary tables about the internal economic or financial return, the net present worth, or the benefit-cost ratio is enough. If you clearly lay out how you arrived at your cash flow or your gross costs and benefits, those who are familiar with the analytical techniques will be able to understand how you carried out the discounting computation.

If you are presenting the results of financial analysis and show the internal financial return, do not fail to specify clearly the point of view you are assuming. The report should read "internal financial return to the farmer's own capital (equity)," "internal financial return to all resources used in the subproject," or some similar specific statement.

6. FINANCIAL ANALYSIS CONSIDERATIONS FOR AGRICULTURAL PROJECTS

Not only is it important to analyze a proposed agricultural project to be certain it will be beneficial from the standpoint of the economy as a whole, it is also critical to assess whether the farmers, private firms, government corporations, and other project entities which are to participate will have sufficient incentive and suitably timed cash flows that they will be able and willing to participate. It is the financial flows on which this assessment can be based which are the domain of financial analysis. Several of the more essential financial analysis applications are discussed in this chapter, but it should be clear that there is much more to financial analysis than can be taken up here.

The objectives of financial analysis are:

1. To insure that there are adequate incentives for farmers and other project participants.

2. To assess the financial impact of the project on farmers and other participants. This assessment is based on an analysis of the participants' current financial position and on projections of their future financial positions as the project is implemented.

3. To provide a sound financing plan for the project.

4. To determine whether the financial requirements of the individual participants in the project are properly coordinated. This determination is made on the basis of an overall financial projection for the project as a whole.

5. To assess the financial management competence, especially of the larger firms and project entities, in order to form a judgment about how well they will be able to discharge their responsibilities for project implementation and what management changes may be necessary.

Just how elaborate the financial analysis must be for a particular project will depend upon the organization of the project and its complexity. Most agricultural projects will probably call for a financial projection based on at least one pattern farm plan assumed for participating farmers. The financial projections for the private firms or project entities may be quite summary in a simply organized project, but a project in which a number of different firms and project entities are concerned may involve a much more complex analysis. An example of a financial analysis prepared by the World Bank for an agricultural project will be found in the Ivory Coast Cocoa Project case study in chapter 7. This would be considered a moderately complicated financial analysis, but by no means one of the most complex prepared for a Bank agricultural project.

Financial projections

A projection of various financial flows is basic to financial analysis.

Pattern farm plans. For most agricultural projects, the proper point from which to begin both the economic and the financial analyses is with a "model" or "pattern" farm plan for an individual farmer. Farm plans usually represent a careful judgment of agriculturalists about the "optimum" or most profitable farming activities and cropping patterns for a farm given reasonable assumptions about such things as the risk farmers are willing to assume and their preferences for subsistence food crop production. These considerations reflect themselves in the rate at which farmers can be expected to adopt new practices, the cropping patterns they will be willing to follow, the yields they can obtain, and the value of their total output. Intuitive judgments based on experience may be supplemented by simple partial budget analysis to test which among alternatives will give the farmer the better income, or judgments may be supplemented by formal programming analysis.

If the project is designed to help farmers add an enterprise to existing holdings--perhaps to plant an orchard or to begin poultry production--then the farm plan may deal only with the added costs and returns from the particular enterprise for which the investment is proposed.

If the project is designed to reorient completely farm production or establish new farmers--as might be the case in a pump irrigation scheme or a land settlement project--then the farm plan will deal with the whole farm and all the farmer's income.

Generally in a project, a half-dozen or so pattern farm plans will be worked out which among them cover the major variations in cropping patterns which can be expected. The farm plans are then used to prepare a financial projection for the pattern farms over the life of the project. The projection shows year by year the value of farm output arising from the project activity (including the value of subsistence crops), the cost of production, loan receipts and repayments, and the cash surplus or deficit. Sensitivity tests should be undertaken to assess the effects of such things as price or yield variation.

Most agricultural projects in developing countries include small farmers and when they do it is important to pay particular attention to the farm family earnings, the total of home consumed food (valued at the farm gate price) plus cash which the family will have to live on during the year. For most small farmers, this is the paramount consideration in deciding whether or not it will be worthwhile to participate in the project. In many countries, too, governments will have minimum income targets for small farmers who participate in the project. The projected farm plan provides the basis for determining if the income goal will be met or if some adjustment to the farm plan--perhaps increasing the average size of holding--will be necessary.

(A more complete discussion of the technique of preparing farm plans and of farm accounts analysis in developing countries will be found in Yang (30).

On the basis of the financial projections derived from the farm plans two directions of analysis can be pursued. One is to aggregate the individual projections to the project level and then to use them as a basis for a discounted measure of project worth--say, the internal economic return. The other is to use the projections as the basis for estimating the financial rate of return to the farmer's own capital.

A typical financial projection based on a plan for a deciduous fruit farm in Iran is given in table 6-1. The form for laying out the financial projection is a convenient one, although there could be many, many others. You will note the treatment not only of crop sales and input costs, but also of investment costs, receipts from loans, loan repayments, interest, and taxes. The method of computing the amount of the loan repayments is discussed on page 146. Examples of two other financial projections based on farm plans will be found in annex 8 of the Ivory Coast Cocoa Project case study, pages 184 to 187.

Projections for firms and project entities and assessing management. Financial projections for private firms, government corporations, and other larger project entities are usually approached in a rather different manner from that for the projections based on farm plans, but the difference is not so much one of concept as it is a recognition that larger firms and entities have more complex management organization, financial structure, and accounting systems.

The points of emphasis in financial projections will differ depending upon whether the firm or project entity involved is essentially financially autonomous or is essentially dependent upon government budget funds. For a private firm or a financially autonomous project entity much of the assessment of financial viability will turn upon whether the firm or entity in the past has been able to meet its obligations and to show an appropriate profit and whether projections for the project implementation period indicate it will continue to be able to do so.

If the project entity is essentially financially dependent, then the emphasis shifts to questions of how well the entity uses the money it receives, whether financial controls and reporting are adequate, and whether the entity is receiving and is likely to continue to receive the money it needs in the proper amounts and at the appropriate times necessary to implement the project on schedule.

Of course, the kinds of project entities vary widely depending upon the project under consideration. Sometimes the entity will be a project authority having complete responsibility for implementation and which operates quite independently of the rest of the government. Sometimes the project will be implemented by a special subdivision of a regular ministry office. Sometimes there will be a division of responsibilities among autonomous semigovernment agencies, regular ministerial agencies and private firms. Whatever the particular pattern to be followed, the financial analyst must prepare suitable financial projections for all the participants and for the project as a whole.

One kind of project entity frequently found in agricultural projects which deserves special attention is the agricultural bank or similar credit agency. The major distinction between a credit agency and other project entities is that the credit agency instead of operating on money earned from production activities or from selling services must operate on the interest spread between what it pays for the money it borrows from the central bank or elsewhere and the interest it receives from farmers to whom it has advanced loans. As a result, the financial analyst must attach particular importance to levels of interest and to the payment record of farmers to whom the credit agency has advanced loans. The financial analyst will expect the credit agency management to be more financially oriented than might be necessary in the case of most private firms or project authorities.

In assessing current and future financial positions, financial analysis relies on three main financial statements: (1) income and expenditure statements, (2) sources and applications of funds statements, and (3) balance sheets.

The income and expenditure statement (also known as the profit and loss statement) summarizes the financial results of operations over a particular period of time, usually a year. It is concerned with recurrent costs in trying to arrive at a determination of the profit or loss for a given year. The analyst will want to

Table 6-1. IRAN: Agricultural Development Fund Deciduous Fruit Farm Financial Projections
(Thousand Iranian Rials)

	Before Development	Year 1	2	3	4	5	6	7
OUTFLOW								
Capital Expenditure								
Land improvement and development	110[a]	245	245	–	–	–	–	–
On-farm irrigation works	1,450[a]	1,770	520	–	–	–	–	–
Agricultural machinery and equipment[b]	200[a]	660	–	60	–	200	–	–
Construction and installations	700[a]	500	–	–	–	–	–	–
Pre-production costs	–	360	500	500	–	–	–	–
Contingencies	250[a][c]	355	125	60	–	–	–	–
A. Sub-total	2,710[a]	3,890	1,390	620	–	200	–	–
Operating Expenses								
Salaries and wages	80	170	300	350	450	500	550	700
Annual inputs	200	170	380	380	650	430	450	500
Taxes[d]	–	–	–	–	–	–	–	–
Other, including contingencies	30	30	70	70	110	90	100	120
B. Sub-Total	310	370	750	800	1,210	1,020	1,100	1,320
Debt Service								
Interest and service charges at 8%	–	109	257	313	330	330 }		
Repayment							791	791
C. Sub-total	–	109	257	313	330	330	791	791
D. Total Outflow (A + B + C)	310	4,369	2,397	1,733	1,540	1,550	1,891	2,111
INFLOW								
Sales								
Wheat	200	–	–	–	–	–	–	–
Pears	170	250	420	590	840	1,090	1,340	1,340
Apples	–	–	–	–	–	320	640	960
Alfalfa hay	–	230	720	900	720	–	–	–
Salvage value[e]	–	–	–	–	–	–	–	–
E. Sub-total	370	480	1,140	1,490	1,560	1,410	1,980	2,300
F. Loan Funds	–	2,720	970	430	–	–	–	–
G. Total Inflow (E + F)	370	3,200	2,110	1,920	1,560	1,410	1,980	2,300
H. Net Cash Balance (G – D)	60	(1,169)	(287)	187	20	(140)	89	189
I. LESS Net Income without								
J. development	60	60	60	60	60	60	60	60
J. Net Benefit (= cash flow)	–	(1,229)	(347)	127	(40)	(200)	29	129

Source of Investment Funds				
Total Capital Expenditure (Line A)	3,890	1,390	620	Internal financial return to farmer's
Borrowed funds (approx. 70%)	2,720	970	430	own capital (equity) = 30%
Farmer's own funds (approx. 30%)	1,170	420	190	

Source: Adapted from IBRD. *Agricultural Development Fund – Iran*. Report No. PA-23a.
Washington: IBRD, 1970. Annex 11.

a. Represents depreciated value of investments, not annual investment expenditures.

b. Tractors are assumed to have a life of eight years; the tractor existing before development is assumed to have a depreciated value of Rls. 100,000 and be replaced in the fifth year. Other machinery is assumed to have a life of 10 years; it is assumed that the machinery existing before development has a depreciated value of Rls. 100,000 and is not replaced when worn out. In the first year of the project one tractor costing Rls. 200,000 and other machinery and equipment costing Rls. 460,000 is purchased.

8	9	10	11	12	13	14	15	16	17	18	19	20
–	–	–	–	–	–	–	–	–	–	–	–	–
–	–	–	–	–	–	–	–	–	–	–	–	–
–	200	–	460	–	–	200	–	–	200	–	–	–
–	–	–	–	–	–	–	–	–	–	–	–	–
–	–	–	–	–	–	–	–	–	–	–	–	–
–	200	–	460	–	–	200	–	–	200	–	–	–
800	900	1,000	1,100	1,200	1,200	1,200	1,200	1,200	1,200	1,200	1,200	1,200
600	700	800	900	1,000	1,000	1,000	1,000	1,000	1,000	1,000	1,000	1,000
–	–	–	–	–	–	–	–	–	–	–	–	–
140	160	180	200	220	220	220	220	220	220	220	220	220
1,540	1,760	1,980	2,200	2,420	2,420	2,420	2,420	2,420	2,420	2,420	2,420	2,420
791	791	791	791	791	–	–	–	–	–	–	–	–
791	791	791	791	791	–	–	–	–	–	–	–	–
2,331	2,751	2,771	3,451	3,211	2,420	2,620	2,420	2,420	2,620	2,420	2,420	2,420
–	–	–	–	–	–	–	–	–	–	–	–	–
1,340	1,340	1,340	1,340	1,340	1,340	1,340	1,340	1,340	1,340	1,340	1,340	1,340
1,600	2,240	3,200	4,480	5,760	5,760	5,760	5,760	5,760	5,760	5,760	5,760	5,760
–	–	–	–	–	–	–	–	–	–	–	–	178
2,940	3,580	4,540	5,820	7,100	7,100	7,100	7,100	7,100	7,100	7,100	7,100	7,278
2,940	3,580	4,540	5,820	7,100	7,100	7,100	7,100	7,100	7,100	7,100	7,100	7,278
609	829	1,769	2,369	3,889	4,680	4,480	4,680	4,680	4,480	4,680	4,680	4,858
60	60	60	60	60	60	60	60	60	60	60	60	60
549	769	1,709	2,309	3,829	4,620	4,420	4,620	4,620	4,420	4,620	4,620	4,798

c. Represents allowance for other capital items not explicitly listed.

d. For new agricultural developments of this type, taxes are forgiven for the first 10 years. For the balance of the period for this type of enterprise they would be negligible.

e. Salvage values are for machinery and equipment only; all other assets including standing trees are assumed to have a zero salvage value.

look at the actual income and expenditure accounts for several recent years if the firm or entity concerned is already in operation, and to project the accounts for the project development period.

For a private firm or a financially autonomous entity, a prime question is whether it has been able to cover its expenses and still realize a profit–and whether the projection of the income and expenditure statement indicates it will continue to be able to do so in the future. Otherwise, the firm or entity will experience difficulty securing the financing it will need to carry out its responsibilities whether through borrowing or through attracting equity participation. In assessing past performance and the future impact of the project on the firm or entity, the analyst often uses ratios to help form his judgments. Among others, he will be looking at the interest coverage--the ratio of profits to interest payments on outstanding debt--the annual return on the net fixed assets in operation, and the ratio of net profits to total sales.

Whether the entity is financially autonomous or financially dependent, many of the aspects to be considered are the same, both in analyzing past performance and in interpreting the projected impact of the proposed project as reflected in the income and expenditure statement. Have receipts for sales been received promptly and in the proper amount? Is all the income properly due in fact accruing to the entity? When the entity has a choice in its pricing policy, has it set prices at a reasonable level?

Turning to a consideration of expenses, are they too high? Are there alternative sources of supply which might be less expensive? Is full advantage taken of discounts available for prompt payment of obligations? Are all expenditures properly chargeable to the entity? Alternatively, are some expenses perhaps too low? Is the salary schedule high enough to attract the caliber of staff needed? Is enough spent on maintenance? Are depreciation policies adequate?

An example of projected income and expenditure statements is found in table 6-2. The table refers to the Perusahan Negara Perkebunan (PNP), the Indonesian state owned estate enterprise.

The second type of financial statement which the analyst will examine is the sources and applications of funds statement. (The sources and applications of funds statement is also known as the cash flow statement. Here we will stick to the term sources and applications of funds to avoid confusion with the definition of cash flow we have developed in connection with our discussion of discounted cash flow analysis of projects. Unfortunately, the elements which enter into the two kinds of streams, both referred to as "cash flow," differ.)

The sources and applications of funds statement takes into account all cash flows in and out for both the recurrent and the capital accounts. The starting point is the net profit or loss from the income and expenditure statement which must be adjusted for noncash items such as depreciation. It will incorporate all capital expenditures, allowances for working capital, loan repayments, and the like, and shows how these costs will be financed. It will also show the cash surplus over the project development period.

The questions the analyst will direct his attention to in his examination of the sources and applications of funds statement revolve primarily around questions of the financing arrangements. He will want to consider how projected expenditures are to be financed. Will the money from the various contributors of investment funds to a project on which the project entity must depend be available in the proper amount and on time? Will expenses be financed out of long term debt? From bank overdrafts? By other short term debts? From earnings? By government subsidy? From equity contributions? As the project proceeds, what will happen to working capital--the sum of inventories, accounts receivable, and the increase or decrease in payables? A particularly useful ratio in considering the sources and applications of funds statement is the debt service ratio, the ratio of cash earnings to interest and repayment of debt.

An example of a projected sources and applications of funds statement is found in table 6-3. It refers to the Sharikat Jengka Sendirian Berhad (SJSB), a Malaysian government corporation charged with timber exploitation in a settlement project area. Another example of a projected sources and applications of funds statement will be found in annex 14 of the Ivory Coast Cocoa Project case study, pages 198 and 199, where the statement has been worked out from the standpoint of the government treasury.

The other major statement which would be examined as part of an assessment of financial management competence and of the financial impact of a proposed project on a firm or project entity is the balance sheet. Critical examination of balance sheets for the immediate past and of projected balance sheets for the project implementation period is essential for forming a judgment about the capital structure of the project entity and the impact the proposed project will have upon it. Here the financial analyst will consider a number of different questions. What is the debt-equity ratio, the relationship of total debt to the equity holding (net worth) in the enterprise? What is the relationship between short-term debt and long-term debt? Will the short-term debt continue to be available as the project proceeds (as might be the case if it is guaranteed by the government), or is there likely to be a refinancing

Table 6-2. INDONESIA: PNP IV Group of Estates Projected Income and Expenditure Statements 1970 Through 1988
(Thousand United States Dollars)

	1970	1971	1972	1973	1974	1975	1976
RUBBER PRODUCTION (MT)	21,739	21,599	21,690	25,872	26,697	27,388	28,333
PROCEEDS (FOB) a/	8,630	8,143	8,177	9,236	9,024	8,709	9,010
Less Export Duty and Cesses b/	1,295	1,221	1,227	1,385	1,354	1,306	1,352
NET PROCEEDS	7,335	6,922	6,950	7,851	7,670	7,403	7,658
OPERATING EXPENDITURE							
Upkeep – Mature Areas c/	418	448	461	499	535	561	590
Fertilizer – Mature Areas d/	269	–	–	291	301	304	308
Tapping Costs e/	622	677	707	777	844	898	955
Transport to Factories f/	16	16	16	19	20	21	21
Foliar Analysis g/	–	–	11	10	10	9	8
Processing Costs h/	890	892	903	1,087	1,133	1,174	1,227
Selling Costs, including Transport to Port i/	159	158	159	190	196	201	208
Inspection Service j/	–	–	–	–	–	52	52
General Charges k/	1,607	1,616	1,624	1,634	1,644	1,654	1,665
SUB-TOTAL	3,981	3,807	3,881	4,507	4,683	4,874	5,034
Contingencies – 10%	398	381	388	451	468	487	503
TOTAL OPERATING EXPENDITURE, EXCLUDING DEPRECIATION	4,379	4,188	4,269	4,958	5,151	5,361	5,537
NET PROFIT BEFORE DEPRECIATION, LOAN INTEREST AND TAXATION	2,956	2,734	2,681	2,893	2,519	2,042	2,121
Less Corporation Tax l/	965	721	667	854	710	539	525
NET PROFIT BEFORE DEPRECIATION AND LOAN INTEREST	1,991	2,013	2,014	2,039	1,809	1,503	1,596

Source: IBRD, *Second North Sumatra Estates Project – Indonesia.* Report No. PA-53. Washington: IBRD, 1970. Annex 15, table 2.

a. Rubber FOB price assumed to be US$397 per ton in 1970; US$377 per ton in 1971 and 1972; US$357 per ton in 1973; US$338 per ton in 1974; and US$318 per ton in 1975 and thereafter (equivalent of CIF New York prices 20, 19, 18, 17, and 16 cents per pound respectively).
b. Equal to 15 percent of FOB value.
c. US$22.50 per hectare of which labor costs are nearly 75 percent. The 1970 daily wage rate of US$0.42 equivalent is assumed to increase by 5 percent compounded annually until 1979 and by 1 percent compounded annually thereafter. By 1988 the daily wage rate is estimated to be US$0.72 equivalent, raising the total cost to approximately US$32.75 per hectare.
d. Assumed to be US$12 per hectare plus 20 percent for port handling and transport to estates. Expenditure 1971 and 1972 regarded as an investment cost.
e. Estimated requirement is 1.1 tappers for every 4 hectares. As labor rates are assumed to rise annually throughout the project life (see note c above), tapping costs rise from just under US$0.03 per kilogram in 1970 to approximately US$0.04 per kilogram in 1988.
f. At US$0.75 per ton of dry rubber production.
g. At US$0.50 per hectare of rubber from age 4 to 19 years.

1977	1978	1979	1980	1981	1982	1983	1984	1985	1986	1987	1988
31,177	34,146	37,274	40,376	42,821	44,697	44,945	46,204	47,080	47,235	47,406	47,149
9,914	10,858	11,853	12,840	13,617	14,214	14,293	14,693	14,971	15,021	15,075	14,993
1,487	1,629	1,778	1,926	2,043	2,132	2,144	2,204	2,246	2,253	2,261	2,249
8,427	9,229	10,075	10,914	11,574	12,082	12,149	12,489	12,725	12,768	12,814	12,744
679	774	866	923	960	983	963	976	974	955	948	950
343	376	406	429	443	450	437	440	436	424	417	415
1,123	1,285	1,454	1,552	1,619	1,662	1,632	1,658	1,658	1,628	1,619	1,626
23	26	28	30	32	34	34	35	35	35	36	35
7	7	7	7	7	7	7	7	7	7	7	7
1,364	1,511	1,668	1,828	1,944	2,034	2,049	2,113	2,159	2,171	2,185	2,179
228	250	273	296	314	328	329	339	345	346	347	346
52	52	52	52	52	52	52	52	52	52	52	52
1,676	1,688	1,700	1,702	1,705	1,708	1,710	1,713	1,716	1,718	1,721	1,724
5,495	5,969	6,454	6,819	7,076	7,258	7,213	7,333	7,382	7,336	7,332	7,334
550	597	645	682	708	726	721	733	738	734	733	733
6,045	6,566	7,099	7,501	7,784	7,984	7,934	8,066	8,120	8,070	8,065	8,067
2,382	2,663	2,976	3,413	3,790	4,098	4,215	4,423	4,605	4,698	4,749	4,677
593	·688	793	962	1,112	1,242	1,311	1,414	1,513	1,586	1,603	1,579
1,789	1,975	2,183	2,451	2,678	2,856	2,904	3,009	3,092	3,112	3,146	3,098

h. Materials assumed to be US$34.05 per ton of dry rubber production plus labor cost of US$6.90 per ton of dry rubber production in 1970 rising to US$12.16 per ton of dry rubber production in 1988.

i. To FOB only. US$7.33 per ton of dry rubber production. Includes transport to port, handling at port, documentation, and Joint Marketing Office expense.

j. US$1.50 per hectare of total planted area. Expenditure 1970 through 1974 regarded as an investment cost.

k. Covers PNB IV head office, estate, and factory overheads. Salaries are assumed to increase by 5 percent compounded annually until 1979 and by 1 percent compounded annually thereafter.

l. At current rate of 45 percent of net profits after deducting loan interest and capital expenditure allowances.

Table 6-3. MALAYSIA: SJSB Actual and Estimated Sources and Applications of Funds
(Thousand Malaysian Dollars)

Year ending September 30,	1970	1971	1972
SOURCES			
Net profit (loss)	M$ (629)	M$ (2,025)	M$ 3,045
Add: Depreciation and Amortization	912	1,915	3,255
Cash Income	283	(110)	6,300
Equity			
MARA	7,000	3,000	—
Pahang State	1,800	1,200	—
Total	8,800	4,200	—
Loan:			
MARA	1,700	(1,700)	—
IBRD Loan 673-MA	—	22,954	2,208
	1,700	21,254	2,208
TOTAL SOURCES	M$ 10,783	M$ 25,344	M$ 8,508
APPLICATIONS			
Buildings and Equipment			
— Forestry	5,660	3,754	—
— Processing	3,485	17,744	1,473
— Administration	96	81	—
	9,241	21,579	1,473
Road Construction	714	—	—
Management Fees and Expenses	2,171	2,373	1,612
Total	12,126	23,952	3,085
Replacements	—	—	—
Debt Service:			
Amortization on IBRD Loan	—	—	—
Increase in Inventories	137	623	185
Increase in Receivables	1,131	1,110	1,930
Less: Increase in Payables	(3,625)	1,020	(820)
Net Increase (Decrease)	(2,357)	2,753	1,295
TOTAL APPLICATIONS	M$ 9,769	M$ 26,705	M$ 4,380
Cash Surplus (Deficit)			
— Annual	M$ 1,014	M$ (1,361)	M$ 4,128
— Cumulative	M$ 1,014	M$ (347)	M$ 3,781
Debt Service			
Cash Income			
Debt Service Coverage			

Source: A.R. Whyte and R.D. Rowe. Memorandum dated November 30, 1970.

	1973	1974	1975	TOTAL
	M$ 5,321	M$ 5,864	M$ 6,508	M$ 18,084
	3,255	3,255	3,255	15,847
	8,576	9,119	9,763	33,931
	–	–	–	10,000
	–	–	–	3,000
	–	–	–	13,000
	–	–	–	
	592	–	–	25,754
	592	–	–	25,754
	M$ 9,168	M$ 9,119	M$ 9,763	M$ 72,685
	–	–	–	9,414
	–	–	–	22,702
	–	–	–	177
	–	–	–	32,293
	–	–	–	714
	592	–	–	6,748
	592	–	–	39,755
	1,530	2,490	2,050	6,070
	–	1,240	2,620	3,860
	70	(45)	(19)	951
	540	–	–	4,711
	(93)	–	–	(3,518)
	517	(45)	(19)	2,144
	M$ 2,639	M$ 3,685	M$ 4,651	M$ 51,829
	M$ 6,529	M$ 5,434	M$ 5,112	M$ 20,856
	M$ 10,310	M$ 5,744	M$ 20,856	
			M$ 3,960	
			M$ 9,763	
			2.5 times	

problem if the short-term debt falls due during a period of economic stress? Is the valuation of assets appropriate for a sound depreciation policy. Is there a suitable cash retention policy which will enable the entity to meet the cost of replacement of its capital assets? Are the stock and inventory levels appropriate? Are there excessive defaults on the repayment of loans made to farmers? Are there other bad debts? If so, what is being done either to recover past due debts or to write them off? What is the liquidity ratio, the relationship between immediate liabilities and liquid assets? (There are normally legal requirements about the liquidity ratio for banks.) What is the current ratio, the relationship between current assets and current liabilities?

An example of projected balance sheets is given for the Malaysian forestry project in table 6-4.

Financial projection for the whole project. In some projects the financial analysis will include a summary table of projected project costs which shows the interrelationships during the project implementation period of all the various financial projections for the pattern farms, private firms, and project entities involved. An example will be found in annex 8 of the Ivory Coast Cocoa Project case, pages 184 to 187. In many projects, however, the financial projection for a single project entity will serve as a summary for the whole project. This might be the case for example, where there is a project authority responsible for project implementation.

Assessing incentives

The most important objective of financial analysis is to insure there are adequate incentives for farmers and others who participate in the project.

For farmers, two kinds of incentives can be singled out for special attention. By far the most important for most farmers is the farm family net benefit--the home consumed production plus the net cash income after repayment of interest and principal--which will be available to the farmer if he participates in the project. This permits comparing the incremental benefit to the farmer "with" the project in contrast to the situation which would exist "without" the project. As noted earlier, the farm family net benefit is usually estimated in the financial analysis by projecting a pattern farm plan over the life of the proposed project. Whether the farm family earnings are sufficiently high to provide adequate incentives for farmers to participate in a proposed project is, of course, a matter for informed subjective judgment.

A second kind of incentive to take part in a project is the return a participant can expect to realize on the capital he invests.

Table 6-4. MALAYSIA: SJSB Actual and Estimated Balance Sheets (Thousand Malaysian Dollars)

	1970	1971	1972	1973	1974	1975
	PROVISIONAL. . . . . . .ESTIMATED.					
LIABILITIES						
Share Capital						
– MARA	M$ 8,700 [a/]	M$ 10,000	M$ 10,000	M$ 10,000	M$ 10,000	M$ 10,000
– Pahang State	1,800	3,000	3,000	3,000	3,000	3,000
– Pahang Development Corporation	–	–	–	–	–	–
Total	10,500	13,000	13,000	13,000	13,000	13,000
Surplus (Deficit)	(629)	(2,654)	291	4,837	9,774	15,607
Total Equity	9,871	10,346	13,291	17,837	22,774	28,607
Debt – IBRD Loan-673-MA	–	22,954	25,162	25,754	24,514	21,894
TOTAL LIABILITIES	M$ 9,871	M$ 33,300	M$ 38,453	M$ 43,591	M$ 47,288	M$ 50,501
ASSETS						
Fixed Assets						
Timber rights	–	–	–	–	–	–
Forestry	5,660	9,414	9,414	10,944	13,434	15,484
Processing	3,485	21,229	22,702	22,702	22,702	22,702
Administration	96	177	177	177	177	177
	9,241	30,820	32,293	33,823	36,313	38,363
Less: Depreciation	650	2,565	5,820	9,075	12,330	15,585
	8,591	28,255	26,473	24,748	23,983	22,778
Roads	714	714	714	714	714	–
Less: Amortization	262	262	362	462	714	–
	452	452	352	252	–	–
Total Net Fixed Assets	9,043	28,707	26,825	25,000	23,983	22,778
Current Assets						
Cash and Bank balances	1,014	(347)	3,781	10,310	15,744	20,856
Accounts receivable, deposits, prepayment, etc.	1,131 [b/]	2,241	4,171	4,711	4,711	4,711
Inventories	137	760	945	1,015	970	951
	2,282	2,654	8,897	16,036	21,425	26,518
Less: Current Liabilities	3,625	2,605	3,425	3,518	3,518	3,518
Net Current Assets	(1,343)	49	5,472	12,518	17,907	23,000
Deferred Assets						
Management Fee	1,856 ⎫					
Management Expenses	315 ⎭	4,544	6,156	6,073	5,398	4,723
Total	2,171	4,544	6,156	6,073	5,398	4,723
TOTAL ASSETS	M$ 9,871	M$ 33,300	M$ 38,453	M$ 43,591	M$ 47,288	M$ 50,501

Source: A.R. Whyte and R.D. Rowe. Memorandum dated November 30, 1970.

a. Includes M$1,700 advanced against share capital.
b. Excludes M$2 million recoverable from IBRD loan which would leave a net position of M$0.7 million.

For a small farmer, of course, this may be a relatively unimportant consideration since he may contribute very little or even no capital to the project.

On the other hand, for larger farmers and for most of the other participants in the project, the major incentive for participation will be the prospect of an attractive return to the capital (that is, to the equity) which each invests in the project. Thus, a principal concern of financial analysis is to estimate the rates of return to capital for each participant and to form a judgment as to whether that rate will be sufficient to attract participation.

Estimating internal financial return. As noted in some detail in Chapters 1 and 4, and elsewhere, in financial analysis we look at the return to the investment from the standpoint of the individual farmer or other entity participating in the project in contrast to economic analysis where we take the point of view of the economy as a whole. (Sometimes a financial rate of return will be estimated for all resources used in a project as a means of testing the financial viability of the project.) All values are taken at market prices, taxes are treated as costs and subsidies as income, and interest on repayment of borrowed money is a cost (see figure 4-1, page 68). However, the methodological techniques for estimating financial returns are identical to those used for estimating economic returns.

Of the three discounted measures of project worth we have discussed for use in economic analysis, the benefit-cost ratio is almost never used for analysis of private investments, that is, for financial analysis. Net present worth analyses are common but give no ranking among those alternative projects or other investment opportunities which have positive net present worths. (For the financial analysis of a private firm, the appropriate discount rate for finding the net present worth of a proposed investment will be a weighted average of the rate at which the firm will be able to borrow money for its proposed undertaking combined with an acceptable price-earnings ratio on equity shares.) The internal financial return—computed using the internal rate of return technique—is perhaps the best measure for investments made by individual entities for reasons closely parallel to those advanced in the discussion about internal economic return. It is a common corporate investment analysis measure.

When reporting the internal financial return, it is especially important to specify precisely from what point of view the calculation was made and just whose equity is assumed to be receiving the return. Otherwise, considerable confusion can result.

Computation of the internal financial return is illustrated in the financial projection for the Iranian deciduous fruit farm in table 6-1.

An excellent detailed discussion of investment analysis for individual entities will be found in Merrett and Sykes (19).

Leverage (gearing). Note that the return to the investment an individual farmer or other participant in a project realizes is substantially dependent upon the particular financing terms which are available. This is in sharp contrast to the economic return where the financing is normally not a consideration and does not affect the choice between alternative investments. The higher the proportion of borrowed capital a farmer or other investor can use, the higher the rate of return which he can realize on his own capital investment (and the higher the risk to which he exposes his own capital, of course). This is true because he pays a fixed interest for the borrowed money and any return to capital in excess of that fixed interest is available for remuneration to his own capital.

The ability of an individual investor to change his own internal financial return through the use of borrowed capital is termed "leverage" in American usage and "gearing" in British usage. Within the limits of the risk he can afford to bear on his own capital investment, it is clearly in the interest of the individual investor to drive his own equity down as far as he possibly can and to increase his borrowed capital to the maximum extent he can. But note that if he only contributes, say, 5 percent of the total capital but bears all the risk, a slight fluctuation in yields or prices might wipe out his whole capital investment while the lending agency might lose nothing.

When we plan a project we can consciously manipulate the leverage provided through favorable credit terms to farmers or other financial entities and thus substantially alter the incentive structure of the project. A balance must be achieved. On the one hand we want credit terms to be favorable enough to secure participation. On the other hand, we are concerned that no large farmer or other project entity be able to take undue advantage of the leverage provided by a government loan for a high proportion of the total investment cost at an attractive interest rate to drive the rate of return on his own capital to a windfall level above the minimum return necessary to attract his participation. This obviously would be unfair to others who cannot participate in the project and would mean tying up scarce government resources instead of mobilizing capital resources available elsewhere in the society.

The financial analysis will address itself to this question by examining what influence proposed financing terms will have on the internal financial return which various participants realize. In table 6-1, for example, is the 30 percent internal financial return which the farmer will receive on his own capital contribution sufficient to induce him to participate? Alternatively, is it perhaps too high? If you feel 30 percent is more than would be necessary to secure the farmer's participation, the financial analysis can test the influence on the rate of return of making the leverage less favorable by reducing the proportion of the investment which can be financed by borrowed capital from 70 percent to 50 percent. This does, in fact, reduce the internal financial return to the farmer's own capital from 30 to 25 percent. Is this sufficient to secure the farmer's participation? Is it still excessive? These questions are a matter of judgment; the financial analysis does not give the answer. Other aspects of the leverage could also be tested. The interest rate could be increased to reduce leverage or lowered to increase leverage. Similarly, the rate at which borrowed capital must be repaid can be varied to test the effect on the internal financial return to the equity of project participants.

One limit to the amount of leverage which can be provided in designing an agricultural project is found when participants are given 100 percent financing. An example might be a land development project such as those in Latin America or Southeast Asia where a number of governments have decided for many reasons to encourage new settlement by landless laborers. These countries are quite glad to make this possible using public funds and without asking the new settlers to make any capital contribution at all, although they commonly ask the new settler to repay the government with interest for the capital and operating expense incurred to establish his new holding. In a narrow, technical sense we might say the settlers in these projects receive an "infinite" return to their capital since they will receive part of the return arising from the use of capital without being asked to contribute any of their own. (The fact that they must repay the capital expenditure necessary to create their holdings does not affect this argument.) Yet no one is bothered that these settlers receive this return. It is more than offset by the reality that settlers make a real resource contribution through their labor and management skills and that their absolute incomes are modest.

Computing loan repayments

Table 6-5 illustrates how to compute the constant annual amount necessary to repay a loan with interest using the capital recovery factor (also called the partial payment factor or the annual payment factor). Although the total amount of each installment is the same each year, it consists of varying amounts of interest and principal repayment. Two alternatives are given, one assuming the interest during the grace period will be paid when it falls due and the other assuming the interest due during the grace period will be added to the principal ("capitalized").

Incidentally, an estimate of the annual repayment of capital and interest which a government must make to the World Bank for a project loan can also be computed using the capital recovery factor. However, the exact amount of the repayment will be somewhat different because Bank loan payments are due semiannually and computed according to a set formula for rounding the principal repayment and then adding the amount of interest due.

Joint cost allocation

Once it is determined a multipurpose project is economically justified (see pages 126 to 128), there arises the financial analysis question of determining an equitable charge for the goods and services produced.

This complication arises, of course, because there are joint costs in a multipurpose project which must be allocated. The technique most often used to allocate joint costs is termed the "separable costs-remaining benefits" method.

General principles of cost allocation. There are several general principles or guidelines of joint cost allocation which underly the rationale of the separable costs-remaining benefits method.

In general, no project purpose should be assigned costs in excess of the value of its benefit or be supported by the benefits of another purpose. Thus, the charge for irrigation water should not be greater than the contribution of that water to the benefits of the project. Similarly, we generally feel no purpose should be subsidized by another purpose: power users in most cases should not be charged high rates to make irrigation water available at low cost to farmers.

All the costs incurred for one purpose only should be allocated wholly to that purpose. The cost of canals is wholly allocated to the irrigation purpose and the cost of the transmission lines wholly allocated to the power purpose. These "separable costs" are the minimum which can be charged to this purpose. If the cost of the canals alone exceeds the benefit from the irrigation water, then clearly the project should not include an irrigation component.

On the other hand, no purpose should be assigned costs any greater than would be incurred if that function were to be supplied by the most economic alternative single purpose project. The alternative single purpose project establishes the maximum which can be charged for any one purpose. It is not equitable to allocate to the power component a cost more than that of the alternative thermal plant which could provide the same electrical service nor to charge the irrigation component more than the cost of an alternative single purpose pumping scheme.

Separable costs-remaining benefits method. To illustrate application of the separable costs-remaining benefits method for

Table 6-5. IRAN: Agricultural Development Fund Deciduous Fruit Farm Computation of Interest and Repayment of Principal
(Thousand Iranian Rials)

I. ASSUMING INTEREST DURING GRACE PERIOD PAID AS IT FALLS DUE

Loan term for 12 years at 8 percent interest with grace period extending through 5th year. Interest to be paid annually on outstanding principal during grace period. Repayment of principal to begin at end of 6th year and to be completed by end of 12th year. Loan disbursements made evenly throughout year.

	Years					
	1	2	3	4	5	6-12
Loan Funds	Rls. 2,720	Rls. 970	Rls. 430	—	—	—
Interest on first year loan [a]	109	218	218	218	218	—
Interest on second year loan	—	39	78	78	78	—
Interest on third year loan	—	—	17	34	34	— [b]
Total interest	109	257	313	330	330	
Annual repayment at 8% from 6th through 12th years [b]						791
Total debt service	Rls. 109	Rls. 257	Rls. 313	Rls. 330	Rls. 330	Rls. 791

II. ASSUMING INTEREST DUE DURING GRACE PERIOD ADDED TO PRINCIPAL ("CAPITALIZED")

Loan term for 12 years at 8 percent interest with grace period extending through 5th year. Interest due during grace period added to principal ("capitalized"). Repayment of capital plus accumulated interest due to begin at end of 6th year and to be completed at end of 12th year. Loan disbursements made evenly throughout the year.

Year of Disbursement	Amount of Loan	Interest Due on Disbursement Made During Year a/	Principal and Interest Outstanding at End of Year	Compound Interest Factor c/	Principal and Interest Due at End of 5th Year
1	Rls. 2,720	+ Rls. 109	= Rls. 2,829	x 1.360	= Rls. 3,847
2	970	+ 39	= 1,009	x 1.260	= 1,271
3	430	+ 17	= 447	x 1.166	= 521
Total					Rls. 5,639

Combined annual installment of interest and principal repayment due from 6th through 12th years b/ :

Rls. 5,639 x .192 072 = Rls. 1,083

a. Since it is assumed the loan will be evenly disbursed throughout the year, the interest due at the end of the year is computed by taking the annual rate of interest on half the amount of the loan. For the first year this is Rls. 2,720,000 ÷ 2 = Rls. 1,360,000 x .08 = Rls. 108,800.

b. The annual installment necessary to pay the interest due and to repay the principal in seven equal payments is computed by using the capital recovery factor for seven years at 8 percent and multiplying it by the total value of the loan outstanding. For the case assuming the interest during the grace period to be paid as it falls due this is .192 072 x Rls. 4,120,000 = Rls. 791,337.

c. The compound interest factor is for the number of years after the end of the year in which the disbursement is made since the interest accumulated during the first year is already accounted for in column 3. Hence, for the loan disbursed during the first year interest is due for a period of four years and the compound interest factor for four years is entered in the column.

joint cost allocation, we may turn again to the United States multipurpose river basin development summarized in table 5-9, page 127. (For simplicity, we will assume that the economic and financial values are identical.)

The analysis is set out in table 6-6. The first part of the table gives the basic data about the project which will be needed to allocate costs. The technical information about costs would be supplied by engineers and other technicians. First are the total costs for the project as a whole which are to be allocated among the three purposes. Included are both the construction cost (stated at its present worth as of the beginning of the project) and the annual operation, maintenance, and replacement cost (OM&R) necessary to operate the project.

Next are the separable costs given by purpose, both for construction at its present worth and for the OM&R charges. Separable costs are those expenditures which could be avoided if one purpose were excluded from the project. It is possible to find that no portion of the joint costs is solely and clearly traceable to a particular purpose. In measuring the separable costs, each purpose should be treated as if it were the last increment added to a project serving all the other multiple purposes in order to avoid favoring one purpose over another.

Then come the alternative costs for each purpose, both for construction at present worth and for the annual OM&R charges. As noted, the alternative costs are the costs of the most economic single purpose project which can provide the same benefit as the multipurpose project. The alternative does not have to be located at the multipurpose project site, but it should be capable of producing its benefit in essentially the same geographic area as that where the benefits from the multipurpose project are to be utilized. The alternative project may be of an entirely different physical nature as would be the case if the alternative to a multipurpose river development were pump irrigation and a thermal generating plant. Of course, the most economic single purpose alternative might cost more than the benefits which it would generate; even the most economic alternative might be unjustified as a separate project.

The annual benefits for each purpose are given and totaled. The power benefit is assumed to be the annual cost of providing the same amount of electricity by means of the most economic single purpose alternative project. This is a simplification to avoid the problems associated with valuing electricity (see page 128). It implies that the real benefit of power--whatever that may be-- is greater than the present worth of the single purpose alternative. The effect of this assumption is to set the maximum which can be charged for power equal to the benefit of the most economic alternative single purpose project which is what the analytical technique would do in any case.

The discount rate is either the financing cost of the project if it is to be constructed using loan funds or the government borrowing rate if the project is to be financed from current government budget allocations.

The life of the project and the length of the construction period are part of the technical data to be supplied by those responsible for designing the project.

Finally are derived the factors for converting between annual costs and present worth values. The factor to convert annual values to present worth equivalents is computed from the present worth of an annuity factor for 2.5 percent as indicated, following the same procedure as was discussed in connection with discounting (see pages 57 to 60). The capital recovery factor necessary to convert present worths to annual costs for a period beginning at some time in the future cannot be computed directly from the capital recovery factors given in standard tables in a manner similar to the computation of the present worth of an annuity factor. Instead, advantage may be taken of the fact that the capital recovery factor for any period is the reciprocal of the present worth of an annuity factor for that period. Following this approach, we find the capital recovery factor for the fourth through the hundredth years at 2.5 percent to be $1/33.758 = .029\ 623$.

Part II of table 6-6 lays out the joint cost allocation computation. Note all values are stated at their present worth equivalents. We may follow the analysis line by line.

1. <u>Costs to be allocated.</u> This is the total cost of the project broken down into construction costs at their present worth taken from line i and the present worth of the OM&R costs for the project computed by taking the value of $206,000 supplied in line ii and multiplying it by the present worth of an annuity factor for the fourth through the hundredth years of 33.758 giving $206,000 x 33.758 = $6,954,000 to the nearest thousand dollars. It is these costs which are to be allocated among the various purposes.

2. <u>Benefits.</u> These are the annual benefits given in line vii multiplied by the present worth of an annuity factor for the fourth through the hundredth years at 2.5 percent. Thus, the annual flood control benefit of $271,000 x 33.758 = $9,148,000 to the nearest thousand.

3. <u>Alternative costs.</u> The costs for the most economic alternative single purpose projects with the same benefits as the project are taken from part I. The alternative construction costs

**Table 6-6. UNITED STATES: Summary of Joint Cost Allocation for a
Multipurpose River Basin Project
Illustrating Separable Costs-Remaining Benefits Method
(Thousand United States Dollars)**

Line	Item	Flood Control	Irriga- tion	Power	Total
			Purpose		
	I. BASIC INFORMATION				
	Project costs to be allocated				
i.	Construction (at present worth)				$15,796
ii.	Annual OM&R (Operation, maintenance) and replacement)				206
	Separable costs				
iii.	Construction (at present worth)	$ 2,089	$ 5,640	$ 3,978	11,707
vi.	Annual OM&R	5	134	61	200
	Alternative costs				
v.	Construction (at present worth)	8,106	9,232	4,085	21,423
vi.	Annual OM&R	22	220	226	468
vii.	Annual project benefits	271	380	347	998

Discount rate: 2.5 percent

Life of project: 100 years

Length of construction period: 3 years

Factor to convert annual costs or benefits to present worth:

Present worth of an annuity factor for 100 years at 2.5 percent	36.614
LESS present worth of an annuity factor for 3 years at 2.5 percent	−2.856
Present worth of an annuity factor for 4th through 100th years at 2.5 percent	33.758

Factor to convert present worth of costs or benefits to annual costs for years 4 through 100:

Capital recovery factor for 4th through 100th years at 2.5 percent = Reciprocal of the present worth of an annuity factor = $\frac{1}{33.758}$ = .029 623

are given in line v. The annual OM&R costs for the alternative single purpose projects are converted to their present worth using the present worth of an annuity factor.

4. Justifiable expenditure. The lesser of the benefit on line 2 or the alternative cost on line 3 is taken as the justifiable expenditure for each purpose, and their sum entered as the total justifiable expenditure. We noted this earlier: the amount to be allocated to a particular purpose is limited on the one hand by the benefits it will produce and on the other hand by the cost of the most economic single purpose alternative.

5. Separable costs. The separable costs are taken from part I. The separable construction costs for each purpose are given in

Line	Flood Control	Irriga- tion	Power	Total
		Purpose		

II. JOINT COST ALLOCATION
(All values at present worth)

Line	Flood Control	Irriga-tion	Power	Total
1. Costs to be allocated				
a. Construction (i)				$15,796
b. Annual OM&R (at NPW) (ii) x 33.758				6,954
1. Total (1a) + (1b)				22,750
2. Benefits (at NPW) (vii) x 33.758	$ 9,148	$12,828	$11,714	33,690
3. Alternative costs				
a. Construction (v)	8,106	9,232	4,085	21,423
b. OM&R (at NPW) (vi) x 33.758	743	7,427	7,629	15,799
3. Total (3a) + (3b)	8,849	16,659	11,714	37,222
4. Justifiable expenditure (lesser of (2) or (3)	8,849	12,828	11,714	33,391
5. Separable costs				
a. Construction (iii)	2,089	5,640	3,978	11,707
b. OM&R (at NPW) (iv) x 33.758	169	4,524	2,059	6,752
5. Total (5a) + (5b)	2,258	10,164	6,037	18,459
6. Remaining justifiable expenditure (4) - (5)	6,591	2,664	5,677	14,932
7. Percentage distribution of (6)	44.14%	17.84%	38.02%	100.00%
8. Remaining joint costs (total from lines indicated allocated according to line 7)				
a. Remaining joint construction costs (1a) − (5a)	1,805	729	1,555	4,089
b. Remaining joint OM&R (at NPW) (1b) − (5b)	89	36	77	202
8. Total (8a) + (8b)	1,894	765	1,632	4,291
9. Total allocated cost				
a. Construction (5a) + (8a)	3,894	6,369	5,533	15,796
b. OM&R (at NPW) (5b) + (8b)	258	4,560	2,136	6,954
9. Total (9a) + (9b)	$ 4,152	$10,929	$ 7,669	$22,750

Line	Item	Flood Control	Irriga-tion	Power	Total
			Purpose		

III. ANNUAL COSTS

Line	Item	Flood Control	Irriga-tion	Power	Total
10.	Annual costs				
	a. Construction (9a) x .029 623	$ 115	$ 189	$ 164	$ 468
	b. OM&R (9b) x .029 623	8	135	63	206
	10. Total (9a) + (9b)	$ 123	$ 324	$ 227	$ 674

Source: Adapted from United States. Department of the Interior. Bureau of Reclamation. *Reclamation Instructions Series 110 – Project Planning.* Washington: Department of the Interior, 1959. p. 116-5.19.

line iii. The present worth of the separable annual OM&R is derived by multiplying the value in line iv by the present worth of an annuity factor. The separable costs are totalled in line 5. Normally, the total separable cost for each purpose will be the minimum allocation which can be charged to that purpose.

     6.   Remaining justifiable expenditure. The separable cost of each purpose given in line 5 is deducted from the justifiable expenditure given in line 4 to determine the remaining justifiable expenditure for each purpose and for the project as a whole. In the case of the irrigation purpose for example, the separable cost of $10,164,000 is subtracted from the justifiable expenditure of $12,828,000 leaving a remaining justifiable expenditure of $2,664,000. (Of course, if the value for any purpose is negative, it means that the present worth of the benefit at the discount rate being used is less than the present worth of the cost. If one purpose is not to subsidize another, then any purpose with a negative justified expenditure should be omitted from the project.)

     7.   Percentage distribution. The percentage distribution of the remaining justifiable expenditure in line 6 is calculated and entered in line 7.

     8.   Remaining joint costs. The total separable cost given in the last column in line 5 is subtracted from the total project cost shown in line 1 to give the total remaining joint cost which is entered in the last column of line 8, $22,750,000 - $18,459,000 = $4,291,000. This total remaining joint cost is then allocated to the individual purpose according to the percentage distribution of the remaining justifiable expenditure given in line 7. In effect, what we are now doing is allocating the joint costs of the project to each purpose in proportion to the excess over the separable costs which we would be justified in spending to realize the benefits.

     To allocate the remaining joint construction costs the same procedure is followed. The total of the separable costs for construction in line 5a is subtracted from the total construction costs in line 1a and allocated according to the percentage distribution shown in line 7. The same is done for the OM&R costs.

     9.   Total allocated costs. The total allocated cost for each purpose is the sum of the separable cost in line 5 and the distributed remaining joint cost for that purpose given in line 8. The total allocated cost for the power component is thus $6,037,000 + $1,632,000 = $7,669,000. The total allocated construction cost is found by adding the separable construction cost in line 5a to the distributed remaining joint construction cost in line 8a. The total allocated cost for the OM&R for each purpose is determined by adding the separable OM&R costs in line 5b to the remaining joint OM&R costs, line 8b.

10. <u>Annual costs.</u> Part III of table 6-6 gives the annual costs for each purpose. These are determined by multiplying the total allocated cost in line 9 by the capital recovery factor for the fourth through the hundredth year at 2.5 percent as computed in part I. Thus, the annual cost for irrigation is determined by multiplying the total allocated cost by the capital recovery factor, $10,929,000 x .029 623 = $324,000 to the nearest thousand. The annual OM&R cost for irrigation may be determined separately in a like manner, $4,560,000 x .029 623 = $135,000 to the nearest thousand. An equitable annual charge to users of irrigation water in the project would thus be $324,000 of which $189,000 would go toward construction costs and $135,000 would be for the OM&R charge. If it were determined that the government would bear the capital costs and that farmers would be asked to pay only the operation, maintenance, and replacement charge, then farmers would have to pay only the $135,000 annual OM&R cost.

Note that the separable costs-remaining benefits method only specifies what would be an equitable financial charge; what the beneficiaries actually will be asked to pay is, of course, another matter. In United States practice, for example, flood control costs are met from general tax revenues, not by payments from beneficiaries, and it is likely power users will be charged the normal rate for the area served by the multipurpose project and not the rate determined by the annual cost of the project power component.

7. CASE STUDY: IVORY COAST COCOA PROJECT

To illustrate application of economic and financial analysis techniques to an agricultural project in a real life situation, we may examine the Ivory Coast cocoa planting and rehabilitation project outlined in this chapter. Of course, all projects have features of their own which a case study of another project cannot hope to deal with. You will need to adapt the analytical techniques to each instance.

This case is drawn from World Bank appraisal report No. PA-41a dated May 4, 1970. The report was prepared by A. Robert Whyte, Peter F. Betsche, and Hans Kordik of the Bank staff, and Philip S. Hammond, a consultant to the Bank. The economic and financial analysis is principally the work of Mr. Whyte.

In the interests of saving space, much of the discussion devoted to technical agricultural topics and to organizational problems contained in the original report has been omitted from this case study since the material is not essential to an understanding of the economic and financial analysis. The subject matter and length of the sections omitted has been indicated, however, so that the case does indicate the full contents and length of the original report.

Since this project is in its early stages, it is too soon to report any information about operational experience.

(It is interesting to note that there has been some question raised in the World Bank about the international incidence of benefits which might arise from this project. No question is raised about the total benefits nor about the advantages of the project for the Ivory Coast. It has been suggested, however, that given the inelasticities of demand for cocoa on the world market, one result of significantly increased supplies might be to reduce costs to consumers. The international benefits might then be divided between consumers, largely in developed countries, and the producers in the Ivory Coast, perhaps at the expense of reduced incomes to other cocoa producing nations.)

Analytical procedures

The method by which the analysis for this project was worked out is indicated in an exceptionally clear manner in the report and its annexes.

Flow of cost and benefit streams from farm budget to internal economic return. Note how the buildup of costs and benefits flows smoothly from the farm budgets in annex 13 to the computation of the internal economic return (termed economic rate of return) in annex 15. The internal economic return was computed separately for the new planting aspect of the overall project and for the rehabilitation aspect. In order to make the investment costs clear and to facilitate following the buildup of the financial flows during the life of the project, the analyst has included a project cost summary in annex 8, table 2 which shows all costs except family labor for the project establishment period from 1970 to 1977. Hence, for the early period of the project, the analyst aggregates cost per hectare for each individual item given in the farm budgets in annex 13 by the appropriate area to be planted according to the schedule for planting and rehabilitation as shown in annex 5. We can see how this works if we take the cost of nursery materials of CFAF 2,000 (CFAF 277.71 = US\$1) given in the farm budget for 1 hectare for the first year (t_1) which is 1970 as given in annex 13, table 1, line 1. Since nursery costs are incurred in the year prior to planting, the appropriate number of hectares by which the farm budget must be expanded is the area of 3,790 hectares to be planted in 1971 as shown in annex 5. Thus, CFAF 2,000 x 3,790 hectares = CFAF 7.6 million. The result is entered in the 1970 column in annex 8, table 1. The total 1970 cost of CFAF 31.8 million is then carried to the project costs entry for 1970 in internal rate of return computation in annex 15.

Another illustration of the buildup may be seen in the case of the fertilizer cost shown in the farm budget for new planting, annex 13, table 1. For the second year (t_2) which is 1971, there is a fertilizer cost of CFAF 4,950 per hectare. Here the appropriate weight is the rea to be planted in 1971 since fertilizer costs are incurred in the year planting takes place. Hence, CFAF 4,950 x 3,790 hectares = CFAF 18.76 million as shown in annex 8, table 1 (where it was rounded down to CFAF 18.7 million). The new planting and the rehabilitation entries are carried separately to the project costs summary in annex 8. The totals for new planting and for rehabilitation are carried from annex 8 to the internal economic return table, annex 15.

Because the analyst has chosen not to show family labor as a project cost in annex 8, the cost of family labor is carried directly from the farm budgets in annex 13 to the internal economic return calculation in annex 15. Thus for project year 1 for the first 3,974 hectares to be planted (which is 1970), 30 man days x CFAF 250 x 1.15 (allowing 15% for contingencies) = CFAF 8,625 which the analyst has rounded to CFAF 8,630 because he is working to the nearest CFAF 10. The family labor cost per hectare is multiplied by the planting target for 1971 since the work is to be done preparing planting stock for the area to be planted in 1971. Thus, CFAF 8,630 x 3,790 = CFAF 32.7 million which is carried directly to the internal economic return computation in annex 15.

Treatment of phasing. Note there is a phasing problem as the project proceeds since there are new areas undertaken each year. The method by which this was handled is illustrated in table 7-1. The phasing of this project is such that it never "turns steady," and the cash flow differs for each year.

Table 7-1. IVORY COAST: Cocoa Project Fertilizer
Cost Buildup for 1974 Illustrating Treatment of Phasing

Year Area Planted	Project Year for Farms in this Planting Group	Area Concerned (ha.)a	Fertilizer Cost Per Hectare (CFAF)b		Project Total (CFAF Million)
1971	5	3,790	x	19,500	=	73.9
1972	4	4,820	x	14,550	=	70.1
1973	3	4,900	x	9,600	=	47.0
1974	2	5,320	x	4,950	=	16.3
Total fertilizer cost carried to annex 8					=	217.3

a   From annex 5.
b   From annex 13.

Treatment of subsidies and credit. The analyst has carefully laid out his farm budgets in annex 13 to facilitate the computation of economic and financial rates of return. The prices shown in the farm budget are the full costs without subsidies. Then the analyst has shown separately the amount of the subsidy which is to be subtracted from the costs to obtain the price which the farmer pays.

The same device is used to separate out the credit arrangements and to avoid confusion between real costs and the lending operation. The amounts of credit received by farmers and the repayments are shown separately in the farm budget in annex 13 in order to indicate clearly the influence of credit upon net farm cash income (termed "income after credit repayments"). This means the true costs of the project to the society can easily be carried directly from the farm budget to the economic rate of return calculation in annex 15, while the farm cash income can also be shown on the table and, when adjusted for the imputed family labor costs, can become the basis for estimating the internal financial return to the farmer's own investment.

Sensitivity analysis. As he shows on pages 176 and 177, the analyst tested the project for sensitivity to higher and lower prices and to a 25 percent reduction in yields. He felt these were the major elements to which the project was likely to be sensitive and did not test the project for other elements, as, for example, a slowdown in implementation.

Internal financial return to the farmer's own investment. The analyst has computed the internal financial return (termed financial rate of return) to the participating farmer's own investment for both those farmers undertaking new planting and those undertaking rehabilitation of existing stands. Because of the way in which the analyst laid out his initial farm budgets, he is able to transfer sums directly from the budgets in annex 13 to the internal financial return computation in annex 16, table 2. The analyst did not choose to show the sensitivity of the internal financial return to a 25 percent reduction in yield, although it can be readily computed from the information tabulated in annex 13.

The analyst has also computed the internal financial return (termed financial return) to the government as shown in annex 16, table 1.

Financial projections for project entities. The project appraisal includes several tables analyzing the financial position of project entities and anticipated financial flows.

Annex 4, table 1 gives the balance sheets for 1968 and 1969 for the Société d'Assistance Technique pour la Modernisation Agricole de la Côte d' Ivoire (SATMACI).

Annex 9 shows the cash flows for project financing. Note how clearly it relates the sources and timing of funds needed to implement the project to the total project costs as given in annex 8. The table has been built up by taking the total project costs in annex 8 and deducting from it the amount of farmer contributions based on the farm budgets in annex 13 and the amount of the World Bank disbursements as shown in annex 10. This leaves as a residual that amount of the total cost of operating the project which must be financed from Government funds. Taking 1971 as an example, we first find the amount of the farmer contribution to project costs. For the 3,790 hectares planted in 1971 as given in annex 5 and now in the second project year, we find the farmer contribution to total costs in 1972 to be 3,790 hectares x CFAF 8,350 = CFAF 31.6 million. For the 4,820 hectares to be planted in 1972 as shown in annex 5 and, for which preparation must be made in 1971, the farmer contribution as shown in annex 13, table 1, is 4,820 hectares x CFAF 3,450 = CFAF 16.6 million. Adding these, CFAF 31.6 + CFAF 16.6 = CFAF 48.2 million which is the amount of the farmer contribution in 1971 as shown in annex 9. From annex 10 we can tell the estimated World Bank disbursement is CFAF 98.5 million for new plantations. We know from annex 8, table 1, that the total project cost for 1971 for new planting is CFAF 229.2 million, and subtracting from this the CFAF 48.2 million farmer contribution and the CFAF 98.5 million World Bank disbursement we arrive at the amount which must be financed from government funds of CFAF 82.5 million as shown in annex 9.

Annex 10 was built up by estimating the amount of expenditure each year as indicated in annex 8 which would be eligible for Bank financing. The details about eligibility were agreed upon in loan negotiations between the Ivory Coast and the Bank. The elements of the computation are clearly set forth in annex 10. If we take the cost of fertilizers, for example, it was agreed that 100 percent of the CIF cost would be eligible for financing under the Bank loan. For 1974 this amounts to CFAF 141.2 million. This figure cannot be derived from the information given in the report since we do not have the CIF equivalent price of the fertilizer costs shown in the farm budgets, annex 13, which was the basis upon which the analyst built his estimate. As another element in the buildup of items eligible for financing under the World Bank loan, we may look at the agricultural extension costs for 1974. Here, it was agreed that 80 percent of the total costs could be financed from the loan. Annex 8, table 1, shows the 1974 extension costs for new planting to be CFAF 58.5 million, so the amount of the loan disbursement in 1974 for extension costs as shown in annex 10 is CFAF 58.5 million x .80 = CFAF 46.8 million.

Annex 14 gives the sources and applications of funds for the government shown separately for new plantations and for rehabilitation. This clearly summarizes in one table the total impact implementing the project will have on the treasury. The demands the project will make for funds during the years 1970 through 1975 for new plantations and from 1970 through 1973 for rehabilitation are indicated as well as the contribution the project will make to the treasury from 1974 through 1994. This table is, of course, closely linked to the amounts of government funds needed during the development period of the loan as shown in annex 9.

Organization and management of the project entity. Because of the key role which SATMACI will play in the overall implementation of this project, the analyst has included a careful assessment of its organization and management. A separate section has been devoted to organization and management in the main project report (indicated on pages 174 and 175 but omitted here in the interests of saving space), and annex 4 (partially omitted here) devotes five pages to a description of the organizational structure

of SATMACI as well as including a table of organization for the
entity and the balance sheets for 1968 and 1969.

Annex 3 (omitted here) is devoted to a description of the
organization and management of the Banque Nationale pour le
Developpement Agricole, the entity responsible for providing
SATMACI with funds for farmer credit.

Study for stage two project. Note that although $400,000
for a study for a possible second phase is included in the loan,
the analyst has properly excluded these funds from his economic
analysis of the project. These funds, of course, are properly
attributable to the second stage, not the present one.

Contingency allowances. The analyst has correctly included
contingency allowances in his cost streams.

Ivory Coast cocoa project report

Excerpts from the Ivory Coast cocoa project report are
reproduced on the following pages.

CURRENCY EQUIVALENTS

US$1   = 277.71 CFAF

1 CFAF   = US$ 0.004

1 Million CFAF = US$3,601

WEIGHTS AND MEASURES

(Metric System)

1 hectare (ha)   = 2.47 acres

1 kilometer (km) = 0.624 miles

1 kilogram (kg)   = 2.204 pounds

1 metric ton   = 2,204.6 pounds

1 liter   = 1.057 U.S. quarts

ABBREVIATIONS

SATMACI: Société d'Assistance Technique pour la Modernisation Agricole
            de la Côte d'Ivoire
SEDES: Société d'Etudes pour le Développement Economique et
            Social (France)
FED: Fonds Européen de Développement (EEC)
BEI: Banque Européene d'Investissement (EEC)
SODEPALM: Société pour le Développement et l'Exploitation du
            Palmier à Huile (Ivory Coast)
IFCC: Institut Française dedu Café, du Cacao et Autres Plantes
            Stumulantes (France)

CFDT: Compagnie Française de Développement des Textiles
                    (France)
BNDA: Banque Nationale pour le Développement Agricole
                    (Ivory Coast)
CSSPPA: Caisse de Stabilisation et de Soutien des Prix des Productions
                    Agricoles (Ivory Coast)
COFROR: Compagnie Française d'Organisation (France)
CAA: Caisse Autonomé d'Amortissement (Ivory Coast)
BDPA: Bureau pour le Développement de la Production Agricole
                    (France)
BSIE: Budget Spécial d'Investissements Economiques
                    (Ivory Coast)
SACO: Société Africaine de Cacao (Ivory Coast)

SUMMARY AND CONCLUSIONS

This report appraises a project for the plantation and rehabilitation of cocoa in the Ivory Coast. A Bank loan of US$7.5 million is proposed. Cocoa is the Ivory Coast's third largest export earner after coffee and timber and the country's cocoa exports account for about 11 percent of total world trade. When the project reaches full production, output would be increased by some 28,000 tons a year compared with current production of about 150,000 tons.

The project would comprise the planting of about 19,000 hectares of cocoa and the rehabilitation of about 38,000 hectares of cocoa not yet in full production. The project would be carried out on small farms averaging about 7 hectares in size, each farm planting some 2.5 hectares of cocoa. It would include the provision of improved seeds; credit to farmers for seasonal inputs and equipment and the cash required for hired labor; extension services; training facilities; a warehouse; vehicles; prospecting and survey; and a study for a second phase cocoa planting program.

Project costs are estimated at $13.6 million equivalent including interest on the Bank loan during the development period. Of this total US$9.0 million would be for new plantations, US$3.2 million for rehabilitation, $0.4 million for a study for a possible second stage project, and US$1.0 million for interest during development. The proposed loan would finance the foreign exchange costs and US$1.1 million of local currency costs, together amounting to 55 percent of total project costs. The government would contribute 25 percent of project costs and the remaining 20 percent would be met by farmers contributions and reinvestment of farm credit repayments. Procurement of most of the equipment and materials, amounting to US$4.5 million, would be by international competitive bidding.

The project would be implemented by the Société d'Assistance Technique pour la Modernisation Agricole de la Côte d'Ivoire (SATMACI) which is a statutory corporation under the control of the Minister of Agriculture. Farm credits would be channelled through the Banque Nationale pour le Développement Agricole. SATMACI is well managed but the appointment of a project manager and a strengthening of its cocoa extension service would be required for execution of the project. Its financial position has been unsound because of inadequate permanent capital and delays in receipt of funds from the government to finance agreed operations, but the government is taking steps to increase SATMACI's capital and reorganize its operations.

The project would produce substantial foreign exchange earnings and would increase participating farmers' incomes. Annual net earnings of foreign exchange at full production are estimated at US$9 million from new plantations and US$5 million from rehabilitation. Based on the current estimate of long-term cocoa prices of US$0.27 per pound, the economic rate of return from new plantations is estimated at 20 percent and from rehabilitation at 35 percent. A sensitivity analysis shows that even if prices were to fall to US$0.20 per pound, the chances of which are negligible, and yields were reduced by 25 percent, the return would be 8 percent from new plantations and 9 percent from rehabilitation. The financial return to the government from new plantations is estimated at 35 percent and from rehabilitation at over 50 percent. Farmers would have adequate incentives to participate in the project by reason of increased incomes and satisfactory returns on investment.

The project is suitable for a Bank loan to the Government of US$7.5 million for a period of fifteen years including seven years grace.

1. INTRODUCTION

The Government of the Ivory Coast has requested Bank assistance to finance part of the costs of a cocoa planting program and of a rehabilitation scheme for existing cocoa plantations. The objective of these programs is to further diversify agricultural production in the forest areas of the Ivory Coast, to introduce modern methods of cocoa plantation establishment and maintenance, and to increase farmer incomes and the country's foreign exchange earnings.

The project for which assistance is sought includes planting of about 19,000 hectares of cocoa and rehabilitation of about 38,000 hectares of cocoa planted with high yielding varieties and not yet in full production.

This report is based on the findings of a Bank mission which visited the Ivory Coast in November-December 1969, consisting of Messrs. Whyte, Betsche, Kordik (Bank) and Hammond (Consultant). The project was identified by the Bank's Permanent Mission to West Africa in 1965. Preparation was in the hands of the French consultant firm Société d'Etudes pour le Développement Economique et Social (SEDES) assisted by PMWA staff and a Bank preappraisal mission.

The Ivory Coast received three Bank loans for agricultural development in 1969. A total of US$9 million was made available for the establishment of outgrower oil palm and coconut plantations. For a commercial oil palm plantation US$3.3 million was lent. The third loan of US$4.8 million was for the construction of a palm oil mill. Progress on these projects has been satisfactory.

2. BACKGROUND

A. General (Omitted)

(A discussion of the major economic statistics of the Ivory Coast and of the current five year plan. The emphasis is on showing how the cocoa project fits into the overall development program of the nation. - Two pages.)

B. Institutional Structure (Omitted)

(Discusses the responsibilities of the Ministries of Agriculture, Animal Production, and Planning. Points out the Société d'Assistance Technique pour la Modernisation Agricole de la Côte d'Ivoire (SATMACI) will be responsible for the project. Discusses organization for agricultural research, extension, and marketing. Outlines the responsibilities of Banque Nationale pour le Dévelopement Agricole (BNDA). One page.)

C. Cocoa Production (Omitted)

(A discussion of the levels of cocoa production in recent years and problems facing the cocoa industry. One page.)

D. SATMACI

A full description of SATMACI which would be responsible for execution of the project, is given in annex 4. SATMACI was formed in April 1958 as a statutory corporation under the authority of the Ministry of Agriculture. It is governed by a Council of Administration of nine members including the Ministers of Agriculture and Finance and Economic Affairs, and is managed by a Director-General appointed by the Council.

SATMACI's principal activities at present consist of cocoa rehabilitation; rice cultivation, marketing and milling; and livestock operations consisting of beef cattle ranches and a forage production center. A coffee extension service is being introduced. These activities are carried out through a chain of field officers responsible to divisional directors for each activity at headquarters. With the exception of its warehouse operations involving the supply of materials on credit to farmers, which have been financed by a revolving fund since 1967, SATMACI's operations are financed by the government under agreements which determine the activities to be carried out, usually for a period of one year. Thus, though in theory SATMACI is financially autonomous in fact it is almost wholly dependent on government appropriations and functions more or less as a government department.

SATMACI was recently reorganized on lines recommended by the Compagnie Française d'Organisation (COFROR) and its rice operations, on which it suffered substantial losses, will shortly be transferred to a new statutory corporation. The chart attached to annex 4 shows the organization of SATMACI's future operations in cocoa, coffee, and livestock, and the management structure for the Bank project. SATMACI's activities are divided functionally into technical services, commercial operations, and administration, with technical services subdivided under directors responsible for cocoa (including the Bank project) and coffee, and livestock.

SATMACI's technical and financial management is sound and its accounting system is satisfactory. Its current financial position, on the other hand, is bad. The balance sheet as at December 31, 1969 given in the table at annex 4 shows an excess of current liabilities over current assets of about CFAF 155 million, short-term bank loans of CFAF 825 million, and a net worth of only CFAF 290 million in relation to fixed and other noncurrent assets of about CFAF 1,860 million. This position is a result of three main factors:

- use of short-term funds to finance long-term assets;
- losses on rice milling and marketing which have not been met by government funds; and
- delays in receiving government funds in reimbursement for expenditure on agreed activities.

In order to put SATMACI on a sound financial basis, the government has increased its capital by CFAF 775 million. This increase in funds together with transfer of the unprofitable rice operations should eliminate the need for excessive short-term borrowing in the future. However, to ensure the prompt provision of funds for the project, a special project fund will be established.

3. THE PROJECT AREAS (Omitted)

(Describes the areas where planting and rehabilitation would take place. Notes the available transportation facilities. One-half page.)

4. THE PROJECT

A. Definition

The project would consist of the planting of about 18,830 hectares of cocoa and the rehabilitaton of about 38,000 hectares of young cocoa plantations of high-yield potential which are not yet fully productive. It entails:

(1)   provision of improved seeds and materials to establish cocoa nurseries;

(2)   provision of credit to farmers for fertilizer, insecticides, spraying equipment and cash required for hired labor;

(3)   provision of adequate extension services;

(4)   provision of training and training facilities for extension officers;

(5)   construction of a warehouse to facilitate input distribution;

(6)   prospecting and a cadastral survey for program implementation; and

(7)   implementation of a study for a second phase cocoa planting program.

The project would aim at increasing farmer incomes and Government revenues by diversifying agricultural production in the rain forest region. It would bring new land under cultivation, ensure optimum productivity of high yield potential planting material, and increase the yields of already planted cocoa farms by introducing modern cultivation techniques and input use.

The project would be executed by SATMACI under the overall responsibility of the Ministry of Agriculture. Farmer credits would be channelled through BNDA. The Institut Francaise du Cafe, du Cocoa et autres Plantes Stimulantes (IFCC) would supply seeds and would carry out technical training while the French Bureau pour le Developpement de la Production Agricole (BDPA) would carry

out extension training.   A Project Coordinating Committee would
be established to ensure close cooperation between the ministries
and organizations concerned in the project.   The organizational
arrangements for the project are described in section 5 of this report.

B.   Detailed Features

Planting and rehabilitation program

Establishment of cocoa nurseries to provide planting material
would commence in late 1970, and planting of cocoa would start
in 1971 and be completed by 1974.   All cocoa plantings under
the project would be in production by the end of 1977.   The
rehabilitation program would be initiated in 1971, and be completed
in 1974.   Full production of all rehabilitated cocoa plantations
should be reached by 1975.   The anticipated life of cocoa trees
planted under the project would be at least 30 years.   The following
table provides a schedule of project planting and rehabilitation and
annex 5 contains details of the planting and rehabilitation program
by location.

Table 7-2. SATMACI Planting and Rehabilitation Program, 1971-74
(Hectares)

	1971	1972	1973	1974	Total
New planting					
Annual total	3,790	4,820	4,900	5,320	18,830
Cumulative total	3,790	8,610	13,510	18,830	18,830
Rehabilitation					
Annual total	13,000	8,000	9,000	8,000	38,000
Cumulative total	13,000	21,000	30,000	38,000	38,000

Field development

New plantings.   Plantings would take place only on soils
approved by SATMACI soil surveyors as being suitable for cocoa,
and in most cases would be made: (1) on land which has been
used for food crop production for two to three years following its
clearing from forest; and (2) on land covered with secondary forest.

Only light shade would be needed as fertilizer would be
applied annually to project plantings in the first few years of their
growth.   The resulting vigorous growth would cause the canopy of
the cocoa trees to close in the third or fourth year after planting
after which time the degree of shade would be of less importance.

On food cropped farms, plantations would be planted as shade, and on land covered with secondary bush selected trees would be retained for this purpose during the clearing process. Cocoa trees would be planted in lines at a spacing of 3 meters by 2.5 meters giving about 1,300 trees per hectare. The varieties planted would be amelonado-Amazon hybrids, or open - pollinated polyclonal Amazon material, for which seed would be obtained from IFCC seed gardens (see annex 6). Hybrid seed is only now becoming available, but sufficient would be available from some 13,500 hectares of project plantings. Assurances were obtained during negotiations that the project would have preference in biclonal seed supplies over any other cocoa development programs in the Ivory Coast.

Investigations have shown that soils of the project area are generally deficient in phosphorus and potassium, and that applications of these nutrients together with nitrogen result in the more vigorous growth of cocoa seedlings and subsequently in higher yields. A compound fertilizer providing 12 parts of nitrogen, 15 of phosphate and 18 of potash would be applied to project plantings.

Groups of participating farmers would establish central nurseries under SATMACI supervision, and subsequently establish their farms as described above. Following the initial planting, gaps where seedlings had died would be replanted for which a 10 percent provision in seedling supplies has been made. Important maintenance operations thereafter would be keeping the plantings satisfactorily free of competitive weed growth by slashing and weeding, the control of insect pests, and pruning and shaping of cocoa trees. A benzenehexachloride insecticide would be suitable for pest control in most cases, but other appropriate insecticides would be made available to farmers as required. Insecticide spraying would be organized on a group basis and one motorized sprayer would be needed for about each twenty-five hectares of cocoa planted; this sprayer would be owned by the group. Further details of cocoa establishment methods are given in annex 6. It is anticipated that new plantings of cocoa would come into bearing in the third year after planting.

Rehabilitation. Rehabilitation would be confined to existing plantations of young amelonado cocoa which had not reached full bearing, and which thus would quickly respond to improved maintenance methods and efficient pest control measures. Elements of the rehabilitation process would be filling vacancies where cocoa plants had died out, adjusting shade, pruning and shaping the cocoa trees, adequate farm maintenance, and--most important--the control of capsids. The latter would be done on a group basis, and provision is made under the project for one motorized sprayer for each twenty-five hectares of cocoa being rehabilitated by a group of farmers. The insecticide used would be a proprietary benzenehexachloride (that now used is Lindane) which would be applied in two annual sprayings at the beginning and end of August.

Selection of farms and size of holdings (omitted)

(Discusses how SATMACI would select farmers to participate in the project. One page.)

Credit arrangements

All funds required for farm credits would be channelled through BNDA by the Caisse Autonome d'Amortissement (CAA) which would be responsible for providing funds for the project as a whole. BNDA would pass the funds on to SATMACI, which would have full responsibility for administering credits at the farm level, and would receive all farmers' credit repayments and interest from SATMACI. BNDA would then pass on to CAA the portion of farm credits financed by the Bank and retain those financed by the Government for reinvestment in agricultural development. BNDA would keep control accounts for the credit program as a whole.

SATMACI would supply needed materials and equipment on credit and would make cash loans to meet hired labor costs. It would also be responsible for keeping credit records and for credit recoveries. These functions would be carried out by staff and extension workers in each zone and would be supervised by the head office. The procedures would be similar for new plantations and rehabilitation.

Farmers would be selected and formed into groups as described in the section on selection of farms. The formation of effective groups would be vital to a successful credit operation, as farmers in each group would be mutually responsible for each other's debts and no further credit would be made available to groups which had an unsatisfactory repayment record. No credit would be allowed to farmers not in groups.

After a group is formed and extension workers have explained to its members their and SATMACI's respective rights and duties, a group contract would be signed between SATMACI and each member of the group. Copies of the contract, which would set out the obligations of all parties, would be sent to SATMACI head office and to the subprefect of the district. Assurances were obtained during negotiations that the contracts would be satisfactory to the Bank.

Assurances were received during negotiations that, except as the Bank should otherwise agree, the extent and terms of credit would be as follows:

1. New plantations - The full cost of fertilizer, insecticides and and sprayers together with cash totalling CFAF 14,000 per hectare to meet the costs of hired labor would be made available on credit. The cash credits would be paid in three tranches of CFAF 10,000 in the planting year and CFAF 2,000 in each of the next two years. The second and third tranches would depend on satisfactory performance by the individual borrower. There would be a grace period of four years from planting for both interest and principal and repayment would be over the following eight years by equal installments with interest at 5.5 percent.

2. Rehabilitation - Farmers would receive credit for 80 percent of the cost of insecticides and sprayers during the two year period of rehabilitation. Interest at 5.5 percent would be capitalized during this period and repayment would be made over the following two years. These terms are the same as those now in force for rehabilitation.

The low rates of interest for both replanting and rehabilitation credits would be acceptable in view of the high taxation levied on farmers through export duties coupled with the low producer prices relative to market cocoa prices, and the success of existing programs at similar interest rates.

The chief concern in these credit arrangements is that of repayment procedures. The most effective way to recover credits would be for repayments to be deducted from crop proceeds, but this would require SATMACI to have a monopoly of cocoa marketing and it would not be desirable to upset the present system of marketing through the private sector. Consideration has also been given to the possibility of requiring a standard deduction to be made from the fixed price payable to all farmers but this would be extremely difficult to administer because of the wide disparity of credit utilization among farmers. Therefore, the proposed system of collective responsibility by groups coupled with adequate credit control by SATMACI's extension workers and head office staff, together with overall control by BNDA, appears to be the most feasible way to ensure credit recovery and one which gives reasonable assurances of success. This is borne out by the repayment records of such mutual guarantee groups in the past two years which is over 90 percent.

Input supplies (Omitted)

(Discusses the channels through which farmers would receive seed from the main nursery and such input supplies as polythene bags, fertilizers, insecticides, and the like. One-half page.)

Study for stage two project (Omitted)

(Outlines plans for a study for a future expansion of this project. One-half page.)

C.   Cost Estimates and Proposed Financing

Cost Estimates

Project cost estimates are based on current costs but include contingency allowances of 10 percent for materials and 15 percent for SATMACI staff salaries, hired labor and the study for the second stage project (table 7-3). The total cost of the project is estimated at CFAF 3,506 million (US$12.6 million), rehabilitation CFAF 899 million (US$3.2 million) and the stage two study CFAF 111 million (US$0.4 million). Including contingencies, on farm costs would account for about 67 percent and administration costs about 29 percent of new plantation costs, the respective proportions for rehabilitation would be 38 percent and 51 percent. Thus, while the majority of new plantation expenditures would be for farm materials and equipment (75 percent being for fertilizer), more than half of rehabilitation expenditures would be on salaries and overheads for project administration and extension services. These services are essential for the creation of an asset in the case of new plantations or the substantial improvement of an existing asset in the case of rehabilitation and in both cases they give rise, as much as direct farm inputs, to benefits over a long period. Table 7-3 summarizes the local expenditures, foreign exchange, and total costs for the project. Further details are given in annex 8.

Proposed financing

It is proposed that a Bank loan of US$7.5 million would be made to the government to finance the estimated total foreign exchange costs of the project and US$1.3 million of local costs. The loans would be for a period of fifteen years including a grace period of seven years, the disbursement period, and would finance interest on the loan calculated on the basis of the first five years of the new planting project and the first three years of the rehabilitation project. The term of the loan takes into account the period in which the farmers' credits would be recovered - up to

Table 7-3. Summary Project Cost Estimates

Item	Local	Foreign (CFAC Million)	Total	Local	Foreign (US$ Million)	Total	Proportion Foreign Exchange (percent)
NEW PLANTATIONS							
On-farm costs	667.0	835.9	1502.9	2.40	3.01	5.41	56
Administration	513.0	119.3	632.3	1.85	0.43	2.28	19
Buildings and vehicles	3.2	22.4	25.6	0.01	0.08	0.09	88
Survey and prospect	32.0	6.6	38.6	0.12	0.02	0.14	8
Training	10.5	14.9	25.4	0.04	0.05	0.09	59
Contingencies	164.3	106.9	271.2	0.59	0.39	0.98	39
Subtotal	1390.0	1106.0	2496.0	5.01	3.98	8.99	44
REHABILITATION							
On-farm costs	98.6	213.3	311.9	0.35	0.77	1.12	68
Administration	352.8	45.8	398.6	1.27	0.17	1.44	11
Buildings and vehicles	1.1	8.0	9.1	0.01	0.02	0.03	88
Survey and prospect	32.6	5.8	38.4	0.12	0.02	0.14	15
Training	15.6	22.1	37.7	0.06	0.08	0.14	59
Contingencies	70.3	32.9	103.2	0.25	0.12	0.37	32
Subtotal	571.0	327.9	898.9	2.06	1.18	3.24	36
Study for stage 2	19.4	77.8	97.2	0.07	0.28	0.35	80
Contingencies	2.8	11.1	13.9	0.01	0.04	0.05	80
Subtotal	22.2	88.9	111.1	0.08	0.32	0.40	80
TOTAL PROJECT	1983.2	1522.8	3506.0	7.15	5.48	12.63	43
Interest on bank loan	---	264.7	264.7	---	0.95	0.95	100%
Total foreign exchange costs		1787.5			6.43		

1985 for new plantations and up to 1977 for rehabilitation - and the cash flow to the Government from the project.

The Bank loan would finance about 55 percent of total project costs. Remaining project costs would be met by government budgetary allocations, farmers' credit repayments and by farmers' contributions. All project funds would be channelled through CAA, which would then provide funds required for farmers' credits to BNDA for transmittal to SATMACI and meet directly SATMACI's project administration and other costs. For new plantations, farmers would meet the full cost of nursery materials and tools and part of the cost of seeds and plastic bags, the remainder being met by government subsidy, which would amount to CFAF 3,760 per hectare, and about CFAF 7 million (US$25,000) for the project. In the case of rehabilitation, farmers would meet the full cost of tools, and make a down payment of 20 percent on the cost of insecticides and sprayers. Table 7-4 summarizes the financing plan which is shown in more detail in annex 9.

Table 7-4. Financing Plan
(CFAF Million)

	Bank	%	Govern-ment	%	Farmer's Contri-bution	%	Farm Credit Re-payments	%	Total
New Plantations	1289	52	770	31	209	8	228	9	2496
Rehabilitation	440	49	155	17	192	22	112	12	899
Stage Two Study	89	80	22	20	-	-	-	-	111
	1818	52	947	27	401	11	340	10	3506
Interest on Bank Loan	265	100	-	-	-	-	-	-	265
	2083	55	947	25	401	11	340	9	3771

As explained in section 2 of this report, there have been considerable delays in the past in the provision of funds by the Government to meet SATMACI expenditures on agreed programs. In order to ensure the continuous and timely flow of funds for the project, assurances were received during negotiations that the Government would establish a special fund which would be replenished quarterly with amounts required to meet Government contributions in the succeeding quarter. A condition of effectiveness is that an initial deposit of CFAF 25 million shall have been paid into the fund.

Procurement (Omitted)

(Notes that procurement with World Bank funds would follow Bank procedures.   One-fourth page.)

Disbursement

Disbursement of the Bank loan would be made against 100 percent of the CIF cost of imported materials, 80 percent of the costs of project administration and extension services, 50 percent of the cost of hired labor, and 100 percent of the foreign exchange costs of the study together with interest on the loan of US$950,000. Applications for disbursement would be supported by contracts, shipping documents and certified records of expenditures.   The following table which is given in more detail in annex 10 summarizes estimated disbursements:

	US$ million
New Plantation	
Fertilizer	2.15
Insecticides, sprayers and vehicles (100 percent)	0.35
Project staff and extension services (80 percent)	1.13
Hired labor (50 percent)	0.59
Rehabilitation	
Insecticides, sprayers and vehicles (100 percent)	0.49
Project staff and extension services (80 percent)	0.91
Stage 2 Study (foreign exchange costs)	0.32
Interest	0.95
Contingencies	0.61
	7.50

It is recommended that any surplus funds remaining in the Loan Account be cancelled.

Accounts and audit (Omitted)

(Notes farmers' credit accounts kept by SATMACI would be audited. One-fourth page.)

5.   ORGANIZATION AND MANAGEMENT

(A discussion of SATMACI organization.   Touches on extent of responsibility of individual field workers, field organization, warehouse operations, field staff training activities for the project and, expatriate staff. Devotes a paragraph to the methods of coordination between SATMACI, BNDA, the nursery agency, and various ministries. A page is devoted to discussing marketing arrangements for cocoa in the project areas. Two pages.)

6. YIELDS, OUTPUT, MARKETS AND PRICES, FARM INCOMES AND GOVERNMENT REVENUES

A. Yields and Outputs (Omitted)

(A discussion of the yield assumptions underlying the project analysis. One-half page.)

B. Markets and Prices (Omitted)

(A discussion of world cocoa market conditions and the world market price assumptions for this project. One page.)

C. Farm Incomes

Farm budgets per hectare of new plantation and rehabilitation are given in annex 13. They are based on the current farmer's price of CFAF 80 per kilogram and the credit terms outlined in section 4 of this report. Annual farm income per hectare from new plantations is estimated at about CFAF 23,200 (US$80) in year 6 increasing to about CFAF 64,500 (US$230) during the credit repayment period and at about CFAF 75,700 (US$270) thereafter. Farm income from rehabilitated cocoa is estimated at about CFAF 44,100 (US$160) a year compared with about CFAF 26,200 (US$95) from unrehabilitated cocoa. Income per man-day from new plantations is estimated at about CFAF 810 after the credit repayment period and at about CFAF 660 from rehabilitated cocoa. These rates compared favorably with estimated incomes per man-day of about CFAF 790 from oil palm and CFAF 400 from coffee and with a current estate wage rate of about CFAF 250 per man-day.

Annex 13 also shows the estimated farm income per hectare of new plantations on the assumption of a 25 percent reduction in yield. The income would still be satisfactory at CFAF 13,200 (CFAF 281 per man-day) in year 6 rising to CFAF 44,500 (CFAF 571 per man-day) during the loan repayment period and CFAF 55,700 (CFAF 710 per man-day) thereafter. These figures would apply equally to a 25 percent reduction in producer prices.

D. Government Revenues

Revenues to the government from the project would be substantial. Annex 14 shows that, taking into account export duties and the difference between the price paid to farmers and net receipts to CSSPPA from a world price of US$0.27 per pound CIF, the Government would earn a cash surplus from 1976 from new plantations, and from 1974 from rehabilitation. The total surplus over the life of the project is estimated at about CFAF 13,600 million (US$49 million) from new plantations and about CFAF 4,300 million (US$15 million) from rehabilitation. Of the amounts which would accrue to CSSPPA, about CFAF 7,300 million from new plantations and CFAF 2,600 million from rehabilitation, present regulations require that 60 percent would be transferred to a reserve fund against CSSPPA losses, 30 percent would be reinvested through the Budget Spécial d'Investissement (BSIE) in economic and social undertakings, and 10 percent would be transferred to BNDA. Receipts from export taxes would be taken to general government revenues.

7. BENEFITS AND JUSTIFICATION

The project's primary benefit would be the increased production of cocoa for export resulting in satisfactory returns on investments made under the project and higher incomes for participating farmers. Other effects would include the modernization of Ivory Coast cocoa production through the use of new planting material and up-to-date field techniques, the strengthening of extension services, and improvements in the farm credit system.

Based on a world price of US$0.27 per pound it is estimated that at full production the project would contribute about US$9 million a year in net foreign exchange earnings from new plantations, and about US$5 million from rehabilitation, these amounts being the estimated FOB value of exports less debt service on the Bank loan and the foreign exchange costs of farm inputs and administration.

The calculation of the return to the economy from the project is shown in annex 15. It takes into account full labor costs. At the assumed price the return from new plantations is estimated at about 20 percent but the return has also been tested for sensitivity at various prices and with a 25 percent reduction in yield. The results are given in table 7-5. The likelihood of a long-term cocoa price of as low as US$0.20 per pound is negligible and the internal economic returns shown in table 7-5, even with a 25 percent drop in yield, are satisfactory.

Table 7-5. Sensitivity Analysis					
	Internal Economic Return at Stated Price per Pound (percent)				
	US$0.20	US$0.25	US$0.27	US$0.30	US$0.35
New Plantations					
With assumed yields	12	18	20	22	35
With reduction of 25 percent	8	13	15	17	20
Rehabilitation					
With assumed yields	20	31	35	40	49
With reduction of 25 percent	9	20	23	28	36

The internal economic return from rehabilitation has also been calculated at the prices above and with a 25 percent reduction in incremental yield. The results are given in table 7-5.

Annex 16 shows the calculation of the financial returns to the government and on farm units. Based on a world price of US$0.27 per pound the return to the government from new plantations would be 35 percent with full estimated yields and 30 percent with a 25 percent yield reduction. The return on farms would be 16 percent and 11 percent respectively assuming a farm gate price of CFAF 80 per kilogram. The return from rehabilitation would be over 50 percent to both government and farmers with full yields and about 38 percent with 75 percent of incremental yields.

The above calculations show that the returns to the economy from the project would be satisfactory. Net funds accruing to the government would contribute materially to the overall development budget of the country, while at the same time farmers would have adequate incentives through increased incomes and would be relatively prosperous. However, to safeguard the position of farmers, assurances were obtained during negotiations that the Government would inform the Bank of any proposed changes in producer prices which might adversely affect the ability of farmers to repay credits.

8.   RECOMMENDATIONS

The   project is technically, economically, and financially
sound and suitable for a Bank loan fo US$7.5 million for fifteen
years including seven years grace.   The main assurances obtained
during negotiations were:

(1)   the project would receive preference in supplies of
biclonal seeds.

(2)   contracts between SATMACI and farmers' groups would
be satisfactory to the Bank and terms and conditions
of farmers' credits would be as agreed with the Bank.

(3)   the government would establish a project fund to meet
project costs.

(4)   a project manager acceptable to the Bank would be
appointed before December 31, 1970.

(5)   new appointments to the position of Cocoa Director
would be in consultation with the Bank.

The   following would be conditions of effectiveness of the
loan:

(1)   that the government will have established and made the
initial deposit into the project fund;

(2)   that the Project Coordinating Committee will have been
established.

ANNEX 1.   AGRICULTURAL BACKGROUND (Omitted)

(Discuss the major crops of the Ivory Coast and institutional
factors including land tenure affecting agricultural production. Four
pages.)

ANNEX 2.   RESEARCH AND EXTENSION SERVICES
(Omitted)

(Discusses the major institutions responsible for research and
extension in the Ivory Coast. Annex 2, table 1 gives the staffing
requirements for the project from 1971 through 1984 showing the
number to be trained from 1971 through 1974. Three pages plus
table.)

ANNEX 3. LA BANQUE NATIONALE POUR LE DEVELOPPEMENT AGRICOLE (Omitted)

(A description of the organization of BNDA and the part it is to play in financing the project. Two pages.)

ANNEX 4. LA BANQUE NATIONALE POUR LA MODERNISATION AGRICOLE DE LA COTE D'IVOIRE (SATMACI) (Partially omitted)

(A description of the organization of SATMACI and its past programs. Describes recent government measures to improve the financial position of the organization. Five pages. Table 1 reproduced here gives the balance sheets as of December 31, 1968 and 1969. Figure 1 reproduced here is an organization chart.)

ANNEX 5. AREAS OF NEW PLANTINGS AND REHABILITATION

(This annex consists solely of a table which is reproduced.)

ANNEX 6. TECHNICAL ASPECTS (Omitted)

(Part I discusses agronomic aspects of cocoa production in the Ivory Coast with sections devoted to history, climate, soils and ecology, varieties, traditional establishment methods, harvesting, and pests and diseases. Part II of the annex describes the improved cultivation paractices to be undertaken by farmers participating in the project. Sections are devoted to seedling production, land preparation, plantation maintenance, harvesting, anticapsid control, fertilizer, yields, labor requirements, projected yields of different varieties. Five pages plus two tables.)

ANNEX 7. COCOA DEVELOPMENT STUDY DRAFT OUTLINE OF TERMS OF REFERENCE (Omitted)

(A set of draft terms of reference for a study to underlie a future cocoa project. 1 page.)

ANNEX 8. PROJECT COST SUMMARY

(This annex consists of tables 1 and 2 reproduced here.)

ANNEX 9. PROJECT FINANCING

(This annex consists of a table reproduced here.)

IVORY COAST – COCOA PROJECT
SOCIETE D'ASSISTANCE TECHNIQUE POUR LA MODERNISATION
AGRICOLE DE LA COTE D'IVOIRE (SATMACI)
BALANCE SHEETS (CFAF millions)

	As at December 31, 1968	As at December 31, 1969
ASSETS		(provisional)
Fixed Assets – net:		
Headquarters	105	100
Rice buildings and equipment	53	1,026
TOTAL	158	1,126
Assets on account of the State:		
Rice buildings and equipment	423	414
Other equipment	7	–
TOTAL	430	414
Other Assets:		
Bonds, deposits, etc.	18	15
Warehouses – inventories	148	144
" – receivables	126	128
Other	20	32
TOTAL	312	319
Current Assets:		
Depositaries	384	148
Receivables	92	196
Cash	168	181
Expenditures recoverable from the State	489	533
TOTAL	1,133	1,058
Less: Current Liabilities:		
State advances for recoverable expenditures	145	162
Creditors and provisions	272	226
Bank loans	933	823
TOTAL	1,350	1,211
Net Current Assets	(217)	(153)
TOTAL ASSETS	683	1,706

[1] Of which:	Rice Marketing	166
	Combined Harvesting	12
	Other	6
		184

April 29, 1970

	As at December 31, 1968	As at December 31, 1969
LIABILITIES		(provisional)
Capital	150	150
Reserves	20	13
Subventions and allocations	94	312
TOTAL	264	475
Surplus (Deficit)	(119)	(184)$\underline{1/}$
Net Worth	145	291
Loans and other Funds		
Rice Mill Loan – Italy	–	766
Loans – CAA	328	253
Amortization of CAA loan by BSIE	86	180
Participators	–	8
TOTAL	414	1,207
Fund for rural dwellings	–	35
Farmers loan repayment fund	124	173
TOTAL LIABILITIES:	683	1,706

Annex 4
Figure 1

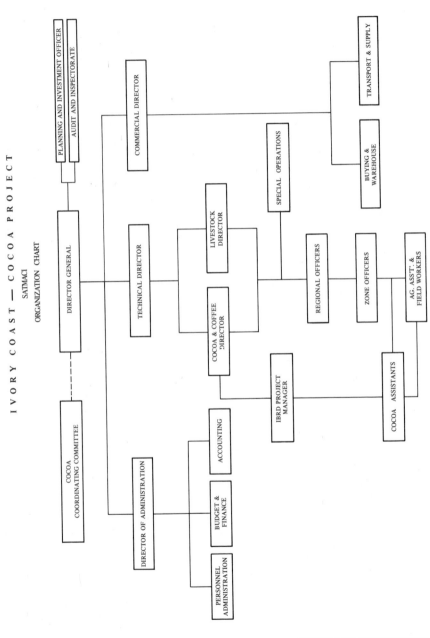

IVORY COAST — COCOA PROJECT

SATMACI

ORGANIZATION CHART

IVORY COAST – COCOA PROJECT   Annex 5
AREAS OF NEW PLANTINGS AND REHABILITATION

(Hectares)

	1971	1972	1973	1974	Total
A. New Planting					
Statistical Zone					
Zone 9	650	890	750	1,030	3,320
Zone 10	600	600	550	650	2,400
Zone 11	300	620	1,000	1,280	3,200
Zone 12	750	750	700	500	2,700
Zone 13	420	600	440	540	2,000
Zone 14	470	760	910	1,170	3,310
Zone 15	600	600	550	150	1,900
Total	3,790	4,820	4,900	5,320	18,830
B. Rehabilitation					
Zone 1	800	800	1,000	–	2,600
Zone 2	1,200	600	1,000	1,600	4,400
Zone 3	2,000	1,600	600	200	4,400
Zone 4	1,600	1,000	1,400	1,000	5,000
Zone 5	2,000	1,400	1,400	1,600	6,400
Zone 6-8	1,800	800	600	600	3,800
Zone 9	200	–	200	–	400
Zone 10	1,000	400	1,600	400	3,400
Zone 11	800	400	200	800	2,200
Zone 14	200	–	–	1,000	1,200
Zone 15	1,400	1,000	1,000	800	4,200
Total	13,000	8,000	9,000	8,000	38,000

April 29, 1970

IVORY COAST – COCOA PROJECT

(CFAF million)

NEW PLANTATIONS	1970	1971	1972	1973
On-farm Costs				
Nursery material	7.6	9.6	9.8	10.6
Hand tools		3.8	8.6	13.5
Plastic bags	11.4	14.5	14.7	15.9
Seeds	5.9	7.5	7.6	8.2
Fertilizer		18.7	60.3	126.1
Insecticide		4.2	9.5	14.9
Sprayers		4.7	6.0	6.1
	24.9	63.0	116.5	195.3
Contingencies 10%	2.5	6.3	11.7	19.5
Hired labor inc 15% contingencies		65.4	83.1	84.5
Sub-total	27.4	134.7	211.3	299.3
Administration Costs				
General administration	2.7	16.5	23.3	37.6
Extension service		33.7	36.7	55.2
General transport	1.1	1.4	1.4	1.5
Project administration		6.9	6.9	6.9
	3.8	58.5	68.3	101.2
Contingencies – 15%	0.6	8.8	10.2	15.2
Sub-total	4.4	67.3	78.5	116.4
Fixed Assets				
Buildings		1.3	2.2	
Vehicles		7.5	0.4	9.0
		8.8	2.6	9.0
Contingencies – 10%		0.9	0.2	0.9
		9.7	2.8	9.9
Survey and Prospection				
Supervision		0.9	0.9	0.9
Survey teams		5.8	5.8	5.8
Materials and overheads		1.8	1.8	1.9
		8.5	8.5	8.6
Contingencies – 15%		1.3	1.3	1.3
		9.8	9.8	9.9
Training				
Personnel		6.1	6.1	5.5
Overhead		0.6	0.6	0.5
		6.7	6.7	6.0
Contingencies – 15%		1.0	1.0	0.9
		7.7	7.7	6.9
TOTAL	31.8	229.2	310.1	442.4

March 2, 1970

PROJECT COST SUMMMARY   Annex 8   Table 1

1974	1975	1976	1977	Total	% Foreign Exchange	CFAF Foreign Exchange
				37.6	90	33.8
18.8	15.0	10.2	5.3	75.2	90	67.7
				56.5	85	48.0
				29.2	40	11.7
217.3	216.4	173.0	103.7	915.5	65	595.0
20.7	16.5	11.2	5.8	82.8	75	62.1
6.7				23.5	75	17.6
263.5	247.9	194.4	114.8	1,220.3		835.9
26.3	24.8	19.4	11.5	122.0		83.6
91.8				324.8		—
381.6	272.7	213.8	126.3	1,667.1		919.5
48.9	43.2	36.3	24.6	233.1	40	93.2
58.5	55.4	55.4	55.4	350.3		—
				5.4	40	2.2
6.9	6.9	4.5	4.5	43.5	55	23.9
114.3	105.5	96.2	84.5	632.3		119.3
17.1	15.8	14.4	12.7	94.8		17.9
131.4	121.3	110.6	97.2	727.1		137.2
				3.5	70	2.5
2.6		2.6		22.1	90	19.9
2.6		2.6		25.6		22.4
0.3		0.3		2.6		2.2
2.9		2.9		28.2	84	24.6
0.9				3.6	66	2.4
9.2				26.6		—
2.9				8.4	50	4.2
13.0				38.6		6.6
1.9				5.8		1.0
14.9				44.4		7.6
5.5				23.2	63	14.6
0.5				2.2	15	0.3
6.0				25.4		14.9
0.9				3.8		2.2
6.9				29.2		17.1
537.7	394.0	327.3	223.5	2,496.0	44	1,106.0

IVORY COAST – COCOA PROJECT

(CFAF million)

	1971	1972	1973	1974
REHABILITATION				
On-farm Costs				
Hand tools	13.0	21.0	17.0	17.0
Insecticides	21.8	35.2	28.5	28.5
Sprayer fuel	10.9	17.6	14.3	14.3
Sprayer	15.3	9.4	10.6	9.4
	61.0	83.2	70.4	69.2
Contingencies 10%	6.1	8.3	7.1	6.9
	67.1	91.5	77.5	76.1
Administration Costs				
General Administration	13.6	15.9	19.5	21.6
Extension service	28.6	46.0	66.2	83.3
Project Administration	4.6	4.6	4.6	4.6
	46.8	66.5	90.3	109.5
Contingencies 15%	7.0	10.0	13.5	16.4
	53.8	76.5	103.8	125.9
Fixed Assets				
Buildings	0.9			
Vehicles	3.0	1.6	2.0	1.6
	3.9	1.6	2.0	1.6
Contingencies 10%	0.4	0.2	0.2	0.1
	4.3	1.8	2.2	1.7
Survey and Prospection				
Supervision	1.8	1.8	1.8	1.8
Survey teams	7.3	7.3	7.3	7.3
Materials and overheads	0.5	0.5	0.5	0.5
	9.6	9.6	9.6	9.6
Contingencies 15%	1.4	1.4	1.4	1.5
	11.0	11.0	11.0	11.1
Training				
Personnel	9.8	2.5	12.2	9.8
Overheads	1.0	0.2	1.2	1.0
	10.8	2.7	13.4	10.8
Contingencies 15%	1.6	0.4	2.0	1.6
	12.4	3.1	15.4	12.4
TOTAL	148.6	183.9	209.9	227.2

March 2, 1970

PROJECT COST SUMMARY

Annex 8 Table 2

1975	1976	1977	Total	% Foreign Exchange	CFAF Foreign Exchange
8.0			76.0	90	68.4
13.4			127.4	75	95.3
6.7			63.8	25	16.0
			44.7	75	33.6
28.1			311.9		213.3
2.8			31.2		21.3
30.9			343.1		234.6
12.3			82.9	40	33.2
68.6			292.7	–	–
4.6			23.0	55	12.6
85.5			398.6		45.8
12.9			59.8		6.9
98.4			458.4		52.7
			0.9	70	0.6
			8.2	90	7.4
			9.1		8.0
			0.9		0.8
			10.0		8.8
			7.2	66	4.8
			29.2	–	–
			2.0	50	1.0
			38.4		5.8
			5.7		0.6
			44.1		6.4
			34.3	63	21.6
			3.4	15	0.5
			37.7		22.1
			5.6		3.3
			43.3		25.4
129.3			898.9	36	327.9

Annex 9

IVORY COAST – COCOA PROJECT
PROJECT FINANCING
(CFAF million)

	1970	1971	1972	1973	1974	1975	1976	1977	Total
NEW PLANTATIONS									
Farmers' credit repayments						44.1	100.2	83.6	227.9
Farmers' contribution to project costs	13.1	48.2	53.7	51.6	39.9	(3.9)	0.6	5.9	209.1
Proposed IBRD loan		98.5	137.9	215.8	286.5	225.6	190.5	134.0	1,288.8
Government funds	18.7	82.5	118.5	175.0	211.3	128.2	36.0		770.2
TOTAL PROJECT COSTS PER ANNEX 8	31.8	229.2	310.1	442.4	537.7	394.0	327.3	223.5	2,496.0
REHABILITATION									
Farmers' credit repayments				30.8	49.8	31.8			112.4
Farmers' contribution to project costs		34.5	52.3	43.0	42.7	19.1			191.6
Proposed IBRD loan		64.0	85.0	99.4	113.6	78.4			440.4
Government funds		50.1	46.6	36.7	21.1				154.5
TOTAL PROJECT COSTS PER ANNEX 8		148.6	183.9	209.9	227.2	129.3			898.9

April 29, 1970

ANNEX 10.   ESTIMATED IBRD LOAN DISBURSEMENTS

(This annex consists of a table reproduced here.)

ANNEX 11.   PROJECT COORDINATING COMMITTEE
(Omitted)

(A brief description of the membership of the project coordinating committee and its main responsibilities.)

ANNEX 12.   SELLING PRICE CALCULATIONS

(This annex consists of a table reproduced here.)

ANNEX 13.   FARM BUDGETS

(This annex consists of two tables reproduced here.)

ANNEX 14.   GOVERNMENT SOURCES AND APPLICATIONS OF FUNDS

(This annex consists of a table reproduced here.)

ANNEX 15.   ECONOMIC RATES OF RETURN

(This annex consists of a table reproduced here.)

ANNEX 16.   FINANCIAL RETURNS TO GOVERNMENT

(This annex consists of two tables reproduced here.)

MAP
(Omitted)

(CFAF million)	IVORY COAST – COCOA PROJECT			
NEW PLANTATIONS	1970	1971	1972	1973
Disbursements of 100%				
C.I.F. cost of imported goods and materials				
Fertilizer		12.2	39.2	82.0
Insecticides		3.2	7.1	11.2
Sprayers		3.5	4.5	4.6
Vehicles		6.8	0.4	8.1
		25.7	51.2	105.9
Contingencies 10%		2.6	5.1	10.6
		28.3	56.3	116.5
Disbursements of less than 100%				
Project Administration - 80%		5.6	5.5	5.5
Extension Services - 80%		27.0	29.4	44.1
		32.6	34.9	49.6
Contingencies 15%		4.9	5.2	7.4
		37.5	40.1	57.0
Hired labor inc. 15% cont. - 50%		32.7	41.5	42.3
Total New Plantations		98.5	137.9	215.8
REHABILITATION				
Disbursements of 100%				
C.I.F. cost of imported goods and materials				
Insecticides		16.3	26.4	21.3
Sprayers		11.5	7.1	8.0
Vehicles		2.7	1.4	1.8
		30.5	34.9	31.1
Contingencies 10%		3.0	3.5	3.1
		33.5	38.4	34.2
Disbursements of less than 100%				
Project Administration - 80%		3.6	3.7	3.7
Extension Services - 80%		22.9	36.8	53.0
		26.5	40.5	56.7
Contingencies 15%		4.0	6.1	8.5
		30.5	46.6	65.2
Total Rehabilitation		64.0	85.0	99.4
Study for Stage 2				
100 of Foreign exchange costs inc. contingencies		20.0	40.0	28.9
Interest and commitment charges	5.0	25.0	40.0	53.0
TOTAL DISBURSEMENTS	5.0	207.5	302.9	397.1

April 29, 1970

ESTIMATED IBRD LOAN DISBURSEMENTS   Annex 10

1974	1975	1976	1977	Total	US$ Equivalent Million
141.2	140.6	112.4	67.4	595.0	2.15
15.5	12.4	8.4	4.3	62.1	0.22
5.0				17.6	0.06
2.3		2.3		19.9	0.07
164.0	153.0	123.1	71.7	694.6	2.50
16.4	15.3	12.3	7.2	69.5	0.25
180.4	168.3	135.4	78.9	764.1	2.75
5.5	5.5	3.6	3.6	34.8	0.12
46.8	44.3	44.3	44.3	280.2	1.01
52.3	49.8	47.9	47.9	315.0	1.13
7.9	7.5	7.2	7.2	47.3	0.17
60.2	57.3	55.1	55.1	362.3	1.30
45.9				162.4	0.59
286.5	225.6	190.5	134.0	1,288.8	4.64
21.3	10.0			95.3	0.34
7.0				33.6	0.12
1.5				7.4	0.03
29.8	10.0			136.3	0.49
3.0	1.0			13.6	0.05
32.8	11.0			149.9	0.54
3.7	3.7			18.4	0.07
66.6	54.9			234.2	0.84
70.3	58.6			252.6	0.91
10.5	8.8			37.9	0.14
80.8	67.4			290.5	1.05
113.6	78.4			440.4	1.59
				88.9	0.32
62.0	79.7			264.7	0.95
462.1	383.7	190.5	134.0	2,082.8	7.50

IVORY COAST – COCOA PROJECT
SELLING PRICE CALCULATIONS

New York, Ghana Cocoa cents/lb	27	27
New York, Ivorian Cocoa cents/lb	26.75	26.75
New York, Ivorian Cocoa $/long ton	599	599
New York, Ivorian Cocoa $/metric ton	589	589
New York, Ivorian Cocoa CFAF/metric ton	163,570	163,570
Common Market preference 5.4%		8,830
CIF price metric ton	163,570	172,400

	(CFAF/ton)
Composite selling price 25% New York, 75% Europe	170,192
Insurance & loss in weight 2.37%	4,036
Brokerage & other charges 1.66%	2,825
Freight plus weighing	7,541
Composite FOB price	155,790
Commitment charge on export duty 0.1%	35
Exporters delivery charges (See below)	21,350

Value to Ivory Coast 134,405

   Guaranteed farmers price 80,000

Value to Government 54,405

   Customs Duty 22.38% [1] FOB value
   -16.73% of Duty Rebated to CSSPPA 29,033

Accruing to CSSPPA 25,372

Exporters Delivery Charges

Collecting and transporting to buying center	6,200
Packing and handling	3,172
Transport	3,500
Storage and grading	3,619
Insurance and general charges	1,589
Quay handling charges	907
Lighterage and other charges	2,109
Port levies	254
	21,350

[1] Assuming that the "mercuriale" price set each year by the Government to assess the tax will be the same as the actual FOB value.

March 24, 1970

IVORY COAST – COCOA PROJECT

(CFAF)

Year	1	2	3	4	5
Production - kg					200
Value @ CFAF 80/kg					16,000
Expenditures					
1. Nursery materials	2,000				
2. Hand tools		1,000	1,000	1,000	1,000
3. Plastic bags	3,000				
4. Seeds	1,550				
5. Fertilizer		4,950	9,600	14,550	19,500
6. Insecticide		1,100	1,100	1,100	1,100
7. Sprayer fuel					
8. Sprayer/Mistblower		1,250			
	6,550	8,300	11,700	16,650	21,600
Contingencies 10%	660	830	1,170	1,670	2,160
Hired labor including 15% contingencies		17,250			
	7,210	26,380	12,870	18,320	23,760
Less: Government subsidy for seeds	1,210				
Government subsidy for bags	2,550				
Financed by credit 100% of items 5, 6 and 8 inc. contingencies		8,030	11,770	17,220	22,660
CFAF 10,000 cash in year 2 for hired labor		10,000			
	3,760	18,030	11,770	17,220	22,660
Farmer's expenditure	3,450	8,350	1,100	1,100	1,100
Cash credits			2,000	2,000	
Income before credit repayment			900	900	14,900
Farmer's Credit					
Financed by credit as above		18,030	11,770	17,220	22,660
Cash credits in years 3 and 4			2,000	2,000	
Total annual credit		18,030	13,770	19,220	22,660
Total cumulative credit					73,680
Credit repayments - 8 years at 5½%					
Income after credit repayments	(3,450)	(8,350)	900	900	14,900
Income after credit repayments per man-day					226
Man-days family labor	30	115	83	78	66
Value @ CFAF 250/day + 15% contingencies	8,630	33,060	23,860	22,430	18,980
Net benefits less family labor	(12,080)	(41,410)	(22,960)	(21,530)	(4,080)
With 25% Reduction in Yields					
Value of production					12,000
Income before credit repayment					10,900
Income after credit repayments					10,900
Income after credit repayments per man-day					167
Man-days family labor					65
Value @ CFAF 250/day + 15% contingencies					18,690
Net benefits less family labor					(7,790)

March 2, 1970

FARM BUDGET – 1 ha NEW PLANTATION

6	7	8	9	10	11	12	13	14-21
500	700	900	1,000	1,000	1,000	1,000	1,000	1,000
40,000	56,000	72,000	80,000	80,000	80,000	80,000	80,000	80,000
1,000	1,000	1,000	1,000	1,000	1,000	1,000	1,000	1,000
1,680	1,680	1,680	1,680	1,680	1,680	1,680	1,680	1,680
840	840	840	840	840	840	840	840	840
1,180			1,180			1,180		400
4,700	3,520	3,520	4,700	3,520	3,520	4,700	3,520	3,920
470	350	350	470	350	350	470	350	390
5,170	3,870	3,870	5,170	3,870	3,870	5,170	3,870	4,310
5,170	3,870	3,870	5,170	3,870	3,870	5,170	3,870	4,310
34,830	52,130	68,130	74,830	76,130	76,130	74,830	76,130	75,690
11,630	11,630	11,630	11,630	11,630	11,630	11,630	11,630	
23,200	40,500	56,500	63,200	64,500	64,500	63,200	64,500	75,690
446	604	681	680	694	694	680	694	814
52	67	83	93	93	93	93	93	93
14,950	19,260	23,860	26,740	26,740	26,740	26,740	26,740	26,740
8,250	21,240	32,640	36,460	37,760	37,760	36,460	37,760	48,950
30,000	42,000	54,000	60,000	60,000	60,000	60,000	60,000	60,000
24,830	38,130	50,130	54,830	56,130	56,130	54,830	56,130	55,690
13,200	26,500	38,500	43,200	44,500	44,500	43,200	44,500	55,690
281	457	550	554	571	571	554	571	714
47	58	70	78	78	78	78	78	78
13,510	16,680	20,130	22,430	22,430	22,430	22,430	22,430	22,430
(310)	9,820	18,370	20,770	22,070	22,070	20,770	22,070	33,260

IVORY COAST – COCOA PROJECT

(CFAF)

Year	1	2
Production - kg/ha	360	420
Value @ CFAF 80/kg	28,800	33,600
Expenditures		
1. Hand tools	1,000	1,000
2. Insecticide	1,680	1,680
3. Sprayer fuel	840	840
4. Mist blower	1,180	——
	4,700	3,520
Contingencies - 10%	470	350
	5,170	3,870
Less: Financed by credit items 2 & 4 including contingencies x 80% year 1 and 2	2,520	1,480
Farmers cash expenditure	2,650	2,390
Income before loan repayment	26,150	31,210
Farmer's Credit		
80% of items 2 & 4	2,520	1,480
Interest at 5.5%	140	230
Cumulative credit	2,660	4,370
Credit repayments		
Income after credit repayment	26,150	31,210
Income per man day	311	372
Man days family labor	84	84
Value @ CFAF 250/day + 15% contingencies	24,150	24,150
Net benefits less family labor	2,000	7,060

March 2, 1970

FARM BUDGET – 1 ha REHABILITATION

3	4	5-13	Without Rehabilitation
600	600	600	360
48,000	48,000	48,000	28,800
1,000	1,000	1,000	1,000
1,680	1,680	1,680	770
840	840	840	340
——	1,180	——	300
3,520	4,700	3,520	2,410
350	470	350	240
3,870	5,170	3,870	2,650
3,870	5,170	3,870	2,650
44,130	42,830	44,130	26,150
2,370	2,370		
41,760	40,460	44,130	
497	604	659	475
84	67	67	55
24,150	19,260	19,260	15,810
17,610	21,200	24,870	10,340

IVORY COAST – COCOA PROJECT
GOVERNMENT SOURCES AND APPLICATIONS OF FUNDS
NEW PLANTATIONS AND REHABILITATION
(CFAF million)

NEW PLANTATIONS	1970	1971	1972	1973	1974	1975	1976	1977
SOURCES								
Crop revenues:								
Export duties [1]						22.0	83.0	175.4
Accruing to CSSPPA [1]						19.2	72.5	153.3
Farmers' credit repayment:								
- to Government								48.0
- to BMDA								25.6
TOTAL SOURCES						41.2	155.5	402.3
APPLICATIONS								
Funds for project	18.7	82.5	118.5	175.0	211.3	128.2	36.0	
Post-development admin. costs						2.4	5.6	8.7
Debt service on proposed IBRD loan [2]							80.0	180.6
TOTAL APPLICATIONS	18.7	82.5	118.5	175.0	211.3	130.6	121.6	189.3
Cash surplus (deficit)	(18.7)	(82.5)	(118.5)	(175.0)	(211.3)	(89.4)	33.9	213.0
Cumulative cash surplus (deficit)	(18.7)	(101.2)	(219.7)	(394.7)	(606.0)	(695.4)	(661.5)	(448.5)

REHABILITATION	1970	1971	1972	1973	1974	1975	1976	1977
SOURCES								
Crop revenues:								
Export duties [1]				22.6	104.5	162.0	223.0	264.8
Accruing to CSSPPA [1]				19.8	91.3	141.6	194.9	231.4
Farmers' credit repayment:								
- to Government						6.4	30.2	14.3
- to BMDA						2.1	10.1	4.7
TOTAL SOURCES				42.4	195.8	312.1	458.2	515.2
APPLICATIONS								
Funds for project		50.1	46.6	36.7	21.1			
Post-development admin. costs				8.4	13.5	88.2	59.5	40.1
Debt service on proposed IBRD loan [2]					21.0	28.0	30.0	54.7
TOTAL APPLICATIONS		50.1	46.6	45.1	55.6	116.2	89.5	94.8
Cash surplus (deficit)		(50.1)	(46.6)	(2.7)	140.2	195.9	368.7	420.4
Cumulative cash surplus (deficit)		(50.1)	(96.7)	(99.4)	40.8	236.7	605.4	1,025.8

[1] Based on world price of 27 US cents/lb.

[2] Excluding interest capitalized.

April 29, 1970

1978	1979	1980	1981	1982	1983	1984-90	1991	1992	1993	1994
299.0	412.8	486.1	531.2	546.7	546.7	3,826.9	546.7	336.7	296.7	154.5
261.3	360.7	424.8	464.3	477.8	477.8	3,344.6	477.8	381.6	259.3	135.0
142.9	142.9	142.9	142.9	142.9	114.1	117.9				
76.2	76.2	76.2	76.2	76.2	60.9	62.9				
779.4	992.6	1,130.0	1,214.6	1,243.6	1,199.5	7,352.3	1,024.5	718.3	556.0	289.5
75.9	55.4	52.0	38.9	29.1	19.3	112.7	12.6	8.9	4.5	
269.3	269.3	269.3	269.3	269.3	269.3	404.0				
345.2	324.7	321.3	308.2	298.4	288.6	516.7	12.6	8.9	4.5	
434.2	667.9	808.7	906.4	945.2	910.9	6,835.6	1,011.9	709.4	551.5	289.5
(14.3)	653.6	1,462.3	2,368.7	3,313.9	4,224.8	11,060.4	12,072.3	12,780.7	13,333.2	13,622.7

1978-83	1984	1985	1986	1987
1,588.8	264.8	174.2	118.5	55.7
1,388.4	231.4	152.2	103.5	48.7
2,977.2	496.2	326.4	222.0	104.4
187.2	20.7	14.3	6.6	
477.0	79.5	39.8		
664.2	100.2	54.1	6.6	
2,313.0	396.0	272.3	215.4	104.4
3,338.8	3,734.8	4,007.1	4,222.5	4,326.9

IVORY COAST – COCOA PROJECT
ECONOMIC RATES OF RETURN (CFAF million)

NEW PLANTATIONS		1970	1971	1972	1973	1974	1975	1976
Costs								
Project costs		31.8	229.2	310.0	442.4	537.7	394.0	327.3
Post-project administration costs							2.4	5.6
Post-project farm costs							16.3	37.1
Family labor		32.7	166.9	292.0	407.9	472.8	385.0	357.4
		64.5	396.1	602.0	850.3	1,010.5	797.7	727.4
Benefits								
Yield – tons							758	2,859
Value at CFAF 134,405/ton							101.9	384.3
Net Benefits		(64.5)	(396.1)	(602.0)	(850.3)	(1,010.5)	(695.8)	(343.1)
Rate of Return	19.9%							

REHABILITATION		1971	1972	1973	1974	1975	1976	1977
Costs								
Project Costs		148.6	183.9	209.9	227.2	129.3		
Post-project administration costs				8.4	13.5	88.2	59.5	40.1
Post-project farm costs				56.0	90.5	129.3	163.8	163.8
Family labor		313.9	507.1	724.5	954.2	915.1	871.0	831.9
		462.5	691.0	998.8	1,285.4	1,261.9	1,094.3	1,035.8
Less Costs without project:								
Farm costs		23.5	55.7	79.5	100.7	100.7	100.7	100.7
Family labor		205.4	315.0	474.0	570.0	570.0	570.0	570.0
		228.9	370.7	553.5	670.7	670.7	670.7	670.7
Incremental Costs		233.6	320.3	445.3	614.7	591.2	423.6	365.1
Benefits								
Yield from rehabilitation - tons		4,680	7,560	11,580	17,280	19,260	21,360	22,800
Yield without project		4,680	7,560	10,800	13,680	13,680	13,680	13,680
Incremental yield		–	–	780	3,600	5,580	7,680	9,120
Value at CFAF 134,405/ton		–	–	104.8	483.9	750.0	1,032.2	1,225.8
Incremental Net Benefits		(233.6)	(320.3)	(340.5)	(130.8)	158.8	608.6	860.7
Rate of Return	35%							

March 2, 1970

1977	1978	1979	1980	1981	1982	1983	1984-90	1991	1992	1993	1994
223.5											
8.7	75.9	55.4	52.0	38.9	29.1	19.3	16.1	12.6	8.9	4.5	–
58.2	81.2	81.2	81.2	81.2	81.2	81.2	81.2	64.8	44.0	22.3	–
357.5	390.2	449.6	488.1	503.5	503.5	503.5	503.5	402.2	273.3	142.3	–
647.9	547.3	586.2	621.3	623.6	613.8	604.0	600.8	479.6	326.2	169.1	–
6,043	10,299	14,218	16,744	18,298	18,830	18,830	18,830	18,830	15,040	10,220	5,320
812.2	1,384.2	1,911.0	2,250.5	2,459.3	2,530.8	2,530.8	2,530.8	2,530.8	2,021.5	1,373.6	715.0
164.3	836.9	1,324.8	1,629.2	1,835.7	1,917.0	1,926.8	1,930.0	2,051.2	1,695.3	1,204.5	715.0

1978-83	1984	1985	1986	1987
31.2	20.7	14.3	6.6	–
163.8	107.8	73.3	34.5	–
831.9	481.5	327.4	154.1	–
1,026.9	610.0	415.0	195.2	–
100.7	66.3	45.0	21.2	–
570.0	395.0	255.0	126.4	–
670.7	461.3	300.0	147.6	–
356.2	148.7	115.0	47.6	–
22,800	22,800	15,000	10,200	4,800
13,680	13,680	9,000	6,120	2,880
9,120	9,120	6,000	4,080	1,920
1,225.8	1,225.8	806.4	548.4	258.1
869.6	1,077.1	691.4	500.8	258.1

IVORY COAST – COCOA PROJECT
FINANCIAL RETURNS TO GOVERNMENT

	1970	1971	1972	1973	1974	1975	1976	1977
NEW PLANTATIONS								
Project Costs:								
Farm subsidies	14.3	18.1	18.4	20.0				
Other costs	4.4	94.5	98.8	143.1	156.1	121.3	113.5	97.2
Total	18.7	112.6	117.2	163.1	156.1	121.3	113.5	97.2
Post-project Administration						2.4	5.6	8.7
Total costs	18.7	112.6	117.2	163.1	156.1	123.7	119.1	105.9
Benefits:								
Customs duties and CSSPPA retentions[1]						41.2	155.5	328.7
Net Benefits	(18.7)	(112.6)	(117.2)	(163.1)	(156.1)	(82.5)	36.4	222.8
Financial Return	35.3%							

		1971	1972	1973	1974	1975	1976	1977
REHABILITATION								
Project Costs		81.5	92.4	132.4	151.1	98.4		
Post-project Administration				8.4	13.5	88.2	59.5	40.1
Total		81.5	92.4	140.8	164.6	186.6	59.5	40.1
Incremental Benefits:								
Customs duties and CSSPPA retentions[1]				42.4	195.8	303.6	417.9	496.2
Net Benefits		(81.5)	(92.4)	(98.4)	31.2	117.0	358.4	456.1
Financial Return	52%							

[1] Based on world price of 27 US cents/lb.

March 2, 1970

1978	1979	1980	1981	1982	1983	1984-90	1991	1992	1993	1994
75.9	55.4	52.0	38.9	29.1	19.3	16.1	12.6	8.9	4.5	–
75.9	55.4	52.0	38.9	29.1	19.3	16.1	12.6	8.9	4.5	–
560.3	773.5	910.9	995.5	1,024.5	1,024.5	1,024.5	1,024.5	718.3	556.0	289.5
484.4	718.1	858.9	956.6	995.4	1,005.2	1,008.4	1,011.9	709.4	551.5	289.5

1978-84	1984	1985	1986	1987
31.2	20.7	14.3	6.6	–
31.2	20.7	14.3	6.6	–
496.2	496.2	326.4	222.0	104.4
465.0	475.5	312.1	215.4	104.4

IVORY COAST – COCOA PROJECT
FARM UNIT FINANCIAL RETURNS (1 Ha)
(CFAF million)

YEAR	1	2	3	4	5	6	7	8	9–21
NEW PLANTATIONS									
Costs									
On farm costs less subsidies	3450	26380	12870	18320	23760	4310	4310	4310	4310
Family labour	8630	33060	23860	22430	18980	14950	19260	23860	26740
	12080	59440	36730	40750	42740	19260	23570	28170	31050
Benefits									
Value of production with assumed yields					16000	40000	56000	72000	80000
Net Benefits	(12080)	(59440)	(36730)	(40750)	(26740)	20740	32430	43830	48950
Rate of Return	16.0%								

REHABILITATION	YEAR	1	2	3	4	5	6	7–13
Costs								
Farm cost of rehabilitation		5170	3870	3870	5170	3870	3870	4270
Family labour		24150	24150	24150	19260	19260	19260	19260
		29320	28020	28020	24430	23130	23130	23530
Less: Farm costs without rehabilitation		2650	2650	2650	2650	2650	2650	2650
Family labour		15810	15810	15810	15810	15810	15810	15810
Incremental cost		10860	9560	9560	5970	4670	4670	5070
Benefits								
Value or production with rehabilitation		28800	33600	48000	48000	48000	48000	48000
without rehabilitation		28800	28800	28800	28800	28800	28800	28800
Incremental benefits			4800	19200	19200	19200	19200	19200
Net Benefits		(10860)	(4760)	9640	13230	14530	14530	14130
Rate of Return		56%						

8. SOURCES OF ASSISTANCE
FOR PROJECT PREPARATION

For specialized assistance in preparing complex agricultural projects, many governments will wish to turn to one of the international agencies or to engage the services of a commercial consulting firm.

United Nations Development Programme

One of the principal purposes of the United Nations Development Programme (UNDP) is to facilitate and promote new capital investments in developing countries. It finances preinvestment activities including surveys of physical resources and of possibilities for their improved use; analyses of national economic sectors including agriculture as a basis for formulating coordinated investment programs or defining priorities; feasibility studies of investment projects; applied research; manpower training; technical education; and the like.

Major organizational and operating changes have recently been introduced in UNDP. Organizationally, there are now four regional bureaux at UNDP headquarters, each headed by an assistant administrator. These regional bureaux have complete responsibility for operations and planning in the countries in their regions: Asia; Africa; Latin America; and Europe, Mediterranean and Middle East.

Operationally, the major change became effective at the beginning of 1972. UNDP has projected its resources for five years and then divided this total up among all developing countries so that each has a five-year indicative planning figure within which all its UNDP projects must fit. Then, on the basis of this planning figure, each country is expected to develop a UNDP Country Program including a list of projects for which UNDP assistance is contemplated.

In the past, UNDP has not itself carried out the preinvestment activities it has financed. Instead, it has made use of the United Nations, the UN specialized agencies, and occasionally other institutions. In agriculture, FAO has normally been the Participating and Executing Agency for UNDP activities. The World Bank has on occasion taken this responsibility, generally in cases such as credit projects where it has special experience to offer.

Each of the developing countries has a Basic Agreement with the UNDP which sets forth the general terms and conditions applicable, in principle, to all UNDP financed activities. Then for each specific activity, a tripartite Project Document (formerly called the Plan of Operation) is prepared and agreed to by the country receiving assistance, the UNDP, and the Participating and Executing Agency. This specifies the arrangements for executing the activity, details of the obligations of the three parties, details of the reports to be prepared, provision for suspension and termination, and details of the financial contributions provided by the UNDP and the Government concerned.

For each activity it has undertaken in a country, the UNDP has normally allocated a specific sum to meet all or part of the foreign exchange costs and certain of the local costs. The Government receiving assistance has contributed some of the local currency costs and, in some cases, has contributed towards the foreign exchange costs.

Requests for UNDP assistance are submitted through the United Nations Resident Representative in the country involved.

Reports of many UNDP preinvestment and feasibility studies are available through the UNDP in New York. They provide a ready source of examples for those considering similar activities.

FAO-development bank cooperative programs

Since 1964, the Food and Agriculture Organization has been developing an Investment Centre staffed by a specialized team of experts to help identify and prepare agricultural projects in close cooperation first with the World Bank and more recently with the Inter-American Development Bank, the Asian Development Bank, the African Development Bank, and with a number of private banks interested in financing agricultural projects.

The Investment Centre staff is especially useful for bringing to bear a comparative knowledge of similar projects in other countries under roughly comparable conditions and for its familiarity with the special requirements of lending institutions. Normally the Investment Centre helps with project identification and preparation in two distinct stages. The first is a preliminary view of the possible project in order to gain an immediate idea of what activities should or should not be included, to assess the information which is available or would have to be obtained to prepare a sound analysis, to gain an idea of the administrative and organizational problems, and to be sure a project has appropriate priority within the overall development program of the country. An identification mission generally remains in the country about two weeks. If a government then wishes further assistance, the Centre may make specialists available to help with project preparation or may advise governments to retain consultants. At this stage the technicians assist in preparing detailed critical analyses of the technical, economic, and financial data and assumptions. The mission helps marshall the available data for the economic and financial analysis and for preparing the project for presentation to the financing agency. The time for project preparation, of course, is dependent upon the complexity of the project, and the Centre may send several missions, particularly if there are serious data gaps.

The simplest way for a country to obtain assistance under these FAO-bank Cooperative Programs is to make direct application to FAO or to the appropriate bank. This may be done either formally to the Director-General of FAO, through personal contact with the FAO Country Representative, or informally to the Director of the FAO Investment Centre or to a staff member of a development bank. The application may be made by letter, or by personal contact at such convenient opportunities as during a visit of a bank staff member to the country, bank annual meetings, FAO Conference, and the like. There is no fixed timetable for considering and approving applications for assistance, although in the nature of the activity there is generally a considerable lag between the first letter or conversation and the time the project is actually ready for work to begin, so that it is important to make contacts early and to be sure there is a "pipeline" of projects under active preparation at all times.

In the case of FAO-bank cooperative programs, the major portion of the cost is borne by the international agencies although in some instances the government involved may be asked to provide local transportation and similar services.

World Bank assistance

Under certain circumstances, World Bank assistance may be available to help with project identification, preparation, and implementation.

World Bank economic missions, sector survey missions, operational missions and resident missions may bring to a government's attention projects which seem to offer prospects for good returns and which appear to deserve priority. Project supervision missions in the course of their work on particular projects may identify the possibility of later stages or similar projects which might be financed by a Bank loan.

Once potential projects have been identified, the Bank in some instances is able to render assistance in preparation. (It should be clear that Bank assistance of any form in preparing a project does not constitute a commitment for Bank Group financing of the resulting project.) The Bank may be able to give advice on the planning of feasibility studies by specifying the information which has to be gathered (often by providing questionnaires), by defining the studies needed to provide this information, by establishing the relative urgency and emphasis to be given to different aspects of the studies, and by advising how these studies can best be organized and presented and, where appropriate, financed. As the feasibility study is proceeding, the Bank may help assure that it is progressing along the right lines and will cover the necessary aspects. This assistance may range all the way from occasional visits to formal participation in steering committees.

The Bank maintains permanent missions at Nairobi for East Africa and in Abijan for West Africa which help identify promising projects and in certain cases are able to assist governments prepare projects for presentation to the Bank.

Sometimes, it is possible to finance project preparation studies either by government agencies or by commercial consultants with funds from a Bank loan or IDA credit. Most commonly this method is used when a loan or credit is being made to a borrower who wishes to finance costs for preparing subsequent phases of a project or additional related projects that are likely also to be financed by Bank loans or IDA credits. Of course, funds from a loan or credit are commonly used to finance technical assistance directly related to the implementation of the project for which a loan or credit was made.

Consulting firms

Many governments will want to engage commercial consulting firms for project preparation assistance to take advantage of the specialized technical expertise of their staffs and to benefit from the experience the firms have gained while preparing similar projects in other countries.

Much more than just technical competence or experience needs to be considered when deciding whether to engage a consulting firm. Many Government agencies are already fully occupied and simply do not have the staff time available to devote to proper project preparation. By engaging a consulting firm, either national or international, it is possible to have a qualified staff able to devote its full time to careful project preparation for however long is needed to do the job properly.

Even when the overall project preparation is to be carried out by a government agency, there may be narrow technical assessments where outside expertise is desirable--a soils analysis for an irrigation project, a market analysis for a specialty crop to be exported, or tests on possible species to be planted for pulpwood.

When an international firm is engaged, its costs may appear to be quite high, especially when the salaries paid by a European or North American firm are contrasted with those of a developing country agency. It is important to remember, however, that if the firm does indeed do a good job it may save any added costs many times over by preparing a more efficient project design and by avoiding the delays or even the outright loss of capital which inadequate technical preparation may incur.

A common drawback of international consulting firms is that the expertise they gain while preparing a project is lost to the nation when their work ends. Sometimes this drawback can be reduced by turning to local consultants. Consulting firms of suitable competence increasingly are to be found in developing countries, and more might grow were there a conscious policy to encourage them and to assure them an opportunity to compete for suitable work. When national consulting firms are used, the advantages of having a group of people who can focus on project preparation without the pressures of day-to-day routine administration are realized while at the same time the specialized skills the consultants learn in the course of their work remain in the country and can be again available in the future. In some cases where a national consulting firm does not have the full range of expertise which will be needed to prepare a project, it may be able to draw upon a foreign associate for particular specialized skills, using its own resources for the less esoteric work.

The work of a consulting firm can hardly be better than its terms of reference and the administrative supervision of its work as the project is being prepared. There must be a detailed description of the objectives of the project and considerable precision about the level of detail which is expected. Terms of reference for agricultural projects commonly run from five to ten pages, but may extend to thirty or forty pages.

Once a suitable set of terms of reference is ready, it may be circulated to three or four consulting firms which seem to have the expertise called for with a request that they prepare proposals for undertaking the work. Probably it is best if these proposals are not expected to include the financial terms--only a statement of how the firm would propose to go about preparing a project, their methodology, their plan of operations, and which experts they propose to assign to the task and their experience and qualifications. The objective should be to select the consultants on the basis of experience and willingness to assign highly qualified staff, not on price. One criterion to which particular attention should be paid is whether the firm proposes to assign its own staff to the project and whether a senior member of the firm will have personal responsibility for the work of the consulting team. Care must be exercised that the consultants are independent from potential suppliers if capital equipment or construction will be an important component in the project. Once the most appropriate firm is selected on the basis of its proposal, then discussions can proceed about the costs. If these seem out of line, another firm may be invited to open talks about its proposal and costs.

In evaluating consultants' proposals, an informal scoring system may be useful. A total of one hundred points is allocated, say twenty to experience with similar projects, twenty to the plan of operations proposed, twenty to the competence and qualification of the team leader, and twenty for the other members of the team, perhaps varying in weight depending on whether the agriculturist's contribution will be more critical than the economist's, and so forth. The purpose of the weighting system is to enable those reviewing the proposals to evaluate them in the first instance on an agreed set of criteria within which there is an agreed weighting of the importance of various factors. For each project, obviously, consideration needs to be given to whether the weighting system adequately reflects the importance of the various components of experience, plan of operation, and personnel skills in the proposed study.

APPENDIX. THREE PLACE DISCOUNT TABLES

For most computations of discounted measures of project worth the three place discount tables on the following two pages are sufficient. They will permit estimations to the nearest whole percentage point for internal rate of return, three significant digits for net present worth, and a tenth of a ratio point for benefit-cost ratios--as much precision as the underlying data will justify in agricultural projects (see page 90).

For final presentation, there are instances where the intervals between percentage points in these tables will not permit computation of the internal rate of return to the nearest percentage point (pages 80 to 82). For the final check in these cases resort will have to be made to more detailed tables.

If the opportunity cost of capital to be used for computing net present worth or the benefit-cost ratio is not given in these tables, a more detailed table will be needed.

A number of suitable, more detailed compounding and discounting tables are available. A convenient set designed with the needs of project analysis in mind is Compounding and Discounting Tables for Project Evaluation (8).

A-1. DISCOUNT FACTOR—How much 1 at a future date is worth today.

Year	1%	3%	5%	6%	8%	10%	12%	14%	15%	16%	18%
1	0.990	0.971	0.952	0.943	0.926	0.909	0.893	0.877	0.870	0.862	0.847
2	0.980	0.943	0.907	0.890	0.857	0.826	0.797	0.769	0.756	0.743	0.718
3	0.971	0.915	0.864	0.840	0.794	0.751	0.712	0.675	0.658	0.641	0.609
4	0.961	0.888	0.823	0.792	0.735	0.683	0.636	0.592	0.572	0.552	0.516
5	0.951	0.863	0.784	0.747	0.681	0.621	0.567	0.519	0.497	0.476	0.437
6	0.942	0.837	0.746	0.705	0.630	0.564	0.507	0.456	0.432	0.410	0.370
7	0.933	0.813	0.711	0.665	0.583	0.513	0.452	0.400	0.376	0.354	0.314
8	0.923	0.789	0.677	0.627	0.540	0.467	0.404	0.351	0.327	0.305	0.266
9	0.914	0.766	0.645	0.592	0.500	0.424	0.361	0.308	0.284	0.263	0.225
10	0.905	0.744	0.614	0.558	0.463	0.386	0.322	0.270	0.247	0.227	0.191
11	0.896	0.722	0.585	0.527	0.429	0.350	0.287	0.237	0.215	0.195	0.162
12	0.887	0.701	0.557	0.497	0.397	0.319	0.257	0.208	0.187	0.168	0.137
13	0.879	0.681	0.530	0.469	0.368	0.290	0.229	0.182	0.163	0.145	0.116
14	0.870	0.661	0.505	0.442	0.340	0.263	0.205	0.160	0.141	0.125	0.099
15	0.861	0.642	0.481	0.417	0.315	0.239	0.183	0.140	0.123	0.108	0.084
16	0.853	0.623	0.458	0.394	0.292	0.218	0.163	0.123	0.107	0.093	0.071
17	0.844	0.605	0.436	0.371	0.270	0.198	0.146	0.108	0.093	0.080	0.060
18	0.836	0.587	0.416	0.350	0.250	0.180	0.130	0.095	0.081	0.069	0.051
19	0.828	0.570	0.396	0.331	0.232	0.164	0.116	0.083	0.070	0.060	0.043
20	0.820	0.554	0.377	0.312	0.215	0.149	0.104	0.073	0.061	0.051	0.037
21	0.811	0.538	0.359	0.294	0.199	0.135	0.093	0.064	0.053	0.044	0.031
22	0.803	0.522	0.342	0.278	0.184	0.123	0.083	0.056	0.046	0.038	0.026
23	0.795	0.507	0.326	0.262	0.170	0.112	0.074	0.049	0.040	0.033	0.022
24	0.788	0.492	0.310	0.247	0.158	0.102	0.066	0.043	0.035	0.028	0.019
25	0.780	0.478	0.295	0.233	0.146	0.092	0.059	0.038	0.030	0.024	0.016
26	0.772	0.464	0.281	0.220	0.135	0.084	0.053	0.033	0.026	0.021	0.014
27	0.764	0.450	0.268	0.207	0.125	0.076	0.047	0.029	0.023	0.018	0.011
28	0.757	0.437	0.255	0.196	0.116	0.069	0.042	0.026	0.020	0.016	0.010
29	0.749	0.424	0.243	0.185	0.107	0.063	0.037	0.022	0.017	0.014	0.008
30	0.742	0.412	0.231	0.174	0.099	0.057	0.033	0.020	0.015	0.012	0.007
35	0.706	0.355	0.181	0.130	0.068	0.036	0.019	0.010	0.008	0.006	0.003
40	0.672	0.307	0.142	0.097	0.046	0.022	0.011	0.005	0.004	0.003	0.001
45	0.639	0.264	0.111	0.073	0.031	0.014	0.006	0.003	0.002	0.001	0.001
50	0.608	0.228	0.087	0.054	0.021	0.009	0.003	0.001	0.001	0.001	0.000

20%	22%	24%	25%	26%	28%	30%	35%	40%	45%	50%
0.833	0.820	0.806	0.800	0.794	0.781	0.769	0.741	0.714	0.690	0.667
0.694	0.672	0.650	0.640	0.630	0.610	0.592	0.549	0.510	0.476	0.444
0.579	0.551	0.524	0.512	0.500	0.477	0.455	0.406	0.364	0.328	0.296
0.482	0.451	0.423	0.410	0.397	0.373	0.350	0.301	0.260	0.226	0.198
0.402	0.370	0.341	0.328	0.315	0.291	0.269	0.223	0.186	0.156	0.132
0.335	0.303	0.275	0.262	0.250	0.227	0.207	0.165	0.133	0.108	0.088
0.279	0.249	0.222	0.210	0.198	0.178	0.159	0.122	0.095	0.074	0.059
0.233	0.204	0.179	0.168	0.157	0.139	0.123	0.091	0.068	0.051	0.039
0.194	0.167	0.144	0.134	0.125	0.108	0.094	0.067	0.048	0.035	0.026
0.162	0.137	0.116	0.107	0.099	0.085	0.073	0.050	0.035	0.024	0.017
0.135	0.112	0.094	0.086	0.079	0.066	0.056	0.037	0.025	0.017	0.012
0.112	0.092	0.076	0.069	0.062	0.052	0.043	0.027	0.018	0.012	0.008
0.093	0.075	0.061	0.055	0.050	0.040	0.033	0.020	0.013	0.008	0.005
0.078	0.062	0.049	0.044	0.039	0.032	0.025	0.015	0.009	0.006	0.003
0.065	0.051	0.040	0.035	0.031	0.025	0.020	0.011	0.006	0.004	0.002
0.054	0.042	0.032	0.028	0.025	0.019	0.015	0.008	0.005	0.003	0.002
0.045	0.034	0.026	0.023	0.020	0.015	0.012	0.006	0.003	0.002	0.001
0.038	0.028	0.021	0.018	0.016	0.012	0.009	0.005	0.002	0.001	0.001
0.031	0.023	0.017	0.014	0.012	0.009	0.007	0.003	0.002	0.001	0.000
0.026	0.019	0.014	0.012	0.010	0.007	0.005	0.002	0.001	0.001	0.000
0.022	0.015	0.011	0.009	0.008	0.006	0.004	0.002	0.001	0.000	0.000
0.018	0.013	0.009	0.007	0.006	0.004	0.003	0.001	0.001	0.000	0.000
0.015	0.010	0.007	0.006	0.005	0.003	0.002	0.001	0.000	0.000	0.000
0.013	0.008	0.006	0.005	0.004	0.003	0.002	0.001	0.000	0.000	0.000
0.010	0.007	0.005	0.004	0.003	0.002	0.001	0.001	0.000	0.000	0.000
0.009	0.006	0.004	0.003	0.002	0.002	0.001	0.000	0.000	0.000	0.000
0.007	0.005	0.003	0.002	0.002	0.001	0.001	0.000	0.000	0.000	0.000
0.006	0.004	0.002	0.002	0.002	0.001	0.001	0.000	0.000	0.000	0.000
0.005	0.003	0.002	0.002	0.001	0.001	0.001	0.000	0.000	0.000	0.000
0.004	0.003	0.002	0.001	0.001	0.001	0.000	0.000	0.000	0.000	0.000
0.002	0.001	0.001	0.000	0.000	0.000	0.000	0.000	0.000	0.000	0.000
0.001	0.000	0.000	0.000	0.000	0.000	0.000	0.000	0.000	0.000	0.000
0.000	0.000	0.000	0.000	0.000	0.000	0.000	0.000	0.000	0.000	0.000
0.000	0.000	0.000	0.000	0.000	0.000	0.000	0.000	0.000	0.000	0.000

A-2. PRESENT WORTH OF AN ANNUITY FACTOR—

How much 1 received or paid annually for X years is worth today.

Year	1%	3%	5%	6%	8%	10%	12%	14%	15%	16%	18%
1	0.990	0.971	0.952	0.943	0.926	0.909	0.893	0.877	0.870	0.862	0.847
2	1.970	1.914	1.859	1.833	1.783	1.736	1.690	1.647	1.626	1.605	1.566
3	2.941	2.829	2.723	2.673	2.577	2.487	2.402	2.322	2.283	2.246	2.174
4	3.902	3.717	3.546	3.465	3.312	3.170	3.037	2.914	2.855	2.798	2.690
5	4.853	4.580	4.330	4.212	3.993	3.791	3.605	3.433	3.352	3.274	3.127
6	5.795	5.417	5.076	4.917	4.623	4.355	4.111	3.889	3.784	3.685	3.498
7	6.728	6.230	5.786	5.582	5.206	4.868	4.564	4.288	4.160	4.039	3.812
8	7.652	7.020	6.463	6.210	5.747	5.335	4.968	4.639	4.487	4.344	4.078
9	8.566	7.786	7.108	6.802	6.247	5.759	5.328	4.946	4.772	4.607	4.303
10	9.471	8.530	7.722	7.360	6.710	6.145	5.650	5.216	5.019	4.833	4.494
11	10.368	9.253	8.306	7.887	7.139	6.495	5.938	5.453	5.234	5.029	4.656
12	11.255	9.954	8.863	8.384	7.536	6.814	6.194	5.660	5.421	5.197	4.793
13	12.134	10.635	9.394	8.853	7.904	7.103	6.424	5.842	5.583	5.342	4.910
14	13.004	11.296	9.899	9.295	8.244	7.367	6.628	6.002	5.724	5.468	5.008
15	13.865	11.938	10.380	9.712	8.559	7.606	6.811	6.142	5.847	5.575	5.092
16	14.718	12.561	10.838	10.106	8.851	7.824	6.974	6.265	5.954	5.669	5.162
17	15.562	13.166	11.274	10.477	9.122	8.022	7.120	6.373	6.047	5.749	5.222
18	16.398	13.754	11.690	10.828	9.372	8.201	7.250	6.467	6.128	5.818	5.273
19	17.226	14.324	12.085	11.158	9.604	8.365	7.366	6.550	6.198	5.877	5.316
20	18.046	14.877	12.462	11.470	9.818	8.514	7.469	6.623	6.259	5.929	5.353
21	18.857	15.415	12.821	11.764	10.017	8.649	7.562	6.687	6.312	5.973	5.384
22	19.660	15.937	13.163	12.042	10.201	8.772	7.645	6.743	6.359	6.011	5.410
23	20,456	16,444	13.489	12.303	10.371	8.883	7.718	6.792	6.399	6.044	5.432
24	21,243	16.936	13.799	12.550	10.529	8.985	7.784	6.835	6.434	6.073	5.451
25	22,023	17,413	14.094	12.783	10.675	9.077	7.843	6.873	6.464	6.097	5.467
26	22.795	17.877	14.375	13.003	10.810	9.161	7.896	6.906	6.491	6.118	5.480
27	23.560	18.327	14.643	13.211	10.935	9.237	7.943	6.935	6.514	6.136	5.492
28	24.316	18.764	14.898	13.406	11.051	9.307	7.984	6.961	6.534	6.152	5.502
29	25.066	19.188	15.141	13.591	11.158	9.370	8.022	6.983	6.551	6.166	5.510
30	25.808	19.600	15.372	13.765	11.258	9.427	8.055	7.003	6.566	6.177	5.517
35	29.409	21.487	16.374	14.498	11.655	9.644	8.176	7.070	6.617	6.215	5.539
40	32.835	23.115	17.159	15.046	11.925	9.779	8.244	7.105	6.642	6.234	5.548
45	36.095	24.519	17.774	15.456	12.108	9.863	8.283	7.123	6.654	6.242	5.552
50	39.196	25.730	18.256	15.762	12.234	9.915	8.304	7.133	6.661	6.246	5.554

20%	22%	24%	25%	26%	28%	30%	35%	40%	45%	50%
0.833	0.820	0.806	0.800	0.794	0.781	0.769	0.741	0.714	0.690	0.667
1.528	1.492	1.457	1.440	1.424	1.392	1.361	1.289	1.224	1.165	1.111
2.106	2.042	1.981	1.952	1.923	1.868	1.816	1.696	1.589	1.493	1.407
2.589	2.494	2.404	2.362	2.320	2.241	2.166	1.997	1.849	1.720	1.605
2.991	2.864	2.745	2.689	2.635	2.532	2.436	2.220	2.035	1.876	1.737
3.326	3.167	3.020	2.951	2.885	2.759	2.643	2.385	2.168	1.983	1.824
3.605	3.416	3.242	3.161	3.083	2.937	2.802	2.508	2.263	2.057	1.883
3.837	3.619	3.421	3.329	3.241	3.076	2.925	2.598	2.331	2.108	1.922
4.031	3.786	3.566	3.463	3.366	3.184	3.019	2.665	2.379	2.144	1.948
4.192	3.923	3.682	3.571	3.465	3.269	3.092	2.715	2.414	2.168	1.965
4.327	4.035	3.776	3.656	3.544	3.335	3.147	2.752	2.438	2.185	1.977
4.439	4.127	3.851	3.725	3.606	3.387	3.190	2.779	2.456	2.196	1.985
4.533	4.203	3.912	3.780	3.656	3.427	3.223	2.799	2.468	2.204	1.990
4.611	4.265	3.962	3.824	3.695	3.459	3.249	2.814	2.477	2.210	1.993
4.675	4.315	4.001	3.859	3.726	3.483	3.268	2.825	2.484	2.214	1.995
4.730	4.357	4.033	3.887	3.751	3.503	3.283	2.834	2.489	2.216	1.997
4.775	4.391	4.059	3.910	3.771	3.518	3.295	2.840	2.492	2.218	1.998
4.812	4.419	4.080	3.928	3.786	3.529	3.304	2.844	2.494	2.219	1.999
4.844	4.442	4.097	3.942	3.799	3.539	3.311	2.848	2.496	2.220	1.999
4.870	4.460	4.110	3.954	3.808	3.546	3.316	2.850	2.497	2.221	1.999
4.891	4.476	4.121	3.963	3.816	3.551	3.320	2.852	2.498	2.221	2.000
4.909	4.488	4.130	3.970	3.822	3.556	3.323	2.853	2.498	2.222	2.000
4.925	4.499	4.137	3.976	3.827	3.559	3.325	2.854	2.499	2.222	2.000
4.937	4.507	4.143	3.981	3.831	3.562	3.327	2.855	2.499	2.222	2.000
4.948	4.514	4.147	3.985	3.834	3.564	3.329	2.856	2.499	2.222	2.000
4.956	4.520	4.151	3.988	3.837	3.566	3.330	2.856	2.500	2.222	2.000
4.964	4.524	4.154	3.990	3.839	3.567	3.331	2.856	2.500	2.222	2.000
4.970	4.528	4.157	3.992	3.840	3.568	3.331	2.857	2.500	2.222	2.000
4.975	4.531	4.159	3.994	3.841	3.569	3.332	2.857	2.500	2.222	2.000
4.979	4.534	4.160	3.995	3.842	3.569	3.332	2.857	2.500	2.222	2.000
4.992	4.541	4.164	3.998	3.845	3.571	3.333	2.857	2.500	2.222	2.000
4.997	4.544	4.166	3.999	3.846	3.571	3.333	2.857	2.500	2.222	2.000
4.999	4.545	4.166	4.000	3.846	3.571	3.333	2.857	2.500	2.222	2.000
4.999	4.545	4.167	4.000	3.846	3.571	3.333	2.857	2.500	2.222	2.000

BIBLIOGRAPHY

You may find it interesting to look into some of the literature on project analysis both to find more formal treatments than in this book and to find discussions of practical applications.

1.   Adler, Hans A. *Economic Appraisal of Transport Projects: A Manual with Case Studies.* Bloomington: University of Indiana Press, 1971.

      Similar to this book but for transportation projects.

2.   Bierman, Harold, Jr., and Smidt, Seymour. *The Capital Budgeting Decision.* New York: The Macmillan Company, 1960.

3.   Bruno, Michael. "The Optimal Selection of Export-Promoting and Import-Substituting Projects." In *Planning the External Sector: Techniques, Problems and Policies, Report on the First Interregional Seminar on Development Planning,* Ankara, Turkey, 6-17 September 1965, pp. 88-135. United Nations publication number ST/TAO/SER.c/91. New York: United Nations, 1967.

      A thorough summary of the theoretical and practical problems associated with computing the internal foreign exchange rate.

4.   Eckstein, Otto. *Water Resource Development: The Economics of Project Evaluation.* Cambridge: Harvard University Press, 1958.

      A theoretical discussion of the issues and problems of project analysis. Classic in its field, but stiff going and written for professional economists.

5.   Food and Agriculture Organization. *Selected Bibliography on Project Analysis.* Rome: Food and Agriculture Organization, 1969.

      A well selected, annotated bibliography ranging beyond narrow questions of agricultural projects. Although the list includes several works in French language, it unfortunately includes not one Spanish language entry.

6.   Food and Agriculture Organization. *General Guidelines to the Analysis of Agricultural Production Projects.* Agricultural

Planning Studies no. 14. Rome: Food and Agriculture Organization, 1971.

> Contains good general discussion of points to be covered in preparing project evaluations, including a summary statement about economic and financial analysis. Complements the outlines below (7).

7. Food and Agriculture Organization/International Bank for Reconstruction and Development Cooperative Programme. *Outlines for Projects to be Presented for Financing.* Rome: Food and Agriculture Organization, 1967.

> Useful general check list.

8. Gittinger, J. Price, ed. *Compounding and Discounting Tables for Project Evaluation.* Washington: Economic Development Institute of the International Bank for Reconstruction and Development, forthcoming.

> A set of discount tables compiled with project analysis needs particularly in mind.

9. Grant, Eugene L. and Ireson, W. Grant. *Principles of Engineering Economy.* 5th ed. New York: Ronald Press, 1970.

> A standard, thorough text in the field which discusses many questions of application. (The material cited in table 4-3 is from the fourth edition.)

10. Hammel, Werner, and Hemmer, Hans-Rimbert. *Grundlagen der Cost-Benefit-Analyse bei Projekten in Entwicklungsländern.* (Basic Principles of Cost-Benefit Analysis of Projects in Developing Countries.) Frankfurt: Kreditanstalt für Wiederaufbau, 1971.

> A manual prepared by the German bilateral technical and economic aid agency to govern analysis of projects submitted to it for financing. Adapts a modified Little-Mirrlees valuation methodology (17). A revised version with an English translation is being prepared.

11. Henderson, P.D. "Some Unsettled Issues in Cost-Benefit Analysis." In *Unfashionable Economics, Essays in Honour of Lord Balogh,* edited by Paul Streeten, pp. 275-301. London: Wiedenfeld and Nicolson, 1970.

> Raises a number of "unsettled issues" about cost-benefit analysis theory and its application to project analysis.

12. Hertz, David B. "Investment Policies that Pay Off." *Harvard Business Review* 46 (1958): 96-108. (Reprinted in *Capital Investment Decisions,* edited by the Editors of the Harvard Business Review, pp. 145-156. Cambridge: Harvard Business Review, 1964.)

Interesting discussion of uncertainty in discounted cash flow analysis. (Other articles in the volume of reprints deal with investment analysis techniques and are useful for those interested in more thorough discussions of applications.)

13.. Hirschman, Albert O. *Development Projects Observed.* Washington: The Brookings Institution, 1967.

It's a good thing you don't know how difficult projects are to carry out or you would never have the courage to try. Fortunately, the "hiding hand" beneficially conceals the difficulties from us and we do embark on development efforts. Or, at least, that is how Hirschman sees it. He then continues to examine ways of reducing some of the difficulties. An excellent, provocative, easily read book for those concerned with projects of all sorts.

14. Kao, Charles H. C., Anschel, Kurt R., and Eicher, Carl K. "Disguised Unemployment in Agriculture: A Survey." In *Agriculture in Economic Development*, edited by Lawrence Witt and Carl Eicher, pp. 129-144. New York: McGraw-Hill, 1964.

Excellent short discussion of the whole question of the marginal value product of labor in agriculture.

15. King, John A. *Economic Development Projects and their Appraisal.* Baltimore: The Johns Hopkins Press, 1967.

A study by a World Bank staff member of a number of projects, discussing mostly problems of implementation. The introduction discusses the aspects of project appraisal as viewed by the World Bank.

16. Krutilla, John V., and Eckstein, Otto. *Multiple Purpose River Development.* Baltimore: The Johns Hopkins Press, 1958.

Serious, theoretical study of economic efficiency and social cost in the context of the United States setting, supplemented with a group of critical case studies of American river projects. Again, written with professional economists in mind.

17. Little, Ian M. D., and Mirrlees, James A. *Social Cost Benefit Analysis.* Vol. II of *Manual of Industrial Project Analysis in Developing Countries.* Development Centre Studies. Paris: Development Centre of the Organisation for Economic Co-Operation and Development, 1969.

A highly influential and to some extent controversial work proposing a method of determining the "present social value" of alternative industrial projects. Notable for the complex valuation methodology which is developed in considerable detail (for a discussion and evaluation see pages 43 to 46). Even were one not to accept the valuation proposals, the questions raised in setting them forth are provocative. The chapters on the need for benefit-cost analysis; policy objectives; and plans, project choice, and project design are themselves worthwhile, cogent statements.

18. McKean, Ronald N. *Efficiency in Government through Systems Analysis with Emphasis on Water Resources Development.* New York: Wiley, 1958.

> A classic in the field which clearly sets forth the issues. Recommends use of internal rate of return rather than benefit-cost ratio.

19. Merrett, A. J., and Sykes, Allen. *The Finance and Analysis of Capital Projects.* London: Longmans, 1963.

> Excellent and thorough text on project analysis techniques with emphasis on their application for private firms. Particularly good for questions of methodology.

20. Mishan, E. J. "The Postwar Literature on Externalities." *Journal of Economic Literature* 9 (1971):1-28.

> A highly technical summary of the literature on secondary effects focusing primarily on the relationships of benefits to individual firms in contrast to the society as a whole.

21. Phillips, Richard. *Feasibility Analysis for Agricultural Projects.* Seoul: Ministry of Agriculture and Forestry, Republic of Korea; United States Agency for International Development; and Dunlap and Associates, Inc., 1970.

> Contains detailed illustrations of worksheets for analyzing a number of kinds of agricultural projects, but only for financial analysis. (Single copies available at no charge from USAID, American Embassy, Seoul, Korea.)

22. Prest, A.R., and Turvey, R. "Cost-Benefit Analysis: A Survey." In *Surveys of Economic Theory*, vol. 3, *Resource Allocation*, edited by the American Economics Association and the Royal Economic Society, pp. 155-207. New York: St. Martin's Press, 1966.

> The best general survey with which to begin serious exploration of the issues in connection with measures of project worth.

23.   Reutlinger, Shlomo. *Techniques for Project Appraisal under Uncertainty*. World Bank Staff Occasional Papers no. 10. Baltimore: The Johns Hopkins Press for the International Bank for Reconstruction and Development, 1970.

A sophisticated treatment of uncertainty requiring the use of a computer. Useful where very large investments are involved and suitable, highly skilled manpower can be assigned to the analysis.

24.   United Kingdom. Overseas Development Administration. *Manual of Project Appraisal*. London: Ministry of Overseas Development, 1971.

Very summary in its treatment of project analysis techniques but interesting because of the adaptation of the shadow pricing techniques proposed by Little and Mirrlees (17). A revised version is being prepared.

25.   United States. Agency for International Development. *Guidelines for Capital Project Appraisal*. Washington: Agency for International Development, forthcoming.

A discussion of techniques for project analysis recommending use of internal rate of return and drawing the same distinction between economic and financial analysis as that in this book. In addition to a section on agriculture, the book deals also with projects for water and sewerage, manufacturing, public health, education, transportation, telecommunications, and electric power.

26.   United States, Congress, Senate, *Policies, Standards, and Procedures in the Formulation, Evaluation and Review of Plans for Use and Development of Water and Related Land Resources*, 87th Congress, 2d session, May 29, 1962, Senate Document no. 97.

Defines costs and benefits for United States government agency use and specifies how they are to be used for evaluating water resource projects.

27.   United States. Water Resources Council. "Proposed Principles and Standards for Planning Water and Related Land Resources." *Federal Register* 36 (1971):24144-14194.

28.   van der Tak, Herman G. *The Economic Choice between Hydroelectric and Thermal Power Developments*. World Bank Staff Occasional Papers no. 1. Baltimore: The Johns Hopkins Press for the International Bank for Reconstruction and Development, 1969.

29.   Ward, William A. *An Appraisal of Alternative Models for Estimation of Indirect Employment and Profit Gains Resulting*